THE GARDENING WHICH? GUIDE TO

SUCCESSFUL SHRUBS

THE GARDENING WHICH? GUIDE TO

SUCCESSFUL
SHRUBS

CONSUMERS' ASSOCIATION

Which? Books are commissioned and researched by
Consumers' Association and published by
Which? Ltd, 2 Marylebone Road, London NW1 4DF

Distributed by The Penguin Group:
Penguin Books Ltd, 27 Wrights Lane, London W8 5TZ
First edition 1995

British Library Cataloguing-in-Publication Data

Gardening Which? Guide to Successful Shrubs:
the essential guide to choosing the right permanent plants for your garden

635.976

ISBN 0 85202 553 X

Colour reproduction by FMT Colour, London SE1

Printed and bound in Great Britain by Scotprint, Musselburgh

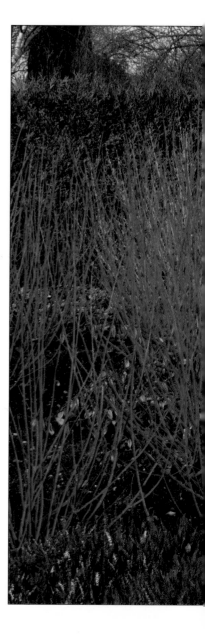

Credits

Text by Elizabeth Dobbs
Design by Susan Dorrington
Edited by Alistair Ayres, Editor *Gardening Which?*
Photographs from *Gardening Which?* library, Gardening Picture Library and
Photos Horticultural

Where to see shrubs

Gardening Which? magazine has a living encyclopaedia of the 200 shrubs most
widely sold at garden centres. Growth rates, times of flowering, berrying,
autumn colour etc. are measured and recorded to provide first-hand information
on the shrubs.

You can visit the shrub collection at the Gardening Which? Demonstration
Garden, Capel Manor, Bullmoor Lane, Enfield, Middlesex EN1 4RQ.
Phone 0181 366 4442 for details of opening times.

Gardening Which? magazine

You can find up-to-date information on all the latest plants, gardening products
and techniques in *Gardening Which?* magazine. It regularly carries out tests and
trials of plant varieties and suppliers, as well gardening equipment and sundries
such as composts and fertilisers. Each issue is packed with ideas, practical advice
and results of the magazine's independent evaluations.

Gardening Which? magazine is available by subscription only. For details and
free trial offer, write to *Gardening Which?*, Consumers' Association, Freepost,
Hertford X, SG14 1YB or freephone 0800 252100.

Contents

How this book works

To select an evergreen shrub, say, just turn to a green-edged page in *The Gardening Which? Guide to Successful Shrubs*. At the top corner, you'll find a chart showing what shape the shrub is and how big it is likely to grow in five, ten and 25 years.

A quick glance at the features calendar shows you when flowers and berries are produced on each shrub in a typical year.

A double frost symbol indicates that the plant is totally hardy, and a cloud and sun symbol shows that the plant is happy in partial shade. Soil requirements and uses are equally easy to check out.

Once you have decided that a plant is suitable, *Successful Shrubs* details the varieties you are likely to find at garden centres and nurseries.

You will also find buying tips to help you get good-quality plants. Growing guides, details of propagation, pruning and potential problems are all included – advice backed up by thorough *Gardening Which?* research.

All the plants are illustrated with colour photographs chosen to represent the plants in their true light rather than to glamorise them

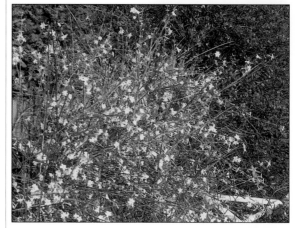

Finding the right plant

Successful Shrubs covers the plants that you are most likely to find at garden centres. The plants are arranged alphabetically, just as you commonly find them in garden centres. Each plant type is colour-coded for quick and easy reference. All the shrubs are illustrated with photographs chosen to represent them in their true light rather than to exaggerate particular features.

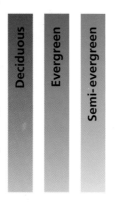

Shape and size

Buying shrubs that get too big for their allotted space is a common problem.

Before buying shrubs, look up and check how big they grow. This way, you can avoid a lot of trouble and effort as a result of unsuitable plants in the future.

Knowing how their shape develops with age also helps greatly when fitting plants into your current garden layout or when planning new beds and borders.

The plant silhouettes on each page indicate the approximate size and shape at five years, ten years and at maturity (for most shrubs around 25 years).

Note that sizes are what you can typically expect; actual sizes can vary considerably according to growing conditions.

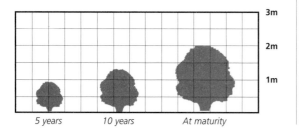

			3m
			2m
			1m
5 years	10 years	At maturity	

Position

Some plants get badly scorched in full sun – many yellow-leaved shrubs, for example – while others grow thin and straggly and may refuse to flower in the shade. Use the symbols below as a quick reference guide to the positions that the plants require.

Sun *Partial or light shade* *Shade* *Needs shelter*

Hardiness

Plants described as very hardy should survive the winter in any part of Britain. Moderately hardy plants can withstand sub-zero temperatures, though may die if they become waterlogged during the winter or are continuously exposed to strong winds. Plants needing winter protection will tolerate temperatures to at least -5°C (20°F), but can be killed by very low temperatures. In most gardens, it is therefore advisable to insulate the roots with a 15cm (6in) layer of bark chippings, bracken, dry leaves or similar. Tender plants are killed by frost and need to be brought indoors over the winter.

Very hardy *Moderately hardy* *Needs winter protection* *Tender*

Soil

Look up the soil symbols to find out the basic requirements of the shrubs that you want to buy. You can save yourself a lot of effort and disappointment by choosing plants that will thrive on the type of soil that you already have in your garden.

The lists in the Shrub Selector at the back of the book suggest shrubs for problem soils, such as heavy clay, sand and boggy conditions.

On light sandy or chalky soils, it's worth adding organic matter to improve retention of moisture and nutrients. On heavy clay soils, you can dig in sharp grit to improve drainage. In both instances, aim to dig in at least a 5cm (2in) layer of material to achieve a noticeable improvement.

If you want to grow acid-loving plants and your soil is not acid, make raised beds or use large containers filled with an ericaceous compost.

Most

Neutral

Acid

Moist

Well-drained

Uses

If you are looking for a shrub for a particular spot in your garden, flick through the book to find plants with the relevant symbol and make your shortlist.

Mixed border

Specimen

Hedge

Screen

Containers

Filler

Ground cover

Focal point

Covering walls and fences

Features calendar

Use the features calendar to help plan for year-round colour and to select good-value plants for your garden.

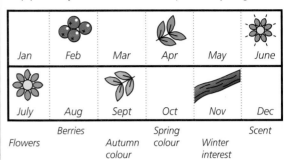

| Jan | Feb | Mar | Apr | May | June |
| July | Aug | Sept | Oct | Nov | Dec |

Flowers — Berries — Autumn colour — Spring colour — Winter interest — Scent

Growing guide

The growing guide provides tips on getting your shrubs off to a good start, and keeping them healthy and looking good. It also gives money-saving advice on propagation, plus pruning details for all the shrubs.

Which variety?

You will often find that the varieties of shrub on offer vary from garden centre to garden centre. You may also be faced with a choice of several different varieties of the same shrub.

In this section, there are descriptions of the varieties most commonly sold at garden centres and nurseries, so you can decide whether it is worth shopping around or if a substitute would be just as good.

As a rule, be wary of plants that are not labelled with the species or variety name. These can often turn out to be inferior types.

BUYING TIPS BOX *Plant quality at garden centres can be very variable. Use the buying tips to help select good specimens.*

Where possible, we have included photographs of the whole plant, as well as of the main features of interest

Shrub care

To avoid the need for soil preparation, choose shrubs that will do well naturally on the type of soil in your garden. If you have a loam or clay loam (i.e. you can mould the wet soil into a ball but it will break up if you try and roll it into a sausage shape), you should be able to grow a wide range of shrubs without any special soil preparation.

Dig out a planting pit in shallow chalky soils

If you have a heavy clay soil (i.e. you can roll it into a sausage shape and bend this into a hoop), it pays to improve the soil before planting. Ideally, dig over the whole bed, incorporating at least a 5cm (2in) layer of sharp grit. You can dig in organic matter too, though it is easier to apply this to the surface and let the worms incorporate it for you. If you just improve the soil in the planting hole, there is a danger that it will fill up with water in winter.

Shrubs can struggle to get established on very free-draining soils unless you can supply constant irrigation, at least for the first spring and summer. To reduce the need for watering and to improve the ability of the soil to retain nutrients, dig in plenty of organic matter, such as spent mushroom compost, before planting. You need to work in at least a 5cm (2in) layer to have any effect.

In chalky areas, the soil is often too shallow to plant shrubs. If the depth of soil is less than 60cm (2ft), dig a planting pit in the chalk using a pickaxe and fill this with a mixture of topsoil and organic matter.

Even if your topsoil is reasonable, you may find that there is a hard pan of clay which restricts drainage. If this is within 60cm (2ft) of the surface, try to break it up to avoid waterlogging problems in the winter.

Planting container-grown shrubs
Water your shrubs thoroughly at least an hour before planting. Dig out a hole roughly twice the size of the rootball and put the soil on a sheet of polythene. Break up this soil and mix in grit or organic matter as necessary. Partly refill the hole so that it is the same depth as the container. Remove the shrub from its pot and gently loosen the

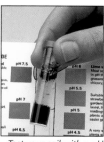
Test your soil with a pH kit if you are not sure whether it is sufficiently acid for plants such as azaleas

roots around the outside. Prune out any pot-bound roots before planting. Finally, fill in the hole, gently firming in the soil around the shrub as you go with your feet. On free-draining soils, leaving a slight depression makes watering easier. On heavy soils, planting on a slight mound helps improve drainage. After planting, water in thoroughly.

Planting bare-rooted shrubs
Before planting, soak the roots in a bucket of water overnight. Hold the shrub in the hole so that the stem is at the depth of the old soil mark. Add a little soil at time, gently shaking the plant up and down, so it filters through the roots. Firm in the soil around the roots with your hands. Once the hole is half-filled, proceed as for container-grown shrubs. If you do not have time to plant bare-rooted shrubs properly straight away, dig a shallow trench for the roots, lay the shrubs on their sides and heap some soil over the roots.

Planting evergreens
Evergreens are best planted in early autumn or late spring. Planting in autumn is best in milder areas as it enables the shrubs to get established with minimal watering. In cold areas with heavy soils, May is generally the best time. To reduce water loss from newly planted evergreens in exposed positions, protect them with a screen of windbreak netting supported on canes for the first year or two.

Watering

Shrubs need to be watered during dry weather for the first couple of years. This means a thorough soaking – e.g. 5 litres (1 gallon) at a time for small shrubs and up to 18 litres (4 gallons) for large shrubs.

Feeding

Unless your soil is very poor, most shrubs can cope without feeding. However, they will get established more quickly if you feed them for the first couple of years. Do not add a fertiliser to the planting hole as this can scorch the delicate new roots. Apply a slow-release fertiliser such as fish, blood and bone at 70g/sq m (2oz/sq yd) in early spring. Shrubs which undergo heavy annual pruning, have a long flowering period, or are grown for large leaves or flowers will benefit from annual feeding.

Mulching

For shrubs to get established quickly, it is important that they do not have to compete for nutrients and water with weeds or other garden plants. Ideally, avoid planting anything else within 60-90cm (2-3ft) within the first year or two. To keep down weeds and help prevent water evaporating from the soil, apply a mulch. You can use a 5cm (2in) layer of bark chippings, a layer of polythene or several layers of newspaper suitably hidden by a thin layer of bark, soil or gravel. Do not use peat as it will not last long, it is not very effective at suppressing weeds and may get blown away by strong winds.

Pruning

Shrubs respond to pruning in different ways, depending on their growth rate and whether they flower on the new shoots or on shoots that are two or more years old. Pruning details are given for each shrub. Also consult *The Gardening Which? Guide to Successful Pruning.*

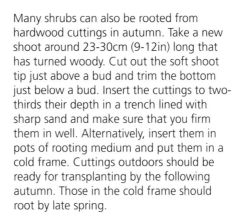

Pruning a dogwood in Spring

Propagation

For most shrubs, the best time to take cuttings is in the summer when the new shoots become flexible enough to bend into a U-shape without breaking. When you take cuttings, make your bottom cut either through the swelling at the base of the side shoot (a basal cutting) or just below a leaf joint (a nodal cutting). Remove the soft tip of the shoot and all but the top two or three leaves. Dip the base of the cutting in a rooting hormone and insert into a rooting medium. An equal mixture of moss peat and sharp sand or a sowing and cutting compost should prove successful for most shrubs. Add a few granules of Osmocote slow-release fertiliser to provide some nutrition once the new roots form. You can either root the cutting in a pot covered with a clear polythene bag or in a cold frame. Cuttings that root before September should be potted up into multipurpose compost. Otherwise, leave this until spring.

Many shrubs can also be rooted from hardwood cuttings in autumn. Take a new shoot around 23-30cm (9-12in) long that has turned woody. Cut out the soft shoot tip just above a bud and trim the bottom just below a bud. Insert the cuttings to two-thirds their depth in a trench lined with sharp sand and make sure that you firm them in well. Alternatively, insert them in pots of rooting medium and put them in a cold frame. Cuttings outdoors should be ready for transplanting by the following autumn. Those in the cold frame should root by late spring.

Shrubs that are difficult to root from cuttings can often be layered. Select a young flexible shoot and peg it to the ground about 15cm (6in) from the tip. Tie the end section to a stake in an upright position. Once the layer has a good root system it can be cut away from the parent and replanted. This can take from six months to two years, depending on species.

For more advice on propagating shrubs and other garden plants, consult *The Gardening Which? Guide to Successful Propagation.*

Using the pot and bag method for spiraea cuttings

Make sure that you firm in hardwood cuttings

Layering is a good way to propagate rhododendrons

This border contains a good mixture of flowering and foliage shrubs with herbaceous perennials as fillers

Using shrubs

There are flowering shrubs like camellias, hydrangeas and magnolias whose flowers alone rival those of any bedding or herbaceous plant. But even these shrubs offer so much more than their flowers. Shrubs create a permanent yet changing shape in the garden. They provide practical features like hedges, and backbone structure to borders, and they can soften harsh landscaping. Some are modest but faithful backdrops, others steal the limelight as focal points.

Whether you want shrubs for their beauty and adornment or as reliable workhorses, you will find many uses and ideas for hundreds of shrubs in this book.

Evergreen *versus* deciduous

Evergreen shrubs do not lose their leaves in autumn. Their year-round colour is a particularly useful feature in winter. However, too many

evergreen shrubs can make for a rather dull garden. Deciduous shrubs add drama as the seasons change: leaves burst forth in spring, flower then turn colour in autumn and fall. Include one evergreen to every two or three deciduous shrubs for a good balance.

Mixed or shrub border

Shrubs can be combined on their own or with other plants (such as bulbs and herbaceous perennials) to create a bed or border that will look interesting throughout the year.

Before planting up a border, it is worth doing a rough sketch to scale on graph paper. Mark on the sketch any sunny or shady spots and any existing features (e.g. walls, trees). You will then get an idea how many shrubs you can fit in. For a quick effect, space shrubs at the distance they spread after five years. This will mean more pruning in the years ahead. The alternative is to

Viburnum plicatum 'Mariesii'

Cornus controversa Variegata'

Hollies are good evergreens for the back of a border

Deciduous azaleas are a focal point when in flower

use the ten-year figure and use quick-growing, temporary shrubs (see 'Fillers' overleaf) or herbaceous perennials to fill the gaps. Once you have fitted your chosen shrubs into the plan, you can then make a quick check for year-round interest. An easy way to do this is to draw a circle to represent each shrub, then colour them in according to their main season of interest.

For the back of the border, choose shrubs with late autumn to early winter features. Among the evergreens, consider those that produce berries, such as pyracantha which makes an excellent wall shrub, or those with variegated foliage, such as elaeagnus or hollies.

For the middle of the border, choose plants that add pockets of colour – long-flowering shrubs like abelias or fuchsias, say, or variegated dogwoods. Towards the front, use smaller, neater shrubs – such as heathers, box or dwarf hebes – planted in groups of three or five. A few large or medium shrubs can be planted near the front to add interest. Examples include bold foliage shrubs such as phormiums and sambucus.

Try to provide something of interest for each season. In a small border, choose shrubs with at least two features of interest – flowers and autumn colour, for example, or coloured winter stems and variegated foliage.

Specimens and focal points

A specimen shrub should have at least one feature of such outstanding beauty that it merits a position where it can be viewed on its own. Examples could be the flowers of magnolias and mock orange (*Philadelphus*) or the new foliage of pieris. A focal shrub is one that has a strong architectural shape that draws the eye. Examples

include the spiky outlines of phormiums and yuccas and the tiered habits of *Cornus alternifolia* 'Variegata' and *Viburnum plicatum* 'Mariesii'. Shrubs such as box can also be trained into shapes or as standards to form focal points.

If well-positioned, these shrubs can highlight the most attractive part of your garden and direct attention away from eyesores.

Before planting specimens and focal points, consider the background. For example, if a specimen shrub has bright, golden foliage this will show up best against a dark background. A Japanese maple with filigree foliage will have more impact if viewed against a plain

Japanese maples and phormiums both make excellent focal points

Box does very well in containers

Brooms are ideal fillers near the front of a border

background, such as a dark fence or hedge. Specimen and focal shrubs should also be in scale with their surroundings and not look as if they have been stuck in as an afterthought.

Fillers

At some stage, there will be gaps in the beds and borders of most gardens. In a newly planted border, there may be gaps which the slow-growing shrubs will not fill for several years. Even in an established border, shrubs can get cut back over winter, thus leaving a gap. A good way to fill these holes is to plant 'filler' shrubs. These are cheap, quick-growing shrubs which can be moved or dug up after a few years. Shrubs worth trying as gap fillers include: brooms, buddleias, kerrias, lavateras, hardy fuchsias, hebes, potentillas, spiraeas and weigelas.

Shrubs for containers

Growing shrubs in containers allows you to extend your range of shrubs to include those that would not otherwise survive in your garden. If your garden has a chalky soil, you can still grow acid-loving shrubs such as pieris and azaleas in containers. Similarly, many silver foliage shrubs, such as *Convolvulus cneorum*, will not survive in a wet, clay soil but would do well in containers in a free-draining compost. Plants that are too

Insulate containers in winter with a duvet made from a dustbin liner stuffed with straw

tender to be grown outside all year round, such as myrtle, can be grown in pots and brought under cover in winter. Shrubs can also look very attractive in containers and you can site them even where there is no soil.

Shrubs that flourish in containers are those that can tolerate drying out occasionally and having their roots restricted. Those that are slow-growing with a good shape and attractive foliage are particularly worthwhile. Many evergreens are suitable including: aucubas (spotted laurel), box camellias, choisya (Mexican orange blossom), euonymus, hebes, pieris, *Rhododendron yakushimanum* and *Viburnum davidii*. Deciduous shrubs are also suitable if they are attractive when out of leaf e.g. Japanese maples or *Magnolia stellata*.

Most shrubs need large containers – 45cm (18in) or more in depth and diameter – to do well. The container also needs to have drainage holes. To make it easier to move around, put the container on a wooden platform with castors before you fill it with compost.

Cover the base of the tub with at least 2.5cm (1in) of drainage material (e.g. crocks or gravel). Most shrubs should do well in a good John Innes No 2 compost. For acid-loving shrubs, use an ericaceous (lime-free) or peat-based compost. When planting up, leave a 5cm (2in) gap between the compost level and the rim to allow for watering.

Shrubs in containers may need daily watering in mid-summer. With acid loving-plants, add a used tea bag or a teaspoonful of aluminium sulphate to the watering can every few weeks. This will prevent alkaline salts building up in the compost.

Forsythia is a good choice for a flowering hedge

You can buy hedging as container-grown plants, but this can be very expensive. Cheaper options are to use bare-rooted plants (watch out for dry roots) or, if you have plenty of time, take cuttings and grow them on.

After planting hedging, cut back all the shrubs by one-third to a half. This will make them branch to produce a dense and bushy hedge.

Feeding is also essential – either add a slow-release fertiliser, such as Osmocote granules, in the spring or provide a weekly liquid feed from April to September.

Large tubs that cannot be moved may need insulating over the winter. Make a jacket from black polythene and stuff it with 5cm (2in) insulating material e.g. straw, bark or newspaper. Tie around the tub and add a covering of bark on the soil surface.

Hedging

Hedges are a common way of marking a boundary, creating privacy or dividing up a garden. In addition to these very practical uses, the style of hedge can be used to reflect the feel of a garden. For example, clipped box edging adds a formal touch to a garden, while spring-flowering *Spiraea* x *vanhouttei* with its arching branches is very informal and colourful.

Where privacy is a priority, choose a dense-growing hedge to create a formal line. Good shrubs for this purpose include the Portugal laurel (*Prunus lusitanica*), which will make a 1.8m (6ft) hedge in five years, and privet (*Ligustrum ovalifolium*), which reaches about 1.5m (5ft) in five years.

Informal flowering hedges take up more space but do not need to be trimmed so often. They also add more colour and seasonal interest than the traditional hedges. Good examples include *Berberis* x *stenophylla* and *Viburnum tinus,* both of which can reach 1.5m (5ft) after five years.

Screening plants

To be effective, screening plants must be evergreen, quick-growing and dense. However, avoid shrubs that grow too tall. For a dark green backdrop consider the Portugal laurel (*Prunus lusitanica*). A paler and slightly less vigorous option would be *Elaeagnus* x *ebbingei*. The large, semi-evergreen cotoneasters have a lot to offer; try *C. franchetii* or the spreading *C.* x *rothschildianus*. In mild gardens, many ceanothus such as 'Autumnal Blue' or 'Gloire de Versailles' will grow quickly, usually flowering in their first summer.

Wall shrubs

A wall and the direction it faces can create a micro-climate that is very different from the rest of the garden. The soil at the base of walls is often poor and dry, so dig an extra-large hole when planting and mix in plenty of well-rotted organic matter.

South- and west-facing walls provide extra

Abelia x grandiflora should survive the winter against a sunny, south-facing wall

Right: winter jasmine will brighten up a north-facing wall

Far right: Vinca minor produces a dense ground cover if clipped annually

shelter, so make the most of them by trying shrubs that are of borderline hardiness in your area. For example, in cold areas *Perovskia atripli-cifolia* would provide late summer flowers and could be grown with other silver foliage plants. In mild areas, warm walls are often suntraps with poor, dry soil. On the plus side, you can grow plants that would normally need lifting or protecting. *Abelia floribunda* is more tender than the familiar *A.* x *grandiflora*. If fan-trained against a warm wall, its larger flowers will be shown to best advantage.

Shrubs for north- and east-facing walls must be tough and adaptable. They need to put up with shade, drought, biting winds and, in winter, rapid thawing out if bright morning sunshine follows freezing during the night.

Japanese quinces (*Chaenomeles*) can endure such conditions, and growing them against a wall gives a better display than if they are left free-standing. *Cotoneaster horizontalis* and pyracantha provide autumn colour against north and east walls and are easy to grow and reliable. For winter colour, consider the winter jasmine.

Ground cover

Many shrubs can be used to cover difficult areas of ground, producing an attractive yet low-maintenance solution to problem areas such as steep banks or shady sites under trees.

Good ground cover shrubs are easy to maintain and grow quickly to form a dense canopy of foliage that keeps down the weeds. They should have a long season of interest, so most are evergreens. *Euonymus fortunei* varieties are good foliage plants. Good flowering ground cover shrubs include cistus, heathers and dwarf hebes.

Clear the area of weeds before planting, keep weeding until the shrubs have grown together. To reduce the need for weeding until the ground cover becomes established, cover the area with black polythene sheeting and plant through it or apply a 5cm (2in) layer of bark chippings as a mulch. If you use black polythene, make holes in it with a fork so that it does not collect water.

When choosing plants, consider their spread in relation to the area to be covered. Some like *Vinca major* root as they spread and can become invasive. Planting ground cover shrubs can work out expensive. To save money, buy or take your own rooted cuttings or small divisions and plant slightly closer than normal.

Right: camellias make good wall shrubs, but avoid east-facing walls where the morning sun can damage the flower buds

Far right: Hebe rakaiensis creates an interesting texture when grown as ground cover

Buying shrubs

Far left: read the display boards as they often contain vital information not included on the plant labels

Left: before buying check that shrubs are not pot-bound

There is no shortage of outlets selling shrubs, but price and quality can vary considerably. The following guide should help you to get the best from the different sources.

Garden centres

Most garden centres stock a reasonable range of shrubs. These will probably have been bought from several wholesale growers rather than grown on site.

As most garden centres are open all year round and supply container-grown stock, in theory, you could buy and plant at any time. In practice, you will probably find the best choice and the best-quality plants in the spring and, to a lesser extent, in the autumn. Certain shrubs tend to be on sale only when they are at their peak of interest. *Caryopteris* x *clandonensis*, for example, is widely sold when in flower in late summer and early autumn, but can be difficult to find at other times of year. Visiting garden centres regularly throughout the year and staggering your purchases is a good way to ensure year-round colour in your garden. In many gardens, spring-flowering shrubs dominate, simply because all the plants were bought in spring.

Be wary of container-grown shrubs that have been left to become starved or pot-bound in the garden centre. Weeds in the pots, faded labels, roots coming out of the pot (or curled round and round inside) are all signs that the plants have been neglected. Inspect growing tips for aphids, and young leaves for notched edges. Check the undersides of the leaves for spots, blotches and other discolouration. Avoid any shrubs with splits in the bark or dieback of the shoots.

Garden centres are now making more use of posters and displays to provide information. Shrubs are generally arranged in an A-Z layout, which makes plants easy to find if you know what you are looking for. Special display areas featuring, say, acid-loving shrubs or shrubs for shade are helpful if you want shrubs for a specific purpose. In general, however, the standard of plant labelling is poor. Many just state the name and price and give little or no essential information on soil, position and size. To avoid buying unsuitable plants, take this book with you when shopping for shrubs.

BUYING TIPS

- Heavily promoted shrubs, in coloured pots with large glossy labels, tend to sell at premium prices. Check out what other similar shrubs are available – you may find one at a lower price that better meets your needs.

- Buy from garden centres with good stock control and a steady turnover. Container-grown plants can be expensive and if left on sale too long can deteriorate rapidly.

- Many garden centres are willing to order shrubs that they do not have in stock.

Specialist nurseries

Shrub nurseries range from large businesses that supply both wholesale and retail to small concerns that specialise in one particular type of shrub – acers or variegated shrubs, for example. Most of the plants sold by shrub nurseries will be smaller than those you will find at garden centres, though in general the prices are lower. Most nurseries will also supply larger plants on request. A few specialise in extra-large plants for instant effect.

Most specialist nurseries are open to visitors but the smaller ones in particular often have erratic opening times, so it pays to telephone before

making a special journey. Visiting specialist nurseries is worthwhile, as you can often get a lot of invaluable advice by speaking to the person who grows the plants. Inspect the quality of the plants as you would at a garden centre. Often turnover is slow and quality cannot always be maintained.

Many offer a mail-order service and some are mail order only. Buying by mail order has the advantages that you are not restricted to what is available locally, you have a wider choice, and the shrubs are delivered to your door. However, buying shrubs by mail order does require some forward planning.

First you have to order a catalogue. Many catalogues are a mine of useful and interesting information, but some of the terms and conditions can be onerous – so read the small print. Most specialists send out their plants between October and March and usually dispatch orders on a first come, first served basis. This means that you need to get your order in by late summer to be sure of getting what you want.

Many shrubs sent by mail order are bare-rooted. These tend to be cheaper than container-grown shrubs, but you need to plant them within a couple of days of arrival, or at least cover their roots with soil. One drawback with mail order is that you have to rely on the efficiency of the nursery. Only *Gardening Which?* magazine regularly tests and reports on the plant quality and service of mail-order nurseries.

Details of specialist nurseries can be found in *The Plant Finder* (available from bookshops), or in catalogues picked up at shows.

This label gives no warning that Gaultheria procumbens will perish unless planted in an acid soil

Hedging plants are often sold in bundles of ten, but it is difficult to tell whether all the plants are of good quality

---

MAIL-ORDER TIPS

- If you do not want to be sent substitutes, make this clear by writing it on the order form.

- Delivery charges can be high, so take this into account when comparing prices with garden centres.

- Keep a copy of your order and any correspondence. Check the plants on arrival, complain promptly if you are not satisfied.

- Make sure that you are clear about the size of plants you are buying. Very small plants may need to be grown on in pots before they are large enough to plant out.

Far left: these two skimmias both cost the same price but are from different garden centres

Left: the spotted laurel on the left should not have been on sale. Look for plants like the one on the right

Cash-with-order advertisements

Newspapers and magazines often carry advertisements that offer plants at bargain prices. Before ordering, make sure that you know what varieties are being offered and the size of plants being supplied. Otherwise, you will not have any right of redress if you end up with tiny, rooted cuttings of a poor variety.

BUYING FROM NEWSPAPER ADS

- Do not rely on the descriptions given in the ad, check with another source.

- Examine plants on arrival. If you are not happy, complain. The Mail Order Protection Scheme (MOPS) covers plants. It gives you some protection if you do not receive your goods or you do not receive a refund on returned goods and the company goes into liquidation.

DIY superstores and high street shops

DIY superstores sell shrubs, but tend to carry most stock in the spring. The plants can be good value but check them over carefully, particularly when buying out of season.

Some high street shops sell a small selection of common shrubs in polythene packs between late October and early March. These are bare-rooted plants, therefore usually cheap, but the choice is limited. The shrubs are also very prone to drying out at the roots and sprouting prematurely in the warmth of the shop. They can be good value if you buy them shortly after they have been delivered to the shop.

KNOW YOUR RIGHTS

Under the Sale of Goods Act 1979 and subsequent amendments, all goods, including plants, must:

- fit their description (e.g. if you bought a named variety of witch hazel which has a red flower that is what you should get)

- be of satisfactory quality (i.e. in good condition; in the case of a shrub, be a healthy, vigorous plant)

- be fit for the purpose (e.g. if you asked for heathers suitable for an alkaline soil, they should be).

In theory, you have up to six years in which to reject shrubs and claim your money back. In practice, the sooner you notify the retailer the better. The law gives you a reasonable opportunity to examine goods once they are delivered. If it takes 18 months, say, to establish whether a shrub is growing properly or is dead, then you can still get your money back within that time. But if you leave it too long , you may lose this right. Many retailers offer 'no quibble' guarantees, typically two years for a shrub.

You may be entitled to compensation even if you are too late for a refund. In the case of a wrongly named plant, this would normally be a replacement or the difference in value between the one you got and the one you ordered, if any. Always check everything carefully as soon as it arrives and complain at the first sight of a problem.

Abelia x grandiflora

Shape and size

			3m
			2m
			1m

| 5 years | 10 years | At maturity |

Position

Hardiness

Soil

NEUTRAL MOIST DRAINED

Uses

Features calendar

Jan	Feb	Mar	Apr	May	June
✿	✿	✿	✿		
July	Aug	Sept	Oct	Nov	Dec

Buying tips *Buy and plant in March or April. The branches can be brittle so look for undamaged specimens.*

Abelia x grandiflora

Growing guide

Abelias have a long flowering season and do not grow very large; two features that make them a good choice for the smaller garden.

They cannot be relied upon to be hardy, so give them a sheltered position. The base of a south- or west-facing fence or wall would be ideal, especially if there are any climbers that have become bare at the base and need covering up.

The hardier types such as *A. x grandiflora* should survive most winters if planted in a sheltered spot. Even if the top growth is killed back, new shoots will usually grow in the spring. As it flowers on both old and new wood, you will not lose out on the summer display. In cold areas, it is best to cut the plant back in late autumn and insulate it with a 15cm (6in) layer of bracken or bark chippings held in place by wire netting. Remove the insulating material in early spring before the new shoots start to grow.

The more tender abelias can be grown in pots and can be moved under cover in winter.

Pruning

Young plants need no pruning for the first three to four years, other than the removal of winter-damaged shoots. Once established, their rather twiggy habit needs to be kept in good shape by regular pruning. In late March or early April, thin out any very dense growth. Once new growth has started, thin out dead and old twigs. After a bad winter, it is best to cut all the shoots back to just above ground level.

Abelia x grandiflora 'Francis Mason'

Propagation

Cuttings are very easy to root throughout the summer. Alternatively, take hardwood cuttings in September and root them in pots in a cold frame or a cool or unheated greenhouse. Plant out the following spring.

Troubleshooting

Generally trouble-free.

Which variety?

A. x *grandiflora* and its yellow variegated variety **'Francis Mason'** are easy to find and the best choice for interest late in the season, as their slightly fragrant, pink and white flowers are often produced until October. Bear in mind that 'Francis Mason' is the more tender of the two.
A. x *grandiflora* **'Goldstrike'** (also sold as 'Aurea' or 'Goldsport') has a more pronounced yellow variegation.

Other good semi-evergreen varieties include:
A. **'Edward Goucher'** A compact shrub with purple-pink flowers from July to September. No scent.
A. floribunda has striking, long, pink-red flowers from June to July. Not scented.

There are also some deciduous abelias:
A. chinensis has scented, very pale pink flowers from July to August. Tender.
A. schumannii has lilac-pink flowers from June to September. Not scented.
A. triflora is the hardiest and most vigorous, but the scented flowers only appear in June.

Close-up of the flowers of Abelia x grandiflora

Abeliophyllum

Shape and size

			3m
			2m
			1m

5 years   10 years   At maturity

Position   Hardiness   Soil

MOST

Uses

Features calendar

Jan	Feb	Mar	Apr	May	June
✿	✿	✿			
July	Aug	Sept	Oct	Nov	Dec

Buying tips *You may have to buy from a specialist nursery. Plants may look weak and twiggy in the container but should improve once planted out.*

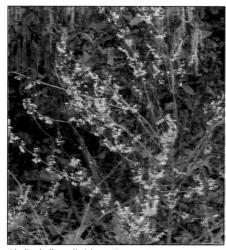

Abeliophyllum distichum 'Roseum'

Abeliophyllum distichum

Growing guide

Abeliophyllum is a very good alternative to forsythia but is harder to find. The winter flowers are the main attraction, but its slow growth and ability to thrive on most soils in sun or partial shade are further useful traits.

In January, tiny mauve flower buds clothe its bare branches. In early spring, they open into star-like white flowers and release a sweet, almond scent. The rest of the year, its twiggy, open habit and light green foliage make it a foil for summer flowers.

It could be incorporated into a border to extend the period of interest in winter. In cold areas, it would be worth training it against a south- or west-facing wall or fence to get the best flowering display. When grown as a wall shrub it can reach 2x2m (7x7ft).

Pruning

No routine pruning is required. Neglected bushes can become very tangled and flower poorly. To improve flowering, cut out one stem in three in spring after flowering. Remove the oldest shoots and the ones that produced the fewest flowers first.

Propagation

Take semi-ripe cuttings and root in a cold frame in summer. Alternatively, try hardwood cuttings in the open in autumn.

Troubleshooting

Generally trouble-free, although flowers may be damaged by hard frosts.

Which variety?

There is only one species **A. distichum**, although you may come across the variety **'Roseum'**, which has pink flowers.

Abutilon megapotamicum

Shape and size

3m
2m
1m

5 years   10 years   At maturity

Position   Hardiness   Soil

MOIST   DRAINED

Uses

Features calendar

Jan	Feb	Mar	Apr	May	June
			✿	✿	✿
July	Aug	Sept	Oct	Nov	Dec
✿	✿	✿			

Abutilon megapotamicum 'Variegatum'

Growing guide

Abutilons are graceful shrubs with showy flowers, but many are tender. They can suffer damage in cold weather and can be short-lived. You may find them as free-standing shrubs in mild areas, but more likely against a warm wall or in a conservatory.

A. megapotamicum has red and yellow lantern-shaped flowers from late spring to the autumn. The leaves are dark green but you may come across varieties with yellow and green variegated foliage. The stems can be trained against a south- or west-facing wall or fence. Tie in new shoots as they grow.

Pruning

Prune in mid-spring once new growth can be seen and any winter damage assessed. Get rid of any frost-damaged and dead shoots. If you need to keep it within bounds, clip back soft growth with shears (secateurs for *A. vitifolium*).

Propagation

Many abutilons are short-lived but they do grow quickly from cuttings or seed. Take softwood cuttings in early summer.

Troubleshooting

Apart from not being reliably hardy, you may find growth is straggly. If so, clip in spring to encourage a bushier appearance. The soft leaves of abutilons are attractive to whitefly, spider mites and aphids. Mealy bug and scale insects can also be a problem.

Which variety?

 A. megapotamicum and its variegated form are among the hardiest. Other abutilons worth trying outdoors in mild areas include:

A. x suntense An upright,

Abutilon megapotamicum flowers

deciduous bush, which can reach up to 4.5m (15ft). It has large, vine-like leaves covered in white hairs and single, blue or mauve hollyhock-type flowers in summer. The variety **'Jermyns'**, with deep mauve flowers is worth looking out for.

A. vitifolium This is a parent of *A. x suntense* and is similar, though it is semi-evergreen and reaches 3x2m (10x7ft) after five years. It has mauve flowers from May to July which combine well with its grey-green foliage. It is quick-growing but short-lived. Fortunately, hardwood cuttings strike easily in autumn or it can be grown from seed. Good varieties include **'Veronica Tennant'** (with deeper mauve flowers) and **'Tennant's White'** (with white flowers).

> ***Buying tips*** *Check that the plants have been hardened off before planting out, and inspect the leaves closely for pests. Best bought in late spring so plants can get established by winter.*

Acanthopanax
(Eleutherococcus)

Shape and size

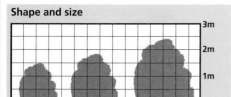

3m
2m
1m

5 years | 10 years | At maturity

Position   Hardiness   Soil

MOST

Uses

Features calendar

Jan	Feb	Mar	Apr	May	June
July	Aug	Sept	Oct	Nov	Dec

Buying tips *The green form is quite rare, though many shrub specialists stock the variegated variety. Look for plants with bright, unblemished leaves and at least three or four strong stems.*

A young plant of Acanthopanax sieboldianus 'Variegatus'

Growing guide

Acanthopanax sieboldianus is an attractive foliage shrub belonging to the same family as *Fatsia japonica*. Like its relative, it adds a lush effect to small or town gardens. The pale green leaves have five lobes with a small curved thorn at the base. In autumn, these turn yellow. It rarely flowers and fruits.

It is hardier than it looks and would do well in a partially shaded spot or could be grown in a container.

Pruning

No pruning is necessary, but you can cut hard back in spring to encourage larger and more attractive new leaves. Feed with a general fertiliser after pruning.

Propagation

Take softwood cuttings in early summer, or semi-ripe cuttings in late summer and root in a cold frame. It is also possible to divide a natural layer in spring or take root cuttings over winter.

Troubleshooting

Generally trouble-free.

Which variety?

There is an attractive variegated variety **'Variegatus'** with creamy-white markings. To maintain a good variegation, it needs to be planted in a sunny spot.

Acer japonicum 'Aureum'
(Acer shirasawanum aureum)

Shape and size

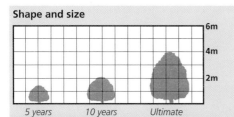

5 years	10 years	Ultimate

6m
4m
2m

Position   Hardiness

Soil

ACID   NEUTRAL   MOIST

Uses

Features calendar

Jan	Feb	Mar	Apr	May	June
July	Aug	Sept	Oct	Nov	Dec

Acer japonicum 'Aureum'

Acer japonicum 'Vitifolium' just starting to change into its autumn colours

Growing guide

The *A. japonicum* varieties tend to have large leaves that are more rounded in outline than *A. palmatum* varieties. Their overall appearance is bolder and their flowers more conspicuous than the delicate appearance of the *A. palmatum* varieties.

A. japonicum 'Aureum' will add dramatic colour to the garden which changes with the season. When the leaves emerge in spring, they are pale yellow. They then deepen to a rich gold in summer. In autumn, the leaves turn orange with red and purple tones. It is slow to establish, so position with care. The ideal site is somewhere that is partially shaded and sheltered from cold winds and scorching sun. The soil should be rich and well-mulched. Providing the conditions are right, place them in a prominent position.

Pruning
None required.

Propagation
Easy to raise from seed, although the seedlings may be nothing like the parent. Harvest before the seeds turn brown and dry. Sow immediately (you do not need to remove the wings). Leave outside for the winter (protect from mice with wire mesh). Transfer to a cold frame in spring. Pot on and plant out the autumn of the second year. Alternatively, sow in pots in spring and keep in the fridge for six to eight weeks.

Troubleshooting
Pink or reddish-orange spots (coral spot) can appear on diseased or damaged wood. Cut out the affected wood. Unnoticed aphid attacks can spoil the foliage.

Which variety?

A. japonicum **'Aureum'** is a widely available variety in garden centres and can be recommended.

A. japonicum **'Aconitifolium'** ('Laciniatum') is faster growing, reaching 2.4m (8ft) in ten years. The leaves are deeply divided and turn from green to scarlet in autumn.

A. japonicum **'Vitifolium'** has broad, fan-shaped leaves, turning from green to shades of orange and purple in autumn. It grows to the same size as 'Aconitifolium'.

Acer palmatum

Shape and size

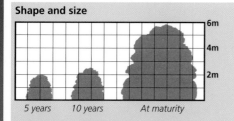

5 years	10 years	At maturity

6m
4m
2m

Position   Hardiness

Soil

ACID   NEUTRAL   MOIST

Uses

Features calendar

Jan	Feb	Mar	Apr	May	June
			🍃	🍃	

July	Aug	Sept	Oct	Nov	Dec
		🍃	🍃		

Acer palmatum 'Osakazuki'

Buying tips

Choose a named variety rather than the parent A. palmatum. Some varieties are grafted, so check the graft has knitted together firmly.

Autumn is a good time to buy as you can select the ones with the best colour.

Acer palmatum 'Sango-kaku' in autumn

Growing guide

The palmate group contains many varieties, most selected for their leaf colour. The soft foliage is vulnerable to late frosts and to sun scorch in summer. Choose a sheltered location, but one where they can act as a focal point.

'Atropurpureum' is a strong-growing upright variety. It is usually grown from seed so individual plants can vary. The leaves generally open to a bright red and this can be seen at its best when backlit by the sun. The bright red soon fades to a duller purple-red or bronze.

Some varieties turn green by mid-summer, but all have good autumn colours.

Pruning

None required.

Propagation

Easy to raise from seed, although there is no guarantee that the seedlings will be like the parent. See page 23 for sowing details.

Troubleshooting

Pink or reddish-orange spots (coral spot) can appear on diseased or damaged wood. Cut out the affected wood. Watch out for aphids on the new leaves. Treat with an insecticide if seen.

Which variety?

There are very many varieties, differing mainly in size and leaf colour. Garden centres only offer a limited selection.

'Atropurpureum' is widely available, but it is worth looking out for the selected form **'Bloodgood'**. This is smaller with a richer, longer-lasting autumn colour.
'Osakazuki' has leaves that turn a dazzling scarlet in autumn. In summer, the leaves are a fresh green and the scarlet fruits hang in bunches below.
'Sango-kaku' ('Senkaki') has pinkish-green foliage that turns orange-yellow in autumn. Its coloured stems are an added attraction in winter.

Acer palmatum 'Dissectum'

Shape and size

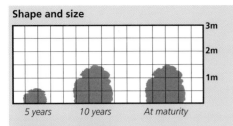

3m
2m
1m

5 years | 10 years | At maturity

Position Hardiness

Soil

ACID | NEUTRAL | MOIST

Uses

Features calendar

Jan	Feb	Mar	Apr	May	June
			🍃	🍃	

July	Aug	Sept	Oct	Nov	Dec
		🍃	🍃		

Acer palmatum 'Dissectum'

Buying tips *It is a good idea to select your tree in October when the autumn colour is at its best. It is worth paying extra for a grafted tree as it will make a better specimen than a seed-raised one.*

Acer palmatum 'Dissectum Ornatum'

Growing guide

The 'Dissectum' group has leaves which are more deeply and intricately divided than the parent species. Most have a semi-pendulous habit and slowly form low hummocks of foliage. As well as superb autumnal tints, the tracery of twigs in winter has its own beauty. They make exquisite small shrubs.

To do well, they need a site where they will get protection from late frosts, wind and sun scorch. An ideal position would be somewhere shaded during the middle of the day but where the evening sun can highlight their colouring. Enrich the soil with plenty of organic matter before planting and mulch with bark chippings every spring.

Pruning

None required.

Propagation

Easy to raise from seed although there is no guarantee that the seedlings will be like the parents. See page 23 for sowing details.

Troubleshooting

Squirrels can devastate them. Prune out any minor attacks of coral spot. Watch out for aphids on the new leaves. Treat with an insecticide if seen. The new foliage is very vulnerable to frost damage when the buds first open. Protect plants with a double layer of horticultural fleece if late frosts are forecast.

Which variety?

The varieties below are described according to their summer foliage colour. All turn gold to orange in the autumn.

'Dissectum Atropurpureum' Mid-purple.
'Dissectum Crimson Queen' Deep purple with very dissected leaves.
'Dissectum Garnet' Dark purple.
'Dissectum Viridis' Fresh green.
'Dissectum Ornatum' Bronze.

Plants raised from seed may vary in colour.

Amelanchier

Shape and size

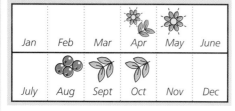

| 5 years | 10 years | At maturity |

Position   Hardiness   Soil

MOST

Uses

Features calendar

Jan	Feb	Mar	Apr	May	June
July	Aug	Sept	Oct	Nov	Dec

Buying tips *There is often confusion between the naming of* A. canadensis, A. lamarckii *and* A. laevis *when these shrubs are sold. All are similar but the true A.canadensis has young leaves that are woolly on both sides.*

Amelanchier flowers

Growing guide

This shrub gives a spectacular display in both spring and autumn, yet it is very easy to grow on almost any soil or in any position, including exposed sites. It is very fast-growing, reaching 2m (7ft) in height and spread after only three to five years, so is best for a medium or large garden or used as a screen.

In spring, the shrub is covered in clouds of white flowers. The young foliage is copper-coloured, becoming a fresh green once the leaves open fully. In autumn, the foliage turns a brilliant, rich orange and red. In some years there maybe reddish fruits, but these are sweet and birds often take them.

Many vigorous shoots emerge from near ground level, so an attractive rounded shape is produced. If all the side branches are removed during the first few years, it can be trained to form a small tree. If you buy an amelanchier as a tree, remove any shoots that form on the trunk.

Pruning

No routine pruning is required. Any weak or crowded shoots can be removed every few years to maintain an open, balanced appearance. The best time to do this is after flowering in the spring.

Propagation

Remove suckers from the base of the shrub or layer shoots near the ground by pegging them down in spring. They should root by autumn.

Troubleshooting

Generally trouble-free. If it gets too large, the whole shrub can be cut hard back in spring. Fireblight can cause blackening and shrivelling on the flowers. Prune out affected shoots and dig up and burn badly infected plants.

Which variety?

Amelanchier canadensis (*A. lamarckii* is indistinguishable) is the best form. You may also come across a compact variety called **'Ballerina'**.

Amelanchier as a garden shrub in autumn colour

Aralia elata
(A. chinensis)

Shape and size

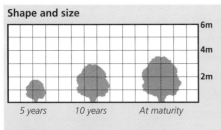

			6m
			4m
			2m
5 years	10 years	At maturity	

Position　Hardiness　Soil

MOIST

Uses

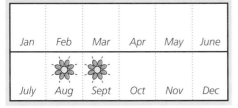

Features calendar

Jan	Feb	Mar	Apr	May	June
July	Aug	Sept	Oct	Nov	Dec

Flowers of Aralia elata

Aralia elata 'Variegata'

Growing guide

This striking shrub from Japan will add an oriental feel to your garden. Aralias make large shrubs or small trees; their size often depends on growing conditions. Thick, spiny stems carry huge leaves up to 0.9m (3ft) in length. It is mainly grown for its shape and leaves, but the white flowers are an attractive feature in late summer and early autumn.

The species is very tolerant of wind but the leaves of the variegated varieties can be ruined by cold winds. If planting these in cold areas, they will need shelter.

To make the most of their architectural shape, use them as focal points in a shrub border or as a specimen plant in a lawn.

Pruning

Do not prune hard unless absolutely necessary as this can stimulate suckering around the base. However, remove any diseased or damaged stems as soon as these are noticed.

Propagation

The species can by raised from seed or a rooted sucker can be transplanted. Variegated forms can only be propagated by grafting on to the species rootstock.

Troubleshooting

Variegated aralias are grafted on to a rootstock of the green-leaved species. Shoots from the rootstock will be green and more vigorous than that of the variegated variety and may dominate the plant. Remove these as soon as they are seen.

Which variety?

The variegated forms are more attractive, but are slightly less hardy.

'Aureovariegata' has golden variegated foliage.
'Variegata' ('Albomarginata') has yellowish-white margins, and sometimes blotching, to the leaves.

Arctostaphylos uva-ursi

Shape and size

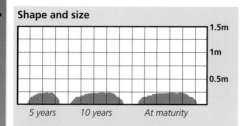

1.5m
1m
0.5m

5 years   10 years   At maturity

Position   Hardiness

Soil

ACID   DRAINED

Uses

Features calendar

Jan	Feb	Mar	Apr	May	June
July	Aug	Sept	Oct	Nov	Dec

Growing guide

This prostrate shrub is a native plant in much of the cooler parts of the northern hemisphere. It is worth considering as a garden plant only if you have a sunny site on an acid soil. It would be ideal for a lime-free, sandy bank.

It can form a useful, evergreen ground cover. Growth is fairly slow, so plant several 0.5m (1½ft) apart for complete cover in three years. In the meantime, mulch between the plants to keep the weeds down.

Single specimens could be grouped together with other acid-loving plants such as azaleas, so long as the site is sunny. In summer, white, bell-shaped flowers nestle in the bright green leaves and these are followed by red berries.

Pruning

Once well-established, A. uva-ursi may need cutting back to keep its spread in check. It is worth taking the time to trim the shoots with secateurs rather than shears. The latter can leave a straight edge which detracts from its appearance.

Propagation

The easiest method is to remove the naturally rooting layers from the parent plant. Another option is to take softwood cuttings in early summer and strike them in a peat-based compost.

Troubleshooting

Generally trouble-free once established.

Which variety?

You are most likely to come across A. uva-ursi. Selected forms and other species are stocked by only a few specialist nurseries.

Buying tips *Widely available from specialist nurseries, but rarely found at garden centres. Look for a large plant that you can divide up into a number of smaller plants.*

Arctostaphylos uva-ursi

Aucuba japonica

Shape and size

		6m
		4m
		2m

5 years   10 years   At maturity

Position

Hardiness

Soil

MOST

Uses

Features calendar

Jan	Feb	Mar	Apr	May	June
July	Aug	Sept	Oct	Nov	Dec

Features in Sept, Oct, Nov, Dec

__Buying tips__ Small plants can be used in window boxes for a year before planting in the garden. Medium-sized shrubs are best for planting in the garden. Look for bright, healthy leaves.

Aucuba japonica 'Picturata'

Aucuba japonica 'Variegata'

Growing guide

All aucubas have an incredible tolerance of poor growing conditions so are ideal for adding year-round colour to dry shady spots. Not only can they survive competition from hedges and conifers, but they also cope well with traffic fumes. The flowers are insignificant; the colour comes from the evergreen, variegated leaves.

Red berries will be produced on female plants if both sexes are growing nearby. There is often confusion about the sex of varieties and some of those often described as male are females that rarely berry.

Pruning

You can do as you please with aucubas. They can be left to grow unpruned, or pruned hard in mid-spring to keep them the required size or they can be clipped into a shape. If grown as a hedge, trim in mid- or late summer. Use secateurs not shears, otherwise the cut leaves will turn brown and look unsightly.

Propagation

Take cuttings from the new shoots in mid- to late summer or hardwood cuttings in the autumn.

Troubleshooting

Generally trouble-free.

Which variety?

A. japonica has plain foliage, but there are many varieties with spotted, blotched and variegated leaves. Widely available ones include:
'Crotonifolia' Narrow, small spots. Female, but often considered male as it rarely berries.
'Maculata' ('Variegata') Large spots and blotches. Female.

Newer varieties that you may come across include:
'Picturata' Yellow blotches on dark green leaves. Male.
'Nana Rotundifolia' Low-growing with shiny green leaves. Female.
'Rozannie' Variegated. New bisexual variety, producing berries on its own.

Azaleas, deciduous

Shape and size

3m
2m
1m

5 years   10 years   At maturity

Position   Hardiness   Soil

ACID   MOIST

Uses

Features calendar

Jan	Feb	Mar	Apr	May	June
				✿	
July	Aug	Sept	Oct	Nov	Dec
		🍃	🍃		

Buying tips Look for a good shape, strong graft union and healthy green leaves. Avoid plants with any yellowing leaves or roots growing through the container. Avoid plants that have been grown in very dry compost.

'Lapwing'

Azalea mollis hybrids mostly have orange flowers

Growing guide

Deciduous azaleas have a more open, bushy habit and tend to be larger than the evergreen azaleas. They are all hardy and many have a bonus of good autumn colour or fragrant flowers.

Azaleas are woodland plants so like the shade of other plants but the deciduous azaleas will thrive in the sun. They have shallow roots and resent deep planting. Cover the top of the rootball with leafmould. Firm gently after planting, but don't stamp down or the roots may be damaged.

Remove dead flower heads if practical. Grip the seed head between finger and thumb and snap off by bending sideways, taking care not to damage new shoots sprouting from the base of the flower stem.

Pruning

Not required. Many deciduous azaleas are grafted and sometimes throw up suckers. Pull off the suckers at their point of origin.

Propagation

Layer branches in July. Wound or nick the stem and treat with a rooting hormone before pegging down. Remove any flowers that form in the spring and detach the rooted layer the following autumn.

Troubleshooting

Leaf hoppers may bore holes in flowers to lay their eggs. This can allow entry to the bud blast fungus, which causes the buds to remain hard and brown. Remove and destroy damaged buds when seen. Pale, waxy swellings on the leaves are due to azalea gall. Pick off the galls before they turn white, and treat with a fungicide.

'Gibraltar'

Which variety?

R. luteum is very hardy and reliable with yellow flowers, a good scent and autumn colour. There are also many hybrids:

GHENT HYBRIDS

Among the best for fragrance and autumn colour. The flowers are small but elegant and appear late, thus missing the frosts. Widely available examples include:
'Daviesii' Cream-white with yellow.
'Nancy Waterer' Golden-yellow, highly scented.
'Narcissiflora' Pale yellow, double, scented.
'Unique' Yellowish-orange.

KNAPHILL AND EXBURY HYBRIDS

Have big flowers in a wide range of colours. Young foliage is often a bronze colour. All are hardy. Widely available examples include:

'Gibraltar' Orange, semi-double.
'Homebush' Pink, scented.
'Lapwing' Yellow with a pink flush, scented.
'Whitethroat' White, double.

MOLLIS HYBRIDS

These have large orange or red flowers which appear in early May before their leaves. They are hardy, but the flowers are at risk from late frosts. Good autumn colour. Widely available examples include:
'Dr M Oosthoek' Reddish-orange.
'Spek's Orange' Pale orange.

OCCIDENTALE HYBRIDS

These tend to flower late and are a good choice if you like soft colours and scented flowers. Widely available examples include:`
'Exquisitum' Pale pink with an orange flush.
'Irene Koster' Pink, highly scented.

Mollis hybrid in autumn colour

Azaleas, evergreen

Shape and size

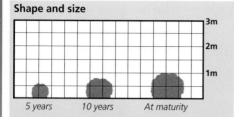

			3m
			2m
			1m
5 years	10 years	At maturity	

Position Hardiness Soil

ACID   MOIST

Uses

Features calendar

Jan	Feb	Mar	Apr	May	June
July	Aug	Sept	Oct	Nov	Dec

Buying tips *Look for a good shape and healthy green leaves. Avoid plants with yellowing leaves or roots growing through the container. Avoid plants grown in dry compost.*

'Mother's Day'

'Hino-mayo'

Growing guide

Evergreen azaleas tend to have a compact habit covered with a mass of flowers. They lack the strong fragrance of the deciduous types and some are much hardier than others.

Orange flowers can fade in the sun, so they need some light shade. A good position is under deciduous, deep-rooted trees such as maples and dogwoods. In the north, where the sun is less strong, they may need a sunnier site to ensure the flowers open well and the wood is ripened. Many will thrive in full sun, if their roots are kept moist.

Evergreen azaleas are ideal in containers if you can keep them watered. Lime-free composts are available, but peat-based multipurpose is sufficiently acidic for their needs. In hard-water areas, use rain water. Alternatively, mix a tea bag or a teaspoonful of aluminium sulphate in 10 litres of water and apply this every three or four weeks to counteract the build-up of alkaline salts in the compost.

Pruning

No pruning is required, but untidy shoots can be cut back to just above the next cluster of buds in early spring.

Propagation

Propagation is slow, so is only for the dedicated gardener. Take cuttings in mid-summer. Root in an open rooting mix. Keep in a cold frame, once rooted pot on and grow on for two years before planting out in autumn.

Troubleshooting

See deciduous azaleas on page 30. Whitefly can also be a problem and you may need to use insecticide.

'Palestrina'

Which variety?

In the hundreds of varieties you are likely to come across the following types:

Kaempferi hybrids are taller and more upright than kurumes. Flowers are single and medium-sized. Generally better for colder areas than kurumes. Most have good autumn colour.
'Atlantica' Pale lilac.
'Fedora' Pale and dark pink.
'John Cairns' Dark orange.
'Orange Beauty' Soft orange.

Kurumes are slow-growing and compact, forming masses of small flowers. Most need the protection of a sheltered wall in cold areas.
'Addy Wery' Scarlet.
'Blaauw's Pink' Pink. Very hardy.
'Hatsugiri' Crimson-purple. Low-growing, 0.6x1.2m (2x4ft).

'Hino-crimson' Crimson.
'Hino-mayo' Bright pink.
'Mother's Day' Rose-red.
'Rosebud' Pink.

Vuyk hybrids have large flowers, often 5-8cm (2-3in) across, on small bushes. Generally hardy and reliable.
'Blue Danube' Blue-purple.
'Palestrina' White. One of the least hardy in this group.
'Vuyk's Rosyred' Red. Later flowering than most.

'Salmon's Leap'. This has attractive variegated leaves and deep pink flowers. Thought to be hardy but only recently introduced.

'Orange Beauty'

Azara dentata

Shape and size

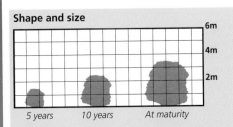

5 years   10 years   At maturity

Position

Hardiness

Soil

DRAINED

Uses

Features calendar

Jan	Feb	Mar	Apr	May	June
July	Aug	Sept	Oct	Nov	Dec

Buying tips *Fairly slow-growing, so it is worth getting a decent-sized specimen. Try nurseries specialising in conservatory plants.*

Close-up of the flowers of Azara serrata

Azara serrata and ceanothus enjoy the same conditions

Growing guide

Azaras are a group of South American plants. Although not widely available their evergreen foliage and yellow flowers make them worth considering.

A. serrata is fairly tender, so requires the protection of a warm wall in most areas. It will withstand frosts but may be killed if winter temperatures dip below -5°C (23°F) for long periods. The easiest way is to grow it as a free-standing bush in front of a wall, but it can also be fan-trained. Alternatively, plant it in a large tub and display it in the conservatory, where you'll benefit from the fragrance of the flowers.

The leaves are a dark, glossy green and make a good foil for the profusion of yellow flowers in June. On close inspection, you will find each flower is tiny, with showy stamens instead of petals.

Pruning

While azaras grown as bushes or small trees require no routine pruning, a specimen trained against a wall will require some tying in and pruning. Select about eight shoots close to the base and tie these to horizontal wires fixed to the wall. Aim for a fan shape. Side shoots will grow from this framework to cover the wall. To avoid the shrub becoming congested, prune back some of the side shoots to the original framework of branches each year in late spring.

Propagation

Take softwood cuttings in mid-summer.

Troubleshooting

Generally trouble-free.

Which variety?

For a bushy azara go for **A. serrata** or **A. dentata**, which is similar. You might also come across **A. microphylla**, which can reach 4.5m (15ft) high or more in mild areas and is considered to be hardier. The flowers appear on the undersides of the branches in March.

Berberis, deciduous

(e.g. Berberis thunbergii)

Shape and size

```
                                          3m
                                          2m
                                          1m
```
5 years   10 years   At maturity

Position   Hardiness   Soil

Uses

Features calendar

Jan	Feb	Mar	Apr	May	June
July	Aug	Sept	Oct	Nov	Dec

Buying tips   *Avoid plants that have dead shoots or leaves. Young plants are generally quick to establish and are a good buy. Choose one with at least four or five stems.*

Berberis thunbergii 'Dart's Red Lady'

Growing guide

All berberis are easy to grow, have thorns and pale yellow through to orange flowers. In addition, the deciduous ones have brilliant autumn leaf tints in hues of orange and scarlet. Particularly showy are varieties with coloured leaves and these need a sunny spot to develop their best colours. Berries (non-poisonous) are another outstanding feature that last well into the winter.

B. thunbergii and its varieties offer a wide choice of sizes, from 'Bagatelle', which grows only 30cm (1ft) high, to those that reach 1.8m (6ft) or more. The smaller ones could be used singly in a container or on a rock garden. Altogether, they can be utilised as an edging (plant 0.5m/1½ft apart) or ground cover. The large ones can add interest to borders or make impenetrable hedges (plant 0.8m/2½ft). There are upright varieties that would make good focal points in small gardens.

Pruning

No regular pruning is needed; just a light thinning or trimming as necessary. This can be carried out in winter after berrying. Drastic pruning, to improve the shape of an old plant say, is best done in February or March. Hedges can be clipped annually in autumn.

Propagation

Take cuttings from the new side shoots in early autumn. Remove the lower spines. Root in compost in a cold frame and cover with thin polythene, burying the sides.

Some (e.g. 'Atropurpurea') come true from seed. Sow ripe berries in pots of peat and sand and leave outdoors over winter. Cover the pot with wire mesh to keep mice out. Pot up the seedlings once they germinate in the spring.

Troubleshooting

Generally trouble-free, but can occasionally succumb to rust. Prune out infected growth and spray with a systemic fungicide.

Berberis thunbergii 'Atropurpurea Nana'

Which variety?

SMALL

(i.e. 0.6x0.6m/2x2ft after ten years and ultimately)

'Atropurpurea Nana' ('Crimson Pygmy', 'Little Favourite') Deep purple-red, red in autumn.

'Aurea' Lime-green, yellow in spring, orange-red in autumn. Best out of full sun to prevent scorching.

'Bagatelle' Similar to 'Atropurpurea Nana' but only half the size.

MEDIUM

(i.e.1.5x1.5m/5x5ft after ten years and up to1.8m/6ft ultimately)

'Atropurpurea' Red-purple, turning orange-red in autumn. One of the best for berries and hedging.

'Dart's Red Lady' Deep purple, turning red in autumn.

'Golden Ring' Purple leaves that develop a gold margin, turning red in autumn.

'Harlequin' Speckled cream and purple, turning crimson-pink in autumn.

'Red Chief' Purple-red, turning orange, red and purple in autumn. Red-purple stems add winter interest.

'Rose Glow' Purple with pink flecks.

UPRIGHT

(i.e.1.2x0.6m/4x2ft)

'Helmond Pillar' Dark purple, turning orange-red in autumn.

'Red Pillar' Purple-red, turning orange-red in autumn.

OTHERS

B. wilsoniae Grey-green foliage, turning pale orange in autumn. Berries are coral colour. Good for low hedging. 1.2x1.8m (4x6ft) after ten years.

Berberis, evergreen
(e.g. Berberis darwinii)

Shape and size

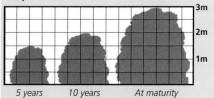

5 years	10 years	At maturity

3m
2m
1m

Position   Hardiness   Soil

MOST

Uses

Features calendar

Jan	Feb	Mar	Apr	May	June
			❀		

July	Aug	Sept	Oct	Nov	Dec

Berberis darwinii

Buying tips *For the best results, buy and plant evergreen berberis in September/October or in April/May. You may find bare-root evergreen berberis hedging on sale - this is best planted in the spring rather than the autumn.*

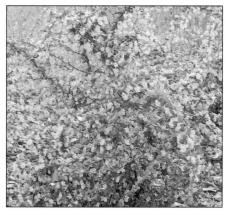

Berberis 'Goldilocks'

Growing guide

The evergreen types are grown for their year-round interest, provided by glossy, often dense, foliage in various shapes, sizes and shades of green. Some are notable spring-flowering shrubs.

B. darwinii is easy to find and grow. As an evergreen with the bonus of orange spring-flowers and purple-black autumn berries, it could be used in a large shrub border where its dark, glossy leaves would make a fine partner for the autumn colour of deciduous berberis. It can be planted as a tall, informal hedge (space plants 0.8m/2½ft apart). You can grow it in sun, but it is just as happy in shade. Consider it for those difficult situations such as against a north-facing wall or on a heavy clay soil in an exposed position. Cut branches are useful for indoor flower arrangements.

Pruning

No regular pruning is needed. They can be trimmed lightly after flowering. Overgrown specimens can be cut back in April, taking out one-third of the stems. They will cope with harder pruning, though this will reduce the number of flowers in the following year.

Propagation

Take softwood cuttings in early summer or hardwood cuttings in autumn. Root them in a cold frame.

Troubleshooting

Generally trouble-free.

Which variety?

B. darwinii is worth looking out for. **'Goldilocks'** is similar, but has larger flower clusters and fewer prickles. It grows up to 4.5m (15ft) high but can be kept to around 1.8m (6ft) by regular pruning.

Berberis x stenophylla

OTHERS
The following are similar in size or taller than *B. darwinii:*

B. julianae Tall, rather dull, plant, but some autumn colour and useful for screening.
B. linearifolia 'Orange King' Eye-catching, orange flowers. Good in moist shade. Can form suckers, which should be removed.
B. x stenophylla Yellow, double flowers make it a good spring-flowering shrub for shady borders. Can also be used as a hedge. There are many named varieties that are smaller than the parent.

SMALLER SHRUBS
(i.e. about 0.9x1.5m/3x5ft after ten years)

B. candidula Light green foliage. Good habit for ground cover, but sparse flowers and berries.
B. lologensis 'Apricot Queen' Like a dwarf *B. darwinii*, but not as hardy.
B. x stenophylla 'Claret Cascade' Purple-red branches, red buds, orange flowers.
B. x stenophylla 'Corallina Compacta' Very slow-growing, 30cm (1ft) high. Red buds and yellow flowers.
B. x stenophylla 'Crawley Gem' Dwarf, 0.6m (2ft). Red flowers, good berries.
B. x stenophylla 'Irwinii' Dwarf, 0.6m (2ft), with arching stems. Yellow flowers.
B. verruculosa Small, shiny leaves. Yellow, semi-double flowers.

Berberis lologensis 'Apricot Queen'

Buddleia (Buddleja)

(e.g. Buddleia davidii)

Shape and size

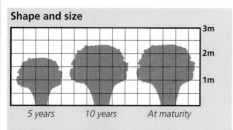

5 years   10 years   At maturity

Position   Hardiness   Soil

MOST   DRAINED

Uses

Features calendar

Jan	Feb	Mar	Apr	May	June
✿	✿	✿			
July	Aug	Sept	Oct	Nov	Dec

Buddleia davidii 'Royal Red'

Buying tips Eelworm can be present in plants on sale. Typical indicators of eelworm presence are: wilted lower leaves, stunted growth, puckered leaves or stunted flower spikes.

Buddleia davidii 'Harlequin'

Growing guide

This familiar shrub is quick-growing and the summer flowers will attract butterflies to your garden. It will grow almost anywhere, so long as the soil drains freely. However, unless you cut it back regularly it soon becomes an unruly shrub with small flowers all at the top of the plant. There are named varieties that offer a wide range of flower colour and are often more compact. There are also less widely grown buddleias that look quite different from the familiar butterfly bush.

With careful pruning and training, buddleias can make very attractive shrubs. *B. alternifolia* can be trained as a weeping standard to create a focal point in the border. The more tender ones can be wall-trained.

Pruning

Each spring (including the first spring after planting), cut back *B. davidii* to within 5cm (2in) of the old wood. Annual hard pruning will also benefit *B. crispa* and *B. fallowiana*, whereas *B.* 'Lochinch' and *B.* x *weyeriana* can be left unpruned until they becomes too large. With *B. alternifolia* and *B. globosa,* cut out a third of the stems after flowering, starting with the oldest.

Propagation

Take cuttings from the new shoots in summer and root in a pot covered with a polythene bag. Alternatively, take hardwood cuttings in November and root in the garden.

Troubleshooting

Stunted growth and malformed flower buds can be a sign of leaf and bud eelworm. A badly-infested plant should be destroyed. Ragged holes or tears in the leaves could be due to capsid bugs. Clearing away debris in the autumn to prevent them overwintering should control them. Otherwise, spray with an insecticide next spring.

Buddleia x 'Lochinch'

Which variety?

It is best to buy a named variety of *B. davidii*. The following are all recommended:

'Black Knight' Has the darkest purple flowers.

'Dartmoor' Long spikes of purplish-red flowers.

'Empire Blue' Violet-blue flowers with orange eye.

'Harlequin' Variegated leaves, red-purple flowers.

'Lochinch' Cross between *B. davidii* and *B. fallowiana*. Compact with grey, downy leaves. Lavender flowers with orange eye.

'Nanho Blue' Deep blue flowers.

'Pink Delight' Bright pink flowers.

'Royal Red' Purple-red flowers.

'White Profusion' White flowers.

OTHER BUDDLEIAS

B. alternifolia Lilac flowers along its arching stems. **'Argentea'** has a silvery sheen to its leaves. 3m (10ft) after ten years.

B. crispa White-felty leaves, lilac flowers in late summer. Needs winter protection. 3m (10ft) after ten years.

B. fallowiana 'Alba' Similar to *B. crispa*, but has white flowers. 1.8m (6ft) after ten years.

B. globosa Semi-evergreen with orange, ball-shaped flowers in May and June. 3m (10ft) after ten years.

***B. x weyeriana* 'Golden Glow'** Golden yellow, ball-shaped flowers from August to September. Neater habit than *B. globosa*. 2.4m (8ft) after ten years. **'Sungold'** is similar.

Buddleia x weyeriana 'Sungold'

Bupleurum fruticosum

Shape and size

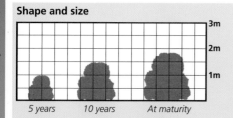

5 years	10 years	At maturity

Position   Hardiness   Soil

DRAINED

Uses

Features calendar

Jan	Feb	Mar	Apr	May	June
✿	✿	✿			
July	Aug	Sept	Oct	Nov	Dec

Buying tips *Fairly slow-growing so look for a large, bushy plant. Most likely to be sold in mild areas of the country.*

Close-up of the flowers

Bupleurum fruticosum in summer

Growing guide

A useful shrub for mild, seaside locations. Several could be planted to create an informal screen. Alternatively, use it in a border where its subtle colouring and soft shape could provide a contrast with sword-shaped leaves, such as those of phormiums. In colder areas, it is best grown as a wall shrub.

In a sunny position, it will form a neat, rounded bush. It will tolerate shade but it is likely to become very leggy. Bupleurum prefers a well-drained soil and is a good choice for chalky soils.

The evergreen foliage is glossy green with a silver underside. The green-yellow balls of flowers are not dramatic, but they last from summer to autumn and the brown seedheads add winter interest.

After planting, give some extra protection, especially on exposed sites, until the plant is established. Once established, it should prove to be moderately hardy.

Pruning

No routine pruning is required, but if desired it can be clipped to shape in spring. To encourage new growth on established bushes, cut out one stem in three.

When grown as a wall shrub, it can become a tangled mass of shoots. To regenerate it, cut down to within 5-10cm (2-4in) of the ground in spring. You will lose one season's flowers but there should be plenty of new growth by the autumn.

Propagation

Take softwood cuttings in early summer and root in a cold frame. It can also be raised from seed.

Troubleshooting

Generally trouble-free.

Which variety?

B. fruticosum is the only species hardy enough to grow permanently outside in Britain.

Buxus sempervirens varieties

Shape and size

	9m
	6m
	3m

5 years   10 years   At maturity

Position

Hardiness   Soil

MOST

Uses

Features calendar

Jan	Feb	Mar	Apr	May	June
July	Aug	Sept	Oct	Nov	Dec

Buying tips *Ready-clipped shapes are very expensive, so it is worth having a go at training your own. If you want a lot for edging, buying young plants in bulk from a specialist nursery will be a lot cheaper than buying at garden centres.*

Edging of Buxus sempervirens 'Suffruticosa'

Buxus sempervirens 'Elegantissima'

Growing guide

A useful shrub for adding structure or formality to the garden, either as an edging or as clipped specimens. It is tolerant of most positions, but it is important to choose a variety that has an appropriate growth rate for the purpose you have in mind.

To edge a small border, look for 'Suffruticosa', 'Blauer Heinz' or 'Elegantissima'. A row of young plants 10cm (4in) high, spaced 10-15cm (4-6in) apart will form a smooth edge in a couple of years.

The more vigorous, cheaper common box can be used for large-scale edging or for hedging – young plants, around 30cm (12in) tall, planted 30cm (12in) apart will make a 0.6m (2ft) high boundary after three to four years.

All box will thrive in containers, where they make good specimens if they are clipped into shapes. They will survive if you forget to water them occasionally, but after prolonged nelect they will start to turn yellow and lose some leaves.

Pruning

Trim once a year, in July for sharp outlines; or just before growth begins in the spring to preserve the new foliage.

Propagation

Box is very easy to propagate from semi-ripe cuttings or hardwood cuttings in August or September. Insert into a sheltered shady border with well-drained soil. They should be ready to lift by June.

Troubleshooting

Box suckers make leaves sticky and cupped like Brussels sprouts. Control with a systemic insecticide in early May and again in June.

Which variety?

Common box is cheap and so is useful for large-scale edging e.g. alongside a drive or path. On a small-scale, use one of the following more compact varieties: **'Suffruticosa'** has a very dense growth, reaching 20x15cm (8x6in) after five years. **'Blauer Heinz'** is similar, but less widely available. Its large, blue-green leaves are a good foil for flowers. **'Elegantissima'** is an elegant, flame-shaped bush, growing 20x20cm (8x8in) after five years.The leaves have white edges but may revert to green if clipped.

You may come across variegated box in a range of different names. These can be useful for brightening up dull corners but shade and clipping will remove the best coloured shoots.

Callicarpa bodinieri 'Profusion'

Shape and size

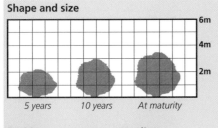

5 years   10 years   At maturity

Position

Hardiness

Soil

ACID   NEUTRAL   DRAINED

Uses

Features calendar

Jan	Feb	Mar	Apr	May	June
July	Aug	Sept	Oct	Nov	Dec

The striking berries of Callicarpa bodinieri 'Profusion'

Buying tips Buy 'Profusion' as it will produce berries prolifically when planted on its own.

Callicarpa viewed from a distance

Growing guide

The striking feature of this plant is the violet berries, which can be seen at their best once the pink purple autumn leaves have fallen. Cut branches make interesting flower-arranging material.

It is fairly tolerant, although if the soil is very alkaline the leaves may suffer from chlorosis. However, think twice before including it if you are short of space. It needs a fair bit of room and it does not have much to offer for much of the year as its flowers are insignificant.

Pruning

Pruning is not usually needed. When young, it has a twiggy, upright shape and shoots freely from the base. With age the branches become more horizontal and if any of these spoil the shape they can be removed in spring.

Propagation

Take softwood cuttings in summer. Root in a pot covered with a polythene bag. Plant out in a sheltered position in the autumn.

Troubleshooting

Generally trouble-free, although the species needs several plants growing together to get a good display of berries.

Which variety?

'Profusion' has the largest most reliable berries and is widely available at garden centres.

Callistemon citrinus

Shape and size

			3m
			2m
			1m
5 years	10 years	At maturity	

Position   Hardiness   Soil

ACID   DRAINED

Uses

Features calendar

Jan	Feb	Mar	Apr	May	June
❀	❀				
July	Aug	Sept	Oct	Nov	Dec

Buying tips *You will probably have to go to a specialist.*

Callistemon subulatus

Callistemon citrinus

Growing guide

Most callistemons are grown as conservatory plants in this country, but there are a few species worth considering for outdoors. For the best results, you need a sunny, sheltered spot against a south- or south-west facing wall. They do well in mild, coastal areas, growing quickly to form a wide-spreading shrub.

C. citrinus is quite hardy and could be grown in a large tub of peat-based compost and brought in over the winter. The eye-catching feature is the distinctive bottle brush flowers, but the leaves also emit a lemon scent when crushed.

Pruning

Any pruning is likely to reduce flowering, as the flowers are produced at the ends of the shoots. However, an old, congested specimen can benefit from having one or two of the oldest shoots removed so the shrub can regenerate from the base.

Propagation

From seed or softwood cuttings taken in late spring or early summer.

Troubleshooting

Generally trouble-free.

Which variety?

You are most likely to come across *C. citrinus* or its variety **'Splendens'** which is not quite as big and has showier flowers. There are hardier species such as *C. rigidus* with red flowers and very stiff leaves. Also, some species have different coloured flowers; those of *C. linearis* have a greenish tinge, while *C. salignus* and *C. sieberi* have creamy-coloured bottle brushes.

Calluna vulgaris

Shape and size

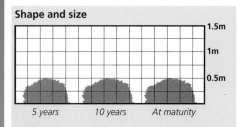

			1.5m
			1m
			0.5m

5 years   *10 years*   *At maturity*

Position   Hardiness

Soil

ACID   MOIST   DRAINED

Uses

Features calendar

Jan	Feb	Mar	Apr	May	June
	✿	✿	🍂		
July	Aug	Sept	Oct	Nov	Dec

Calluna vulgaris 'Peter Sparkes'

Calluna vulgaris 'Gold Haze' with Erica vagans varieties in the background

Growing guide

The common heather or ling grows wild in many parts of Britain. The garden varieties vary from low and spreading, neat hummocks to tall, upright ones. The leaves are tiny, like overlapping scales, quite distinct from the 'needles' of *Erica* species.

Calluna vulgaris varieties flower in summer, but their evergreen foliage, which is brightly-coloured in some varieties, extends their interest through the year. Some varieties even develop leaf tints in autumn and winter. If your soil is acid, they can be grown as ground cover, planted 30-40cm (12-15in) apart. They also make attractive flowering shrubs for rock gardens or tubs.

Calluna vulgaris varieties require a pH6.5 or below; the soil should also be moist but well-drained. A sunny site is needed for the best flowering and foliage displays.

Plant deeply, so that the rootball is covered and the lower branches rest on the soil. Keep the weeds down and do not let the plants dry out.

Pruning

Trim with shears after flowering or in early spring before new growth appears. Cut out any dead, damaged or straggly branches.

Propagation

There are many ways of propagating heathers. Layering is the simplest and can be done at any time of the year. Separate the young plants from the parent after nine months. Small cuttings can also be taken from early to mid-summer and rooted in pots of ericaceous compost.

Troubleshooting

An unsuitable soil is the cause of most problems. If waterlogged, the stems can die back and the roots rot. A raised bed about 30cm (12in) filled with 50:50 peat and soil could be the answer if your soil gets waterlogged in winter.

Heathers can dry out in sandy or compacted soil. Dig in well-rotted organic matter (e.g. composted bark, but not mushroom compost or animal manure) and mulch after planting.

Calluna vulgaris 'County Wicklow'

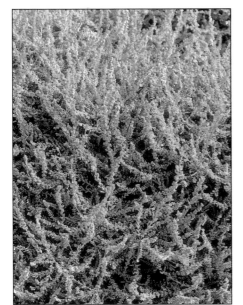

Calluna vulgaris 'Wickwar Flame'

Which variety?

There are hundreds of varieties; the following is a selection of the most widely available.

YELLOW FOLIAGE DEEPENING TO RED IN WINTER:
'Beoley Gold' White flowers.
'Blazeaway' Lilac flowers.
'Gold Haze' White flowers.
'Golden Carpet' A prostrate grower with lilac flowers.
'Golden Feather' Sparse, light pink flowers.
'Multicolor' Sparse, purple flowers.
'Robert Chapman' Lavender flowers.
'Sir John Charrington' Dark red flowers on compact plants.
'Sunset' Pink flowers.
'Wickwar Flame' Mauve flowers.

SILVER/GREY FOLIAGE:
'Silver Knight' Woolly leaves. Pink-mauve flowers.
'Silver Queen' Lavender flowers. Vigorous and spreading.
'Sister Anne' Low-growing with woolly leaves and pink flowers.

SHOOT TIPS COLOURED IN SPRING:
'Spring Cream' Cream shoot tips. White flowers.
'Spring Glow' Red and pink shoot tips. Mauve flowers.
'Spring Torch' Pink-red shoot tips. Mauve flowers.
'Winter Chocolate' Cream shoot tips. Purple-pink flowers.

FLOWERS:
'County Wicklow' Compact with shell-pink flowers.
'Darkness' Crimson flowers on upright plants.
'Elsie Purnell' Lavender flowers on long spikes; good for cutting.
'H E Beale' Bright, rose-pink flowers on 0.6m (2ft) tall plants.
'Kinlochruel' White flowers on compact plants.
'Tib' Lilac-pink flowers on compact plants.
'Peter Sparkes' Rose-pink flowers on long spikes; good for cutting and drying.

Camellia

Shape and size

3m
2m
1m

5 years | 10 years | At maturity

Position   Hardiness   Soil

ACID   DRAINED

Uses

Features calendar

Jan	Feb	Mar	Apr	May	June
	✿	✿	✿		
July	Aug	Sept	Oct	Nov	Dec

Camellia x williamsii 'Anticipation'

Camellia x williamsii 'Donation'

Growing guide

At their best, camellias make beautiful spring shrubs with showy blooms against dark, glossy leaves. Unfortunately, the early spring buds are often damaged by icy winds followed by early morning sun. So although the plants are hardy, the buds may need protection.

The ideal conditions for camellias are a well-drained, acidic soil with plenty of shelter. In the South, they do best in light shade; among other acid-loving shrubs, for example. In the North, they need a sunny but sheltered spot to produce flower buds. Those with long, arching branches like 'J C Williams' make good wall shrubs. A west-facing wall would be a good spot.

Luckily for those who have not got an acidic soil, camellias do well in containers. To get the best flowers, keep slightly pot-bound. Feed regularly from March until June with a dilute liquid feed. In July, switch to a high potash feed, such as a tomato feed, then stop feeding in August. Water often, particularly from July to October when the buds are forming. Use rainwater when possible. If you can, move under cover in severe weather.

Pruning

To keep them neat, prune back straggly branches or unwanted growth to old wood in winter or spring. Deadhead regularly if the flowers do not drop naturally.

Propagation

The easiest option is to layer plants in early spring; they should root by the autumn.

Troubleshooting

Yellowing leaves usually indicate there is too much lime in the soil, but on an acidic soil it could be due to drought. Sooty leaves are due to a mould colonising the sticky secretions left by scale insects or aphids. Bud drop is a sign that the soil was too dry in August and September, when the buds were forming.

Camellia x williamsii 'Debbie'

Which variety?

C. japonica varieties need plenty of sun to promote flower buds and, although perfectly hardy, they tend to put on a poorer display in the North. Easier to please are the *C. x williamsii* varieties as these need less sun to flower. They also shed their dead petals naturally, so do not require deadheading.

Flowering times vary depending on the weather and location and can be up to two months later in the North, or in some years.

C. japonica varieties:
'Adolphe Audusson' Bright red, semi-double, March to April.
'Contessa Lavinia Maggi' Pink with white stripes, double, March to May.
'Elegans' peach-pink anemone March to May.

C. x williamsii varieties:
'Anticipation' Crimson, peony-shaped, March to May.
'Debbie' Deep-rose, pink peony-shaped, February to April.
'Donation' Light pink, semi-double, March to May.
'J C Williams' Rose-pink, single, March to May.
'Leonard Messel' apricot-pink, peony-shaped, February to April.
'Saint Ewe' Large, rose-pink, single, February to March.

New hybrids which are worth looking out for include:
'Jury's Yellow' The nearest yet to a yellow-flowered camellia.
'Les Jury' Has a reddish tinge to the leaves.

Camellia japonica 'Elegans Splendour'

Buying tips You are likely to get the best choice just before Easter. Look for plants with a strong main stem and plenty of side shoots and flower buds. The leaves should be clean, glossy and dark green – not mottled or yellow. Avoid any plants that have lots of roots showing above the surface.

Camellia 'Jury's Yellow'

Caragana

Shape and size

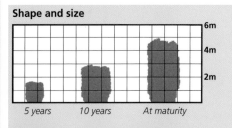

6m
4m
2m

5 years 10 years At maturity

Position

Hardiness

Soil

MOST

Uses

Features calendar

Jan	Feb	Mar	Apr	May	June
			✿	✿	✿
July	Aug	Sept	Oct	Nov	Dec

Buying tips *May not be easy to find except from specialist nurseries.*

Caragana arborescens

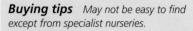

Caragana arborescens 'Lorbergii'

Growing guide

An interesting group of tough shrubs that are related to the pea family. They are worth looking out for if you have a windswept site with poor soil where little else will grow.

Some, such as *C. arborescens,* are tall, fast-growing shrubs, but there are varieties which are grafted on to the top of the main stem of *C. arborescens* to produce small weeping trees. Other species are low-growing shrubs which make good plants for containers or dry banks. All thrive on chalky soils.

All the types have attractive, orange-yellow, pea-like flowers, but *C. arborescens* 'Lorbergii' is worth growing for its foliage alone. The light green, needle-like leaves give the whole plant a feathery appearance.

Pruning

Do not prune. The exception is *C. arborescens* 'Lorbergii' which produces more attractive foliage if all the shoots are cut back by at least two-thirds between late winter and early spring.

Propagation

Take cuttings in mid- to late summer and root in a cold frame. Alternatively, propagate by layering.

Troubleshooting

Generally trouble-free but pruning can result in the shoots dying back.

Which variety?

C. arborescens **'Lorbergii'** is a good foliage variety.
C. arborescens **'Pendula'** makes an attractive, small, weeping tree.
C. arborescens **'Nana'** and **C. frutex globosa** are small, neat shrubs, suitable for a rock garden.

Carpenteria californica

Shape and size

5 years	10 years	At maturity

3m
2m
1m

Position

Hardiness

Soil

MOST

DRAINED

Uses

Features calendar

Jan	Feb	Mar	Apr	May	June
July	Aug	Sept	Oct	Nov	Dec

Carpenteria californica

Buying tips *Some of the plants on sale may be seed-raised. These can be of variable quality and may not flower well. To avoid getting poor specimens, it is worth buying plants when in flower. and choosing ones with plenty of blooms.*

The blooms measure up to 7.5cm (3in) across

Growing guide

A beautiful, summer-flowering evergreen worth growing in mild areas. In other regions, it can be fan-trained on a sunny wall. Plant about 45cm (18in) away from the wall to allow the shrub to develop.

The main feature is the display of scented, white flowers with prominent yellow anthers. In some gardens, this shrub never seems to flower well, while in others it is reliably covered in bloom all summer. Whether this is due to the origin of the plant (see 'Buying tips') or some other factor is a mystery.

Pruning

No regular pruning is required until the shrub is well-established. Once it becomes too large, or the older shoots become thin and bear few flowers, cut out one stem in three in late summer. This will ensure a healthy, young growth.

If the shrub is damaged after a hard winter, cut back to healthy wood.

Propagation

From seed or from softwood cuttings from the tips of the new shoots taken in July or August.

Troubleshooting

Carpenterias can be damaged at temperatures below -5°C (23°F). Although the shoots will generally regrow after a hard winter, flowers will not appear for several years, so it is worth giving it some protection. In most regions, you will need to protect this shrub every winter. In mild areas, it will only need protection for the first couple of years. Insulate the roots with 15cm (6in) of chipped bark and cover the top with a double layer of fleece.

Which variety?

You are only likely to come across **C. californica**.

Caryopteris x clandonensis

Shape and size

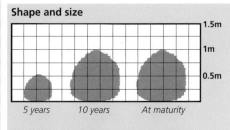

5 years	10 years	At maturity

1.5m
1m
0.5m

Position Hardiness Soil

DRAINED

Uses

Features calendar

Jan	Feb	Mar	Apr	May	June
July	Aug	Sept	Oct	Nov	Dec

Caryopteris x clandonensis 'Ferndown'

Growing guide

This dome-shaped shrub has masses of small blue flowers from August to September. An ideal choice for adding late summer interest to sunny borders, especially in gardens on chalk soils. Its greyish leaves combine well with the flowers and are aromatic.

It seems to be hardier than once thought. It has come through the winter unscathed in *Gardening Which?* trials in Scotland and Northern England, but choose a sheltered site.

In mild areas it can be grown as a low, flowering hedge.

Pruning

Cut back hard each year to 2.5-5cm (1-2in) above ground level in mid- to late spring. This will reduce the amount of dead wood and encourage more flowers.

Propagation

Take cuttings from the shoot tips in July and August. Root in a pot covered in a polythene bag or in a shaded cold frame.

Troubleshooting

Rotting of the stems can occur if you mulch too near the stems.

Which variety?

There is little to choose between the species and its varieties, so choose the shade of flower and foliage you find most attractive.
'Ferndown' Dark violet flowers
'Heavenly Blue' and **'Kew Blue'** both have mid-blue flowers.
'Worcester Gold' similar to species, but with eye-catching, yellow-green foliage.

Buying tips Best time to buy is in spring, so plants can get well-established before winter. However, it is most commonly sold in late summer when the plants are in flower. Look for a bushy, well-rooted plant.

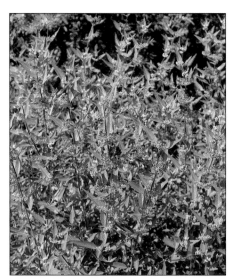

Caryopteris x clandonensis

Ceanothus, deciduous

Shape and size

5 years	10 years	At maturity

3m
2m
1m

Position   Hardiness   Soil

DRAINED

Uses

Features calendar

Jan	Feb	Mar	Apr	May	June
✿	✿	✿			
July	Aug	Sept	Oct	Nov	Dec

Buying tips *Choose plants with vigorous young shoots. Avoid old, leggy or starved plants. Check the plants are not pot-bound. If plants have been kept in pots for more than two years, the roots coil round and will fail to anchor themselves when planted in the garden.*

Ceanothus x pallidus 'Perle Rose'

Ceanothus x delileanus 'Gloire de Versailles'

Growing guide

Ceanothus have a reputation for being tender, but it depends on the variety you choose and where you grow it. Deciduous ceanothus tend to be hardier than the evergreen ones and will survive in most parts of the country if given a sunny position, shelter from cold winds and a fertile, well-drained soil.

They make attractive late summer- and autumn-flowering shrubs, but site them carefully as they are very fast-growing. This can be a virtue if you want a screen but, if planted where space is restricted, it does mean that you will have to keep pruning them.

In a border or against a wall they make ideal shrubs for underplanting with spring- or autumn-flowering bulbs. The flowers have a soft, fluffy appearance so combine well with lilies and other large late summer flowers, as well as coarse-textured foliage plants.

Pruning

In March, trim back all the previous year's shoots to within a few centimetres of the base. A neglected bush needs to be cut right back to a framework of main branches.

Propagation

Take cuttings in September or October and root in a shaded cold frame.

Troubleshooting

Pests and diseases are seldom a problem but the leaves can become chlorotic when plants are grown on thin, chalky soil.

Which variety?

C. x *delileanus* 'Gloire de Versailles' is one of the hardiest and widely available. You may also come across **C. x *delileanus* 'Topaz'** which has brighter blue flowers but is not as hardy. Also two pale pink varieties: **C. x *pallidus* 'Marie Simon'** and **C. x *pallidus* 'Perle Rose'**.

Ceanothus, evergreen

Shape and size

3m
2m
1m

5 years | 10 years | At maturity

Position

Hardiness

Soil

DRAINED

Uses

Features calendar

Jan	Feb	Mar	Apr	May	June
July	Aug	Sept	Oct	Nov	Dec

Ceanothus 'Blue Mound'

Growing guide

Evergreen ceanothus are more particular in their requirements than the deciduous ones. However, if you have the right conditions for them you will get a shrub that, in addition to blue flowers, provides a neat foliage background for other plants.

Choose a sunny spot with a well-drained soil. If your garden is sheltered or you live in a mild area, grow ceanothus as a free-standing shrub. Otherwise, grow them against a wall or fence; plant at least 0.9m (3ft) away if possible. There are drawbacks to growing them as wall shrubs. It tends to make for top-heavy growth, which is vulnerable to being loosened by the wind. Make sure you secure the branches to a strong trellis or training wires and tie in the new shoots twice a year. Also, evergreen ceanothus tend not to live as long when trained against a wall, so always have some cuttings on the go as replacements.

There are a few tougher evergreen ones such as C. thyrsiflorus 'Repens' which will grow in the open, even in colder areas. This makes a useful ground cover plant.

Pruning

Trim back lightly each year after flowering. Avoid cutting into old wood. Keep young plants in check before they grow too large. It is not worth renovating mis-shapen ones.

Propagation

Most are very easy to propagate from stem cuttings in summer. Put them in a pot and cover with a polythene bag. .

Troubleshooting

The leaves can become chlorotic on thin, chalky soils.

Buying tips *Select small young plants and check the roots to make sure they are not coiled around the pot. Such plants are vulnerable to drought and blowing over.*

Ceanothus 'Autumnal Blue'

Which variety?

Choose carefully as they vary in their hardiness, size and flowering time. The following grow around 2m (7ft) after ten years and flower in May-June unless otherwise stated.

MODERATELY HARDY
'Autumnal Blue' A hybrid between an evergreen and a deciduous ceanothus, it is evergreen, fairly hardy and flowers in spring and summer (July to September).
***C. thyrsiflorus* 'Repens'** Good ground cover, 0.5m (1½ft).

SLIGHTLY TENDER
Burkwoodii' Flowers May and September.
'Concha' Bright, deep blue flowers.
'Puget Blue' Dark blue flowers, 0.9m (3ft).
***C. griseus* 'Yankee Point'** Flowers in June, 0.9m (3ft).

FAIRLY TENDER (i.e. top growth may be killed back over the winter)
'Blue Mound' 0.9m (3ft).
C. impressus Dark blue flowers in May 1.5m (5ft).
'Italian Skies' Bright blue flowers in June, 3m (10ft).
'Cascade' Lovely habit as has weeping tips with dark blue flowers, 3m (10ft).

TENDER (i.e. killed in cold winter)
'Trewithen Blue' 4m (13ft).

Ceratostigma willmottianum

Shape and size

5 years	10 years	At maturity

1.5m
1m
0.5m

Position

Hardiness

Soil

MOST | DRAINED

Uses

Features calendar

Jan	Feb	Mar	Apr	May	June
July	Aug	Sept	Oct	Nov	Dec

Buying tips *Plants on sale may look weak in winter and early spring, but once planted out they should establish well.*

Ceratostigma willmottianum showing autumn colour

Ceratostigma plumbaginoides

Growing guide

Ceratostigma willmottianum is ideal for adding autumn colour to the front of a border. It grows each year into a small bush about 0.6m (2ft) or so high. Its bright blue flowers appear in late summer and continue into September, forming an attractive contrast with the red autumnal tint of the foliage.

For the best flowers and foliage, plant in a deep, rich soil. If your soil is thin and poor it is worth digging in some well-rotted organic matter before planting.

Pruning

After planting, cut back the previous year's growth to within 5cm (2in) of the old wood if planting in early or mid-spring. If planting at any other time, wait until the following spring before pruning.

With established plants, cut back the old shoots to living wood – i.e. above where the topmost bud breaks – in spring. After a severe winter, this may mean cutting them back close to ground level.

To prune the low-growing *C. plumbaginoides*, cut back the previous year's growth to the ground in early or mid-spring. In cold areas this growth will probably be killed over the winter anyway.

Propagation

Take softwood cuttings in mid-summer. It is possible to lift and divide them, but if the roots are disturbed too much they take a while to re-establish.

Troubleshooting

Generally trouble-free.

Which variety?

C. willmottianum is the hardiest, but there are two other widely available species:
C. griffithii is lower-growing and slightly less hardy but it has large purple-blue flowers and good autumn colour.
C. plumbaginoides (*C. larpentae*) is the lowest growing, making it a better choice for ground cover, but in a border it can be invasive. Its flowers can last until November in a mild autumn.

Chaenomeles

Shape and size

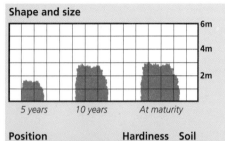

5 years | 10 years | At maturity

6m
4m
2m

Position Hardiness Soil

MOST

Uses

Features calendar

Jan	Feb	Mar	Apr	May	June
		✿	✿		

July	Aug	Sept	Oct	Nov	Dec
	●	●			

Chaenomeles speciosa 'Nivalis'

Chaenomeles x superba 'Chosan'

Growing guide

Flowering quinces are among the most reliable shrubs for early spring flowers. They tolerate virtually any site, although the more sun they get the better they flower. Most varieties flower for six weeks between March and May, but flowers can appear in February if the weather is mild. Varieties such as 'Crimson and Gold', 'Nivalis', 'Pink Lady' and 'Simonsii' tend to flower early.

C. speciosa varieties mostly form large, upright shrubs 3x2.4m (10x8ft), while many of the *C. x superba* varieties are lower-growing at around 1.5x1.5m (5x5ft).

In a border they make good free-standing bushes. A summer-flowering clematis grown over them extends the season of interest. To grow them as an informal hedge, plant 0.6m (2ft) apart.

As wall shrubs, they are useful for draughty, narrow passages, windows, fences or garage walls. Used in this way they can grow a third or half as tall again unless pruned.

Pruning

Pruning is not vital but it does improve flowering and keeps the plants compact. Cut all the previous year's shoots hard back to where there are flower buds during early spring. If training on a wall or fence, prune once a framework has been formed. Cut all the new season's shoots back to within a few centimetres of the main stem each summer. Also cut out any branches growing away from the wall.

Propagation

Take softwood cuttings in early summer, root in pots covered in a plastic bag. Cuttings should root within four weeks.

Chaenomeles x superba 'Crimson and Gold'

Troubleshooting

Aphids can colonise the soft shoot tips in spring and early summer. If this happens, pinch out the affected shoots. Occasionally, flowering quinces can be attacked by fireblight which causes the leaves and shoots to wither and turn brown. Cut off and dispose of affected branches. Dispose of the whole plant if this does not solve the problem.

Which variety?

C. x superba varieties tend to grow wider than they do tall:
'Chosan' Abundant pink flowers.
'Crimson and Gold' Crimson flowers with prominent golden anthers. One of the best reds.
'Knap Hill Scarlet' Orange-red flowers. **'Firedance'** is similar.
'Pink Lady' Pink flowers, lots of fruit. One of the best pinks.
'Rowallane' Large, semi-double, dark red flowers.

C. speciosa varieties tend to grow bigger and more upright:
'Geisha Girl' Subtle pink and yellow flowers.
'Moerloosei' ('Apple Blossom') White-pink flowers.
'Nivalis' Open, rather straggly habit. White flowers.
'Jet Trail' Compact habit. White flowers.
'Simonsii' Low, almost prostrate habit. Semi-double, deep red flowers.

C. japonica is still widely sold, although it has plenty of orange-red flowers it flowers late and forms suckers.

Buying tips *Be wary of buying plants simply labelled as 'Chaenomeles' or 'flowering quince'. These are often seed-raised plants of unpredictable quality.*

The edible fruits are good for making jellies

55

Chimonanthus praecox

(C. fragrans)

Shape and size

	5 years	10 years	At maturity

3m
2m
1m

Position   Hardiness   Soil

DRAINED

Uses

Features calendar

Jan	Feb	Mar	Apr	May	June
July	Aug	Sept	Oct	Nov	Dec

*Right: flowers suffering after a rapid thaw
Below: Chimonanthus praecox trained as a wall shrub*

The flowers of Chimonanthus praecox are best appreciated close up

Growing guide

The main feature of this otherwise rather dull shrub is its fragrant winter flowers. The flowers are pale yellow with a waxy appearance and are borne on leafless stems from December to March. Branches are often cut and taken indoors so the strong, sweet scent can be appreciated.

It can be grown in the open in sheltered gardens, or as a wall shrub against a south- or west-facing wall. As a wall shrub it can grow to 2.7m (9ft) or so.

Pruning

Pruning a young shrub is likely to delay flowering. With an established specimen, cut out one stem in three in early spring to encourage a regular supply of new growth from the base.

Propagation

You can layer shoots in summer, but it can take two years to root and a further seven years to flower.

Troubleshooting

The main problem is that it takes many years to flower.

Which variety?

You are most likely to find the species, but you may occasionally come across the following varieties with showier flowers:
'Grandiflorus' has deep yellow flowers but is less fragrant.
'Luteus' has brighter yellow flowers but is later flowering.

***Buying tips** It may look unattractive in a pot, but once planted it should grow rapidly.*

Choisya ternata

Shape and size

5 years	10 years	At maturity

3m
2m
1m

Position Hardiness Soil

MOST

Uses

Features calendar

Jan	Feb	Mar	Apr	May	June
July	Aug	Sept	Oct	Nov	Dec

'Sundance' needs light shade

'Aztec Pearl'

Growing guide

This shrub is loved for its flowers, which give off a strong, sweet, spicy fragrance like orange blossom.

The white, star-like flowers appear at the end of April, but sometimes there is a second flush in late summer. When not in flower, the bright green, glossy foliage makes a good foil for other flowers. If the leaves are crushed they also give off an aroma.

Cold winds can damage the foliage. In colder areas, choose a warm, sheltered position or grow in a container on the patio and move it into a greenhouse or under a porch over the winter. Growth can be stunted in cold regions.

Pruning

No regular pruning is required except to remove any frost-damaged shoots in spring. To encourage new foliage to shoot from the base on a mature shrub, cut back one in three branches close to the ground after flowering. If you want to encourage a second flush of flowers, cut back shoots that have flowered by 25-30cm (10-12in) after spring flowering.

Propagation

Take cuttings from the new shoots near the base in June and root in pots covered with a polythene bag. Or take cuttings in the autumn and root in a cold frame.

Troubleshooting

Generally trouble-free.

Which variety?

'Aztec Pearl' is a new variety worth growing for its finely-divided foliage and its clusters of flowers. The only drawback is that it is not as scented as the species.

'Sundance' is widely sold and promoted for its bright yellow foliage. However, it can scorch in strong sunlight but turns green in dense shade and it rarely flowers. Also, it can be cut hard back in winter in cold areas even if given a sheltered site.

Buying tips Avoid plants of 'Sundance' that have pale or bleached leaves. Young plants are a good buy as they are quick-growing. Buy in spring or early summer so plants are well-established by winter.

The orange-scented blooms of Choisya ternata

Cistus

Shape and size

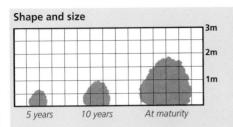

5 years	10 years	At maturity

3m
2m
1m

Position   Hardiness   Soil

DRAINED

Uses

Features calendar

Jan	Feb	Mar	Apr	May	June
July	Aug	Sept	Oct	Nov	Dec

Buying tips *A plant that has been grown 'hard' is likely to establish more reliably than one that has been grown under protection. So a tough, leggy plant might be a better buy than a soft, fleshy one.*

Cistus x purpureus

Cistus 'Silver Pink'

Growing guide

Rock roses are so named because they thrive on the rocky, sun-baked hills of the Mediterranean region. If you have a sunny, dry, sheltered site it is worth considering them for summer colour. The individual flowers are short-lived but new buds come quickly over the summer.

Some of the larger ones grow up to 1.8m (6ft) and would lighten a shrub border dominated by sombre evergreens. The smaller ones can be used to carpet the ground, and are especially useful for softening gravel, stone or paving.

The most vulnerable to frosts is *C. x purpureus*, but its flowers are so beautiful that it is worth growing in a large pot that can be moved under glass over the winter.

Pruning

In March, cut back any shoots that have been damaged by frost. In summer, clip over with shears, cutting two-thirds off each new shoot. Avoid cutting into old wood.

Propagation

Take cuttings in September or October and root in a cold frame.

Troubleshooting

Heavy shade, clay soils, cold winds and wet are more likely to kill them than frost. In exposed areas, old cistus plants should be staked and protected from frost.

Which variety?

Be wary, the following are amongst the most eye-catching and widely available but they will all need winter protection, even in mild parts of the country.
C. 'Silver Pink' Large clear-pink flowers with yellow centres.
C. x purpureus Has a bushy upright habit with rose-purple flowers with a dark blotch. One of the best pinks.

The following are more hardy:
C. x corbariensis White flowers with yellow centres. 0.6x0.9m (2x3ft)
C. x cyprius Can reach 2m (7ft) but is one of the best. It has clusters of maroon-blotched white flowers.
C. x dansereaui 'Decumbens' White flowers with a crimson blotch. At 0.6x1.2m (2x4ft) it makes a good ground cover.
C. laurifolius Can form a 1.8m (6ft) shrub. It has white flowers blotched with yellow and laurel-like leaves.

Clerodendrum trichotomum

Shape and size

				6m
				4m
		▮		2m
5 years	10 years	At maturity		

Position   Hardiness   Soil

MOST

Uses

Features calendar

Jan	Feb	Mar	Apr	May	June
	✿	✿	⚈	⚈	
July	Aug	Sept	Oct	Nov	Dec

Buying tips   *You may have to go to a specialist nursery.*

Clerodendrum bungei

The blue berries of Clerodendrum trichotomum 'Fargesii'

Growing guide

This is a vigorous grower that looks spectacular in autumn. It is fairly easy to grow, doing best in a light, shady site but in time it will reach tree-like proportions.

The flowers are pink in bud, opening out into white stars in late summer. They are fragrant, but avoid crushing the leaves as an unpleasant smell will be released. Bright blue berries contrast with the maroon calyxes.

It is moderately hardy but young plants are vulnerable to winter die-back and this can affect the size and shape of the shrub.

Pruning

No routine pruning is required but remove any frost-damaged tips in the spring.

C. bungei is tender and is invariably cut down by frost. However, in mild areas an established bush will produce new shoots in the spring. Cut the shoot to the ground for larger flowers and foliage.

Propagation

From seed or rooted suckers removed from the parent plant.

Troubleshooting

Protect with a 15cm (6in) layer of bark over winter for the first few years in cold areas.

Which variety?

Of the two species which can be grown outdoors, **C. trichotomum** is the hardiest. Look out for the variety **'Fargesii'** which is said to fruit more freely. **C. bungei** is more tender, the whole plant dies to ground level and comes back the following spring; roots can be damaged in very cold spells. It has large clusters of purple-red flowers with a pungent odour and purple-green foliage. It can be invasive as it spreads underground suckers.

Clethra alnifolia

Shape and size

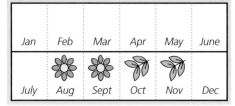

5 years   10 years   At maturity

Position   Hardiness

Soil   Uses

ACID   MOIST

Features calendar

Jan	Feb	Mar	Apr	May	June
July	Aug	Sept	Oct	Nov	Dec

Buying tips *Fairly slow to get established so buy the largest plants that you can afford.*

Clethra alnifolia

Growing guide

A summer-flowering shrub suitable for a wild or woodland garden. It will grow best in light shade on an acid or peaty soil.

The small white flowers are clustered together to form long spikes and are fragrant. The leaves turn a good yellow in autumn.

Pruning

No routine pruning is required but in time a thicket will be formed where the shoots develop from soil level. To keep it under control, cut back some of the oldest shoots and any very thin ones to ground level every couple of years.

Propagation

Take cuttings from the new shoots in July or August. It can also be propagated from seed or from layers from the parent plant.

Troubleshooting

If a very dense thicket is allowed to develop, it can be difficult to remove the weeds growing within the base. Dig up the plant and replant selected pieces with plenty of vigorous new shoots and roots.

Which variety?

C. alnifolia is the most widely-grown but it is worth looking out for named varieties which have more striking flowers. For example, **'Paniculata'** has larger flowers, and **'Pink Spire'** and **'Rosea'** have pink flowers. You may sometimes come across species such as **C. barbinervis** and **C. fargesii** which are noted for their autumn colour.

Clethra fargesii

Colutea arborescens

Shape and size

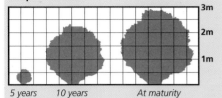

5 years   10 years   At maturity

Position

Hardiness

Soil

MOST

Uses

Features calendar

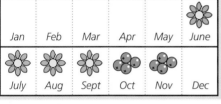

Jan	Feb	Mar	Apr	May	June
July	Aug	Sept	Oct	Nov	Dec

Growing guide

The inflated seed pods that pop when pressed make this an interesting novelty shrub.

It is a bushy, rounded shrub with a long flowering season. *C. arborescens* has yellow flowers and pale green foliage. The flowers are followed by 8cm (3in) inflated seed pods which are green with red or copper tones.

Although not often seen these days, it is easy to grow and would be suitable for a hot, dry spot.

Pruning

Prune out one stem in three in late spring, to help keep the shrub neat and compact. As flowers are borne on the current season's wood, this method of pruning ensures the old wood is replaced by new.

Propagation

Sow seed in spring or take cuttings from the new shoots in July or August and root in a cold frame.

Troubleshooting

In exposed areas, insert a short stake to prevent damage by wind rock. Prune hard back if encroaching on other plants.

Which variety?

You are most likely to come across **C. arborescens**, but there is a rarer one, **C. x media 'Copper Beauty'**, with copper-coloured flowers and greyish green foliage.

Buying tips   *Not easy to find, you may have to buy from a specialist.*

Colutea flowers

The seed pods of Colutea arborescens

Convolvulus cneorum

Shape and size

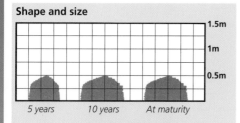

1.5m
1m
0.5m

5 years   10 years   At maturity

Position

Hardiness

Soil

DRAINED

Uses

Features calendar

Jan	Feb	Mar	Apr	May	June
				✿	✿
July	Aug	Sept	Oct	Nov	Dec

Buying tips *Buy in spring or early summer rather than autumn. Small plants should soon establish, so are a good buy.*

Growing guide

This is an attractive, silver-leaved small shrub that deserves to be more widely grown. Although evergreen, it looks most silvery in spring and early summer. The flower buds are pink, these open out into white trumpets in May. Flowering occurs at intervals throughout the summer.

It needs a sunny, well-drained spot so could be grown along with herbs, in a large rockery or at the front of a border. Alternatively, grow it as a single subject in a container.

Pruning

To encourage new silvery leaves and flowers the following year, cut two-thirds off each shoot in late summer.

Propagation

Take cuttings from new shoots in July or August. Root in a cold frame.

Troubleshooting

Old shoots can become long and woody, making the shrub look untidy. Regular pruning can prevent this. Can be short-lived, dying for no apparent reason.

Which variety?

No varieties.

The trumpet-shaped blooms of Convolvulus cneorum

Cordyline australis

Shape and size

| | | | | 6m |
| 4m |
| 2m |
| 5 years | 10 years | At maturity | | |

Position   Hardiness   Soil

DRAINED

Uses

Features calendar

Jan	Feb	Mar	Apr	May	June
July	Aug	Sept	Oct	Nov	Dec

Buying tips *Expensive to buy as plants but cheap and easy to grow from seed. If buying plants, look for unmarked leaves. The odd dead leaf near the base is not a cause for concern but all the new leaves should be bright and healthy.*

The dazzling 'Torbay Dazzler'

Cordylines make ideal container plants

Growing guide

In most areas, *C. australis* and its varieties will be grown in containers to add a tropical touch to patios and brought in over winter. But they can also be used as dot plants to give height and contrast to bedding schemes.

Cordylines must have very well-drained soil, a sheltered spot and full sun. They are an ideal choice for mild seaside areas where they will survive strong, salt-laden winds. In fact, in such areas they can be grown permanently outside without protection.

Once a plant gets too large for a pot, it will have to take its chance outdoors. Before the hard frosts set in, tie up the foliage at the top and wrap several layers of hessian, windbreak netting or fleece around it. Insulate with bubble polythene before slipping a loose-fitting sleeve of polythene over the top to keep it all dry.

Pruning

No pruning is required, but dead lower leaves can be removed to improve the appearance.

Propagation

If a plant becomes too tall or the foliage is rather sparse, cut off the top 10-15cm (4-6in) of the stem in spring. Insert into a mix of two parts peat to one part sharp sand. Keep out of direct sunlight at 18-21°C (65-70°F). After three weeks it should have rooted. Any offsets produced at the base can be separated from the parent and treated the same way.

Troubleshooting

Generally trouble-free.

Which variety?

Varieties are often not named in garden centres.
'Albertii' Variegated red, pink and cream.
'Purpurea' Purple-red leaves.
'Torbay Dazzler' Dark red leaves

Cornus alba varieties
and others for foliage and winter stems

Dogwoods

Shape and size

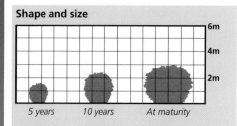

| 5 years | 10 years | At maturity |

6m
4m
2m

Position

Hardiness Soil

MOST

Uses

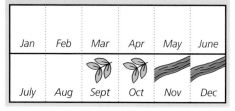

Features calendar

Jan	Feb	Mar	Apr	May	June
July	Aug	Sept	Oct	Nov	Dec

Growing guide

These are thicket-forming, suckering shrubs that can quickly reach 2.4m (8ft) if left unpruned but are usually more compact with regular pruning. They are grown for their coloured winter stems but many varieties are variegated and have outstanding foliage and/or good autumn colour too. *C. alba* 'Spaethii' is useful as, unlike many yellow variegated shrubs, it does not fade in full sun.

If grown for foliage, a single plant can look attractive in a border, but to make a real feature of their winter stems they are best grown in groups of three or more. In a small garden, try a single plant next to a pond where the stems can be reflected in the water.

Pruning

Dogwoods grown for their decorative stems need regular pruning as the old stems become dull. Green-leaved varieties can be cut back hard to within a few centimetres of the ground any time in early spring. Do this every couple of years to stimulate plenty of new shoots. With variegated types, pruning back a third of the stems each year gives the best compromise between good leaf cover and brightly coloured stems. It also means that you don't lose out on the flowers and berries, which are produced only on stems which are two or more years old. Feed plants with a general fertiliser after pruning.

Propagation

Take hardwood cuttings in the autumn or layer shoots near the ground in the spring.

Troubleshooting

Generally trouble-free but can become infected with scale insects. Burn them off with a cigarette lighter or scrub the stems with a toothbrush soaked in methylated spirit. Inspect the stems carefully for signs of re-infection.

Which variety?

The species *C. alba* can provide autumn and winter interest but is bigger and more rampant than the varieties, so go for a variety.

Buying tips *Look for plants with plenty of well-coloured stems. Plants with few stems will take several years to produce a good display in winter.*

Cut out reverted shoots like this plain green one on Cornus alba 'Elegantissima'

Autumn foliage of Cornus alba 'Spaethii'

*Cornus stolonifera 'Flaviramea'
in winter*

Among the best is **C. alba
'Spaethii'** as it has a long period of
interest. The yellow variegation
looks good all summer and is
followed by striking autumn leaf
tints. The red stems then add
interest until leaf burst in the spring.
Equally good, but with a silver
variegation, is **C. alba
'Elegantissima'.**

Other good varieties that you may
come across include:
C. alba 'Aurea' Yellowish-green
leaves. Can scorch in full sun.
C. alba 'Kesselringii' Purple-brown
stems, often described as black.
Some spring interest as the leaves
are reddish when they unfold but
are then plain green.
C. alba 'Sibirica' The brightest red
stems of all the varieties but with
green leaves.
C. stolonifera 'Flaviramea'
Greenish-yellow stems and green
leaves.

Cornus alba 'Sibirica' in front of a yellow-flowered witch hazel

Cornus, for flowers and foliage

Shape and size

			6m
			4m
			2m

5 years　　10 years　　At maturity

Position　　Hardiness

Soil　　　　　　　　　　　Uses

ACID　　MOIST　　DRAINED

Features calendar

Jan	Feb	Mar	Apr	May	June
July	Aug	Sept	Oct	Nov	Dec

Buying tips *All these plants are expensive and slow-growing. However, as their main role in the garden is as feature plants, it is best to get the largest specimen you can afford. Also ensure that you get one with an attractive shape, otherwise it can take many years of training to get it looking good.*

The amazing bracts of Cornus kousa 'Chinensis'

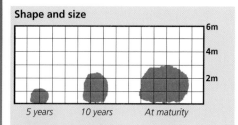

Cornus mas and the flowers in close-up

Growing guide

C. kousa is a large shrub or small tree. Given enough room, it makes a fine specimen with its spreading, tiered branches. In the summer it is covered with white 'flowers' (actually bracts), followed by orange and red autumn leaf tints and, sometimes, strawberry-like fruits.

For large, rounded flowering shrubs there are a couple more alternatives. C. florida is suitable if you live in the southern counties where the longer summers ripen the wood. More reliable is the Cornelian cherry, C. mas which produces yellow flowers in February and autumn colour from the foliage and fruit.

Pruning
No routine pruning required.

Propagation
Easy to layer in spring.

Troubleshooting
C. kousa may take several years after planting to settle down and start flowering.

Which variety?

FOR FLOWERS
C. kousa 'Chinensis' has larger bracts than the species and is a better choice. You may come across **C. nuttallii** which has showier bracts than **C. kousa** but does not make such a good specimen overall.

Cornus alternifolia 'Variegata'

There are many varieties of **C. florida**. One of the best is **'Rubra'** with its rosy-pink bracts in spring. Also look out for: **'Cherokee Chief'** deep rose-red bracts, good autumn colour; **'Rainbow'** white bracts, yellow-green margins on dark leaves, plum-purple in autumn.

There are several variegated forms of **C. mas** which add more interest in the summer months. **'Elegantissima'** (variegated yellow and flushed with pink, slower-growing) and **'Variegata'** (white margins to the leaves).

C. canadensis is a semi-evergreen, low-growing dogwood. Only 20cm (8in) high, it spreads 0.9m (3ft) every five years by means of runners. It has white bracts in summer followed by red berries and some autumn foliage colour. It needs a sandy, open soil and shade.

FOR FOLIAGE
C. alternifolia 'Variegata' (pagoda tree) has tiered horizontal branches and silver variegated leaves.
C. controversa 'Variegata' (wedding cake tree) branches form on a new tier each year, creating a wedding cake effect. Leaves are variegated with broad white margins.

Cornus florida 'Rainbow' in autumn

Corokia cotoneaster

Shape and size

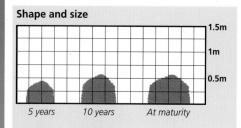

5 years	10 years	At maturity

1.5m
1m
0.5m

Position

Hardiness

Soil

DRAINED

Uses

Features calendar

Jan	Feb	Mar	Apr	May	June
				✿	✿
July	Aug	Sept	Oct	Nov	Dec
		●			

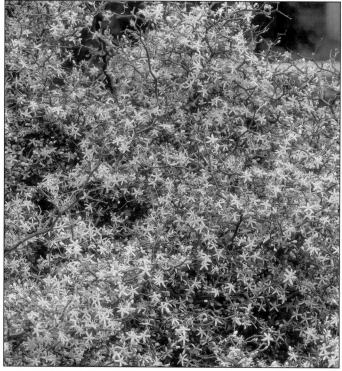

Corokia cotoneaster in early summer

The abundant fruits of Corokia x virgata

Growing guide

The tangled mass of stems earns this shrub the common name of wire-netting bush. When covered in its star-shaped, yellow flowers, it looks quite amazing. Even without the flowers, the intricate contortion of the purple-tinted stems covered in tiny, dark green leaves makes it a plant to behold. After a very hot summer, it may even produce small, round, orange fruits.

Unfortunately, it is not that easy to grow. It is very slow-growing and not reliably hardy. This means that it would be best as a conservatory plant, or in a container on a sunny patio and taken under glass for the winter. Although it will withstand light frosts, it would not be worth risking a mature specimen outdoors for the winter. Choose a pot to match the size of plant and use a John Innes No 2 compost. Feed with Osmocote slow-release granules rather than a liquid fertiliser.

Pruning
No pruning is required.

Propagation
Take cuttings from the new shoots in June and root in a heated propagator. Expect a high rate of failures.

Troubleshooting
The main problem is getting the plant to grow to a reasonable size, which can take several years of nurturing.

Which variety?

Another species you may come across is **C. x virgata**. This is more tender but slightly quicker growing. The basic features are the same as for *C. cotoneaster*, except that *C. x virgata* has grey-green leaves with white undersides, and it produces a good crop of orange fruits every year, even after a poor summer.

> **Buying tips** Buy the largest plant you can find as they are very slow-growing. Rarely found at garden centres.

Coronilla glauca

Shape and size

5 years	10 years	At maturity

3m
2m
1m

Position

Hardiness

Soil

MOST

Uses

Features calendar

Jan	Feb	Mar	Apr	May	June
				✿	✿

July	Aug	Sept	Oct	Nov	Dec
✿	✿	✿	✿		

The flowers of Coronilla glauca

Buying tips   *Does not grow that well in pots so often tends to look a bit weak and spindly at garden centres. However, it soon recovers when planted out in the ground.*

Coronilla likes a sunny wall

Growing guide

This shrub has a very long flowering season, but as it originates from Southern Europe it is not fully hardy. To overcome this, fan train it against a sunny, sheltered wall.

The foliage is grey-green and its flowers are yellow and pea-like with a scent. The flowers open in early May and the peak of the display is in June. From then on it flowers intermittently until the first frosts.

It will thrive in full sun and tolerate any soil, including very alkaline conditions.

Pruning

To encourage a supply of new shoots, and to prevent the plant becoming too woody, cut back a few of the oldest branches to ground level each year.

Propagation

Plant semi-ripe cuttings in a cold frame in summer.

Troubleshooting

Generally trouble-free but sometimes suffers from blackfly attacks. Spray small plants with an insecticide if serious.

Which variety?

C. glauca (*C. valentina glauca*) is a good choice, so is the variety **'Citrina'** with pale yellow flowers. You may also come across **'Variegata'**, which is slightly smaller and with cream-splashed leaves. It is more tender and worth considering in mild areas only.

Corylus

Shape and size

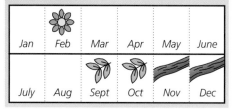

5 years   10 years   At maturity

6m
4m
2m

Position   Hardiness   Soil

MOST

Uses

Features calendar

Jan	Feb	Mar	Apr	May	June
	✾				

July	Aug	Sept	Oct	Nov	Dec
		🍂	🍂	▬	▬

Buying tips *Choose a well-shaped plant and watch out for aphids if buying in the summer.*

Corylus maxima 'Purpurea' showing a reverted stem which needs to be pruned out

The winter catkins of the corkscrew hazel

Growing guide

The native hazel (*C. avellana*) is well-known as an easy-to-please hedge or screening plant. However, there are also ornamental varieties that make interesting garden plants either because of their leaf colour or the form of their stems.

The coloured leaved forms will produce nuts, but if harvesting the nuts is your main reason for growing them, choose a specific fruiting variety like 'Kentish Cob'.

Plants may look a bit uninspiring in the early years, but they would be useful additions to a wild garden. The branching twiggy tops from pruned stems can be used as plant supports in the border or for forced bulbs.

Pruning

Those grown for their coloured leaves benefit from annual pruning. Remove one stem in three to encourage new shoots with brighter foliage.

The corkscrew hazel can have one stem in three cut out once it is established, say after five years. This only needs doing every two to three years, not annually.

Propagation

Remove layers or suckers from the base of the plant.

Troubleshooting

Generally trouble-free, although squirrels are likely to take the nuts. The purple-leaved filbert may produce green stems occasionally. These need to be pruned out to prevent the bush reverting to an ordinary hazel.

Which variety?

C. avellana **'Contorta'** (corkscrew hazel or Harry Lauder's walking stick) slow-growing, reaches up to 3x4m (10x13ft) after 25 years or more. Looks good in winter when the twisted stems are visible and when there are catkins, but is a bit dull in summer when in leaf. Rarely produces nuts.

FOR COLOURED FOLIAGE:
C. avellana **'Aurea'** (golden hazel) Yellow foliage; deep yellow in autumn, lime-green in spring.
C. maxima **'Purpurea'** (purple-leaved filbert) Glossy, deep purple foliage, red-purple catkins and nuts.

Cotinus coggygria

Shape and size

6m
4m
2m

5 years | 10 years | At maturity

Position | Hardiness

Soil | Uses

| MOST | DRAINED | MOIST | |

Features calendar

Jan	Feb	Mar	Apr	May	June
July	Aug	Sept	Oct	Nov	Dec

Buying tips *Check the purple-leaved varieties for mildew.*

Cotinus obovatus in autumn

Growing guide

The smoke bush is a naturally bushy shape, with rounded leaves that make a good backdrop for the haze of flowers. It is a shrub that offers a lot of summer and autumn interest and is best grown as a specimen.

The plumes start in summer as a pale pink and persist into autumn, turning smoky grey. The green foliage turns a vivid orange-yellow in autumn.

It will tolerate any soil, although will establish quicker in a deep, rich soil, so it is worth adding garden compost or well-rotted organic matter to the planting hole. The green-leaved varieties can tolerate some shade, but purple-leaved varieties must have a sunny position.

Pruning

The first spring after planting, shorten all the previous year's growth by one-third. This will help produce a good, shaped bush. Thereafter, the pruning you do depends on what feature of the shrub you want to encourage. Left unpruned the shrub will grow large with masses of flower. At the other extreme, cutting down to a framework of stubs close to ground level, will give you a compact plant with good foliage but few flowers! As a compromise, cutting out one stem in three in mid-spring will give a good display of foliage and flowers.

Propagation

Remove rooted suckers from the parent plant and plant in the autumn.

Troubleshooting

Can be slow to establish. Purple-leaved varieties can turn green if they do not get enough sun.

Which variety?

The green-leaved species is widely sold but there are some good varieties too. **'Flame'** has particularly bright orange autumn colour. Those with reddish purple leaves include: **'Foliis Purpureis'** ('Rubrifolius Group'), **'Grace'**, **'Notcutt's Variety'** and **'Royal Purple'**.

C. obovatus (*C. americanus*) can grow twice the size of *C. coggygria*. It has pink plumes and turns red-purple then orange in autumn.

Cotinus coggygria 'Royal Purple'

Cotoneaster, evergreen

PROSTRATE TYPES: shape and size

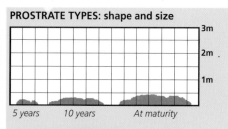

5 years   10 years   At maturity

PROSTRATE TYPES: uses

SEMI-PROSTRATE TYPES: shape and size

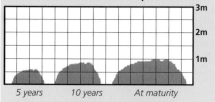

5 years   10 years   At maturity

SEMI-PROSTRATE TYPES: uses

BUSH TYPES: shape and size

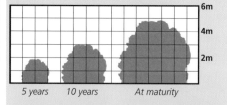

5 years   10 years   At maturity

BUSH TYPES: uses

Position   **Hardiness** **Soil**

MOST

Features calendar

Jan	Feb	Mar	Apr	May	June
July	Aug	Sept	Oct	Nov	Dec

Cotoneaster salicifolius 'Gnom'

Growing guide

Evergreen cotoneasters come in a wide range of shapes and sizes which makes them useful for providing berried shrubs all around the garden. Unlike pyracanthas they have no thorns.

The prostrate types are ideal for covering manholes and steep banks where little else thrives. They will even grow under established shrubs, so could cover up those that have gone bare at the base. Plant with summer-flowering or variegated ground cover like periwinkles, ivies or *Hypericum calycinum* for year-round interest.

The semi-prostrate types can be used to cover large areas. Plant 0.6m (2ft) apart into weed-free ground. They will suppress future weeds once the branches have knitted together. Many within this group like *C. salicifolius* 'Autumn Fire', *C. microphyllus* and *C. conspicuus* 'Decorus' make good wall shrubs too.

The bush cotoneasters can be used in borders to create a contrast of texture by growing them next to plants with different foliage, texture or size. Some, like *C. franchetii*, have enough attractive features to be grown as specimens in an expanse of lawn or in a paved area.

Most bush cotoneasters make good screens or windbreaks as they grow quickly up to 1.8m (6ft). Upright forms such as *C. simonsii* and *C. lacteus* are the best for hedges and will still produce plenty of berries, even when clipped.

Pruning
No routine pruning is needed. To limit the size, trim in mid-spring.

Propagation
Take semi-ripe cuttings in summer. Alternatively, take hardwood cuttings in autumn or winter and insert into compost in a cold frame.

Troubleshooting
They can get fireblight. Symptoms are dead leaves which remain on the branches and dieback. Prune out and burn infected branches. Destroy badly affected plants.

Cotoneaster frigidus 'Cornubia'

Cotoneaster dammeri as ground cover

Which variety?

PROSTRATE TYPES

You are most likely to come across:
C. dammeri a vigorous type, suitable for ground cover or a wall shrub. And many named varieties of **C. salicifolius** like **'Repens'**, some of which are particularly prone to fireblight.

SEMI-PROSTRATE TYPES

C. congestus has a dense, mound-forming habit with blue-green foliage.

C. conspicuus 'Decorus' has arching branches and long-lasting berries.

'Coral Beauty' and **'Skogholm'** are two semi-prostrate *C. x suecicus* varieties that are widely sold. Of the two, 'Coral Beauty' has better berries and makes better ground cover.

C. microphyllus has an open, mound-like habit; berrying can vary.

C. salicifolius 'Autumn Fire' ('Herbstfeuer') is a semi-evergreen so there is some autumn colour. Its lax habit makes it a better free-standing or wall shrub rather than a

ground cover. Prone to fireblight.
C. salicifolius 'Gnom' is compact with good dark green-grey foliage but few berries.

BUSH TYPES

C. salicifolius 'Exburiensis' has yellow berries, as does **'Rothschildianus'** which is similar.
C. franchetii is semi-evergreen. The stems are almost black.
C. lacteus excellent formal hedging plant, berries ripen in December and persist into January.
C. simonsii is a vigorous semi-evergreen; good as a hedge if clipped.
C. x watereri is a very vigorous, semi-evergreen shrub. It can reach 4.8x4.8m (16x16ft) after ten years.
C. frigidus 'Cornubia' is the same size as *C. x watereri*. Usually trained as a single stemmed tree, very abundant berries.

> **Buying tips** *Some stocks of C. microphyllus produce hardly any berries, so buy in flower or when they fruit. Quite a lot of plants are incorrectly named.*

Berries of Cotoneaster x watereri

Cotoneaster, deciduous
(e.g. Cotoneaster horizontalis)

Shape and size

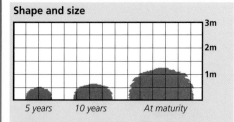

| 5 years | 10 years | At maturity |

3m
2m
1m

Position

Hardiness

Soil

MOST

Uses

Features calendar

Jan	Feb	Mar	Apr	May	June
				🌸	🌸

July	Aug	Sept	Oct	Nov	Dec
		🍃	🍃	🫐	🫐

Cotoneaster horizontalis is good for covering difficult areas

Cotoneaster horizontalis

Growing guide

This makes an excellent wall shrub. The branches form an attractive herring-bone pattern when planted against a wall. This naturally semi-prostrate plant can attain a height of 2.4m (8ft) or more. There is a brilliant autumn display of red leaves and red berries.

It is invaluable in the garden as its toughness can be pressed into service on cold, north- or east-facing walls, or used to camouflage dustbin bays and the like.

Pruning

No routine pruning is needed, but to limit its size cut out one stem in three in late winter or early spring.

Propagation

Take semi-ripe cuttings in summer or hardwood cuttings in autumn or winter.

Troubleshooting

Cotoneaster can get fireblight. Birds often take the berries.

Which variety?

There is a variegated form **C. horizontalis 'Variegatus'** (*C. atropurpureus* 'Variegatus') that is less vigorous than the species. It has attractive green and cream leaves tinged pink in autumn, but does not produce as many berries as the species.

Crinodendron hookerianum
(Tricuspidaria lanceolata)

Shape and size

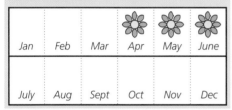

5 years	10 years	At maturity

3m
2m
1m

Position

Hardiness

Soil

ACID   MOIST   DRAINED

Uses

Features calendar

Jan	Feb	Mar	Apr	May	June
July	Aug	Sept	Oct	Nov	Dec

Growing guide

This shrub is fussy about its growing conditions, but, if you can provide them, you will be rewarded with a striking display of red lanterns in late spring to early summer.

As it is not fully hardy, a mild, sheltered spot is needed. It flourishes in an acid soil. You will find the *C. hookerianum* associates well with azaleas, rhododendrons and heathers. The foliage can scorch in the sun, so choose a lightly shaded spot.

Pruning

No routine pruning is required, but to reduce the size of an established bush, cut out one stem in three. The best time to do this is mid-summer.

Propagation

From softwood cuttings taken in early summer.

Troubleshooting

It can be slow to establish and live up to its promise. Likely to be a disappointment unless grown under ideal conditions.

Which variety?

C. hookerianum is the hardiest. Also available is *C. patagua*, which has white, bell-shaped flowers that appear in late summer.

Buying tips *Not widely sold at garden centres, so you may need to go to a specialist.*

Crinodendron hookerianum

Cytisus
(e.g. Cytisus x praecox)

Shape and size

5 years	10 years	At maturity

3m
2m
1m

Position Hardiness

Soil

ACID   DRAINED

Uses

Features calendar

Jan	Feb	Mar	Apr	May	June
			🌼	🌼	
July	Aug	Sept	Oct	Nov	Dec

Buying tips *Small plants are the best value. Avoid old, woody specimens.*

Cytisus x praecox

Cytisus x kewensis hybrid

Growing guide

Cytisus are short-lived plants but have the advantage of growing quickly and providing masses of flowers in spring and early summer. They are a very diverse group, ranging from the Moroccan broom (*C. battandieri*) which can reach 5m (17ft) to 20cm (8in) ground huggers like *C. decumbens*. They also vary in their tolerance to lime (see 'Which variety?' for details).

The information in the icons relates to *C. x praecox* varieties and other similar hybrid varieties that are widely available.

The early flowers which smother the arching stems make them useful fillers in the border. There are soft creamy colours as well as the bright yellows, so one can be chosen to fit an established colour scheme.

Pruning

Cytisus become leggy and produce less flowers after 10-12 years. Cut back the current year's growth by half immediately after flowering. Do not prune the woody branches or you may kill the plant. *C. battandieri* is best not pruned.

Propagation

Seeds germinate very readily, but for named varieties you need to take cuttings. Cuttings from the new growth in summer can be rooted in a cold frame and planted out in spring.

Troubleshooting

Plants can quickly become leggy if shaded by neighbouring plants or if grown in a shady position. Once plants become bare and woody at the base, it is best to replace them. The larger cytisus varieties may need staking in more exposed areas.

Cytisus albus

Which variety?

C. x praecox varieties flower in April to May and cannot tolerate very alkaline soils:
'Albus' (*C. albus*) White flowers.
'Allgold' Yellow flowers.
'Warminster' Creamy-white flowers, acrid scent.

Similar varieties that flower slightly later, in May to June:
'Donard Gem' Compact variety with purple-pink flowers and clover scent.
'Hollandia' Purple-red and cream.
'Lena' Red and yellow flowers. Spreading habit with upright branches. Avoid alkaline soils.
'Zeelandia' Fragrant, creamy-white and lilac flowers.

OTHER CYTISUS:
C. battandieri Pineapple-scented, golden flowers June to July. Can reach 5x5m (17x17ft). Needs a sheltered position, best as a wall shrub. Avoid alkaline soils.

C. x kewensis Creamy-yellow flowers in May, 0.5x1.5m (1½x5ft) Tolerates alkaline. Hybrids may have pink or red flowers

Ground-hugging types for the front of borders or on large rock gardens:
C. x beanii Gold flowers in May on a mound-shaped plant 30x50cm (1x1½ft). Tolerates alkaline soils.
C. decumbens Golden-yellow flowers May to June, flat carpet 20cmx1.5m (8inx5ft). Tolerates alkaline soils

Cytisus battandieri

Other brooms *See Genista and Spartium.*

Daboecia cantabrica

Shape and size

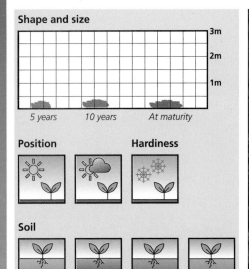

3m

2m

1m

| 5 years | 10 years | At maturity |

Position

Hardiness

Soil

ACID   NEUTRAL   MOIST   DRAINED

Uses

Features calendar

Jan	Feb	Mar	Apr	May	June
				✿	✿

July	Aug	Sept	Oct	Nov	Dec
✿	✿	✿	✿	✿	

Daboecia cantabrica 'William Buchanan'

Buying tips *Most likely to be found at garden centres in areas with acid soils. To save money buy a large plant to propagate.*

Daboecia cantabrica 'Bicolor'

Growing guide

This native of Ireland and Western Europe looks very attractive when planted *en masse* to fill the gaps around dwarf conifers and azaleas. As well as being a good ground cover plant for acid soils, its exceptionally long flowering season makes it well worth considering for containers. The only drawback of growing it in pots is that it needs to be kept moist and will suffer badly if allowed to dry out. The flowers are pitcher-shaped and hang from 15cm (6in) stalks. The species has purple-pink flowers but varieties are available in various shades of pink and purple, as well as white.

Soil conditions are everything to this plant and it is likely to die out within a season unless it gets the right balance of moisture and drainage, and a pH of below 7. It prefers light shade, though will be happy in the sun provided the soil does not get too dry. Although hardy, cold winds in very exposed positions can scorch the leaves, so give it some shelter in windy gardens.

Propagation

Easy to propagate from cuttings taken from the shoot tips throughout the summer. Can also be layered as for heathers.

Troubleshooting

Generally trouble-free.

Which variety?

D. cantabrica is widely available from specialist nurseries. The following varieties are also commonly found (the main difference being flower colour): **'Alba'**, white; **'Atropurpurea'**, purple; **'Bicolor'** white, pink and purple on same plant; **'Praegerae'**, deep purple, low-growing.

Danae racemosa

(Ruscus racemosus)

Shape and size

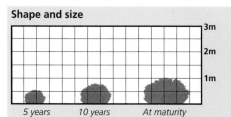

5 years	10 years	At maturity

Position

Hardiness

Soil

MOST

Uses

Features calendar

Jan	Feb	Mar	Apr	May	June
July	Aug	Sept	Oct	Nov	Dec

Danae racemosa

Ruscus aculeatus, the native butcher's broom

Growing guide

Not many plants can cope with dry, deep shade, but this low-growing evergreen can.

Its glossy green leaves are in fact flattened stems (called cladodes) which are specially adapted to conserve moisture. Bearing both male and female flowers, single plants can carry bright red berries in autumn, following hot summers.

It can take several years to settle in but once it starts producing lots of new shoots, it can be clipped to form a low hedge.

Pruning

Routine pruning is not essential but it is worth doing after four or five years to improve the appearance of the shrub. Cut out one stem in three in spring each year. By doing this annually all of the older shoots will be removed before they become unsightly. In their place you will have plenty of young, attractive shoots.

Propagation

Divide in spring or autumn as you would a herbaceous perennial.

Troubleshooting

Generally trouble-free.

Which variety?

Ruscus aculeatus (butcher's broom) is a British native, occasionally found in the South and West. It is similar in appearance but male and female flowers are borne on different plants and both sexes need to be present for the females to produce berries. You may find it at native plant specialists.

Ruscus hypoglossum is lower-growing and more spreading with less pointed tips to the leaves. It produces sparse crops of berries, even when both sexes are present.

Buying tips *Slow-growing to start with, so it is worth getting a large clump.*

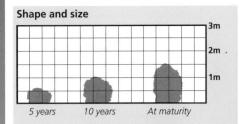

Daphne
(e.g. Daphne odora aureomarginata)

Daphne (side tab)

Shape and size

3m
2m
1m

5 years   10 years   At maturity

Position

Hardiness

Soil

DRAINED   MOIST

Uses

Features calendar

Jan	Feb	Mar	Apr	May	June
July	Aug	Sept	Oct	Nov	Dec

Buying tips Daphnes can be expensive as they are slow-growing and some are grafted. Buy when the shrub is in leaf so you can check for virus symptoms.

Daphne x burkwoodii 'Somerset Gold Edge'

Growing guide

Daphnes have wonderfully scented flowers, attractive foliage and are small enough to fit in any garden. To appreciate their scent, plant around patios or doorways, next to paths or at the front of a border. In sheltered positions, the scent will collect in the air on still days. Unfortunately, they seldom thrive if grown permanently in containers.

All daphnes are poisonous and you should bear this in mind if young children use your garden – especially as many types produce attractive berries.

D. odora 'Aureomarginata' is a typical, widely available representative. However, daphnes do vary in size, flowering time and some are deciduous. They vary in their growing requirements too. Many, like *D. mezereum,* are woodland species that do well in shade. Most can cope with a sunny spot if it is not too hot and dry. They will not withstand drought. Nearly all will thrive in chalk if it is made more moisture-retentive, although their leaves can become chlorotic.

Pruning
No pruning is needed.

Propagation
Most species are easily grown from seed. Alternatively, take cuttings from new shoots in summer, root in a pot covered with a polythene bag or in a cold frame. Take plenty of cuttings as they can be difficult to root. Layering in spring is more reliable, though rooting may take 12-18 months.

Daphne mezereum

Troubleshooting

Viral infections are common. Look for a distortion and yellow flecking or mottling of the leaves. Once a shrub has a virus there is nothing you can do, but try to control the aphids that spread them.

Which variety?

D. x *burkwoodii* **'Somerset'** and variegated forms. Easy and reliable rounded shrubs. Pink flowers from May to June and in late summer. Deciduous.

D. cneorum Small spreader, very free flowering with pink flowers from May to June. **'Eximia'** is an improved form. Evergreen.

D. mezereum Narrow habit. The flower colour can vary from pink to purple. Flowers January to February or March. Often berries. Deciduous. **'Alba'** has white flowers and yellow berries.

D. odora Green-leaved and not as hardy as the variety. Evergreen.

D. odora **'Variegata'** Cream variegated foliage. Pink flowers February to March. Evergreen.

D. tangutica Small, easy-to-grow. Pale, pink-purple flowers in May to June. Evergreen.

Daphne odora 'Variegata'

Decaisnea fargesii

Shape and size

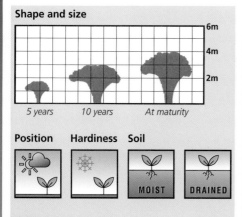

5 years	10 years	At maturity

6m
4m
2m

Position Hardiness Soil

MOIST   DRAINED

Uses

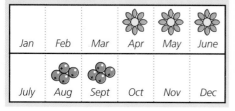

Features calendar

Jan	Feb	Mar	Apr	May	June
			✿	✿	✿
July	Aug	Sept	Oct	Nov	Dec
	●	●			

Decaisnea fargesii

Buying tips *Not widely available, so you may have to go to a specialist.*

The amazing seed pods of Decaisnea

Growing guide

This is a large architectural shrub that would make a good focal point. It also has novelty value, thanks to its metallic-blue bean pods. Following hot, dry summers, these form on shrubs that are several years old. In good years the fruits can be around 30cm (1ft) or more. The greenish flowers are also quite curious, hanging in long strands from the tops of the upright shoots.

To maximise the chances of getting the flowers and fruit, choose a moist, well-drained spot in light shade. Growing it against a wall also seems to improve fruiting.

Pruning

No pruning is required. Weak, old or damaged stems can be removed in spring.

Propagation

Sow seed under glass in late summer.

Troubleshooting

Generally trouble-free, but beans will only be produced on established shrubs and after dry, hot summers.

Which variety?

D. fargesii is the only species available.

Desfontainia spinosa

Shape and size

| 5 years | 10 years | At maturity |

3m
2m
1m

Position

Hardiness

Soil

ACID **DRAINED** **MOIST**

Uses

Features calendar

Jan	Feb	Mar	Apr	May	June
✳	✳	✳	✳		
July	Aug	Sept	Oct	Nov	Dec

Growing guide

This shrub has eye-catching flowers and attractive foliage, but is intolerant. It is only worth considering in mild gardens with an acid or neutral soil and it will do best in a partially shaded position.

Desfontainia is slow-growing and may take several years to establish. The evergreen, holly-like leaves provide a good foil for the tubular flowers. The flowers are scarlet with yellow mouths. The flowering display should last until October providing there is enough moisture at the roots.

Pruning

No routine pruning is required, but any dead or unwanted branches can be removed in spring.

Propagation

Take semi-ripe cuttings in mid-summer or remove rooted suckers from the edge of the clump. Alternatively, sow seeds in a warm greenhouse in spring.

Troubleshooting

If the flowers do not last into the autumn, apply a mulch the following spring and water when dry over the summer.

Which variety?

D. spinosa is the most widely available. You may come across a variety **'Harold Comber'** with red flowers.

Desfontainia spinosa in flower

Deutzia

Shape and size

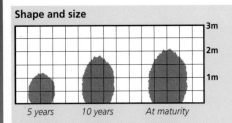

3m
2m
1m

5 years   10 years   At maturity

Position

Hardiness

Soil

ACID   NEUTRAL   DRAINED   MOIST

Uses

Features calendar

Jan	Feb	Mar	Apr	May	June
				✿	✿

July	Aug	Sept	Oct	Nov	Dec

Deutzia discolor 'Major' – a rare, white form

Most deutzias come in shades of pink

Growing guide

This useful group of summer-flowering shrubs is not widely grown, yet would be suitable in any garden where the soil does not get waterlogged or very dry. They vary in height from 0.9-3m (3-10ft) after ten years, so most could be grown in borders or as specimens, even in small gardens.

They flower very freely, mostly in June; some a month earlier or later. The flowers are usually a shade of pink, but each variety looks quite distinct.

Pruning

To encourage flowering, cut out one stem in three in mid-summer, immediately after the flowers have fallen.

Propagation

Take hardwood cuttings in October, root in a cold frame or in a pot

Buying tips Most likely to be found at garden centres in early summer when in bloom.

covered with a polythene bag. Plant out in late spring.

Troubleshooting

Late frosts can sometimes damage the May-flowering varieties. A prolonged dry spell could be fatal.

Which variety?

D. x *elegantissima* 'Rosealind' Makes a small, rounded 0.9m (3ft) bush. Deep pink flowers June to July.
D. *gracilis* Pure white, single flowers in late spring/early summer. Slightly tender.
D. x *hybrida* Large flowers:
'Magicien' Vigorous, upright habit, 1.8x1.5m (6x5ft) with large mauve-pink flowers edged with white.
'Mont Rose' Rose-pink flowers in early summer.
D. x *kalmiiflora* Small shrub with arching branches of pink flowers. Plum-purple foliage in autumn.
D. x *rosea* 0.9x0.9m (3x3ft) with pale pink blooms. The earliest to flower in May. **'Carmine'** is a good form.

Diervilla

Shape and size

5 years   10 years   At maturity

6m
4m
2m

Position

Hardiness

Soil

MOIST

Uses

Features calendar

Jan	Feb	Mar	Apr	May	June
July	Aug	Sept	Oct	Nov	Dec

Buying tips *Widely stocked by specialist nurseries, but may prove hard to find at garden centres.*

Diervilla splendens

Growing guide

A shrub similar to weigela but not as well known. It is easy to grow, and summer flowers, together with autumn colour, make it an attractive shrub.

Use it in a mixed or shrub border, either in the middle or further back; alternatively, it can be planted in groups. Its suckering roots can be used for stabilising the soil on banks etc.

The yellow flowers are borne on clusters at the ends of the shoots. The foliage is green with some yellow or purple-red tints in autumn.

Pruning

Cut out one in three shoots in mid-summer after flowering, removing old or damaged shoots first. This will encourage a bushy shape. Diervillas flower on the current season's growth, so cutting back hard will not affect flowering. You can also prune in spring.

Propagation

The easiest method is to remove suckers from the parent plant. Or take semi-ripe cuttings in summer and root in compost in a cold frame.

Troubleshooting

Diervillas can form spreading clumps which eventually become large and congested. To deal with this, dig up the plant, divide and replant young vigorous portions.

Which variety?

D. x splendens is particularly noted for its flowers and autumn colour. **D. sessilifolia** has smaller flowers.

Drimys winteri

Shape and size

		6m
		4m
		2m

5 years   10 years   At maturity

Position

Hardiness

Soil

ACID

MOIST

DRAINED

Uses

Features calendar

Jan	Feb	Mar	Apr	May	June
July	Aug	Sept	Oct	Nov	Dec

Drimys winteri in March

The scented flowers of Drimys winteri

Growing guide

A conical-shaped tree or large bush which is only worth considering if you have an acidic, woodland soil.

In such conditions it could be planted at the back of a border containing azaleas, witch hazels and heathers. In cold areas, it is worth siting it in the shelter of a wall as the foliage is easily damaged by winter chills.

D. winteri is not a striking shrub, but it does have the special attraction of pleasantly scented bark, leaves and flowers.

Pruning

No routine pruning is required, but any spreading branches can be removed to confine the plant. Any foliage that gets damaged over winter can be cut back the following spring.

Propagation

The easiest method is to take layers from the parent plant. Alternatively, try semi-ripe cuttings in late summer.

Troubleshooting

Leaves may drop and dieback can occur due to cold winds. Careful siting is important, as is protection.

Which variety?

D. winteri is the species most usually found.

> **Buying tips**   Widely stocked by specialist nurseries, but seldom found at garden centres.

Elaeagnus, deciduous

Shape and size

| 5 years | 10 years | At maturity |

3m
2m
1m

Position

Hardiness   Soil

DRAINED

Uses

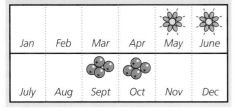

Features calendar

Jan	Feb	Mar	Apr	May	June
				✿	✿

July	Aug	Sept	Oct	Nov	Dec
		🍇	🍇		

Elaeagnus angustifolia

Buying tips *Buy and plant between November to March.*

Elaeagnus commutata

Growing guide

The deciduous elaeagnus seem very much the poor relation to the brighter evergreen varieties. However, they make useful backdrops in mixed borders and make a tough, although not dense, hedge. They seem to do particularly well on sandy soils but will tolerate most others, except for very chalky, poor soil.

Most have willow-like leaves of silver-grey, that turn yellow in autumn. The flowers are insignificant but sweetly scented and there are small fruits in the autumn.

Pruning

Not required, but old shoots can be cut back to soil level to rejuvenate the shrub. If grown as a hedge, trim lightly in late spring. *E. angustifolia* can be trained into a spreading tree by removing the lower shoots from the central leading stem.

Propagation

Take hardwood cuttings in early spring, root in a heated propagator and then grow on in a cold frame until planting out in the autumn.

Troubleshooting

Roots can be damaged by drought, waterlogging or root disturbance, this may lead to foliage dying off. In old specimens of *E. angustifolia*, the branches tend to grow long and heavy and are prone to storm damage. Prune back the tips every few years to prevent this.

Which variety?

E. angustifolia (oleaster) Spiny shrub, with yellow flowers in June and dull orange fruits.
E. commutata (*E. argentea*, silver berry). A suckering shrub with white flowers in May and silver fruit.

Elaeagnus, evergreen

Elaeagnus (side tab)

Shape and size

5 years	10 years	At maturity

3m
2m
1m

Position

Hardiness

Soil

 ACID
 NEUTRAL
 MOIST
 DRAINED

Uses

Features calendar

Jan	Feb	Mar	Apr	May	June
July	Aug	Sept	Oct	Nov	Dec

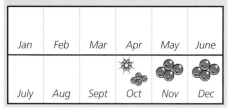

Elaeagnus x ebbingei 'Gilt Edge'

Growing guide

These shrubs are grown mostly for their year-round foliage. They are salt- and wind-tolerant, and have long been used as windbreaks in seaside towns. You can capitalise on this property by using them at the back of a mixed border to shelter other plants, although in cold, exposed places the leaves can scorch. Their foliage will also act as a backdrop to flowers in summer and be a feature in winter.

The plain-leaved *E. x ebbingei* and *E. macrophylla* will show off winter- and early spring-flowering shrubs that flower on bare branches. This group also has the best flowers and scent.

However, the brighter, variegated ones are the most valuable group. They are ideal for shady sites as they retain their markings. Position them where they will catch the winter sun and you will see the benefit from their bright foliage.

They make good hedging plants, space them 38-45cm (15-18in) apart for a formal hedge, or 0.6-1m (2-3ft) for an informal screen.

Pruning

Prune if they grow too big or start to look straggly. New growth can be encouraged by cutting out one stem in three in April. For a neat hedge clip in June and in September if needed. Remove any plain green shoots produced by variegated varieties.

Propagation

Take hardwood cuttings between February and March. Root in a heated propagator, then grow on in a cold frame until the autumn.

Troubleshooting

Elaeagnus are prone to coral spot; cut back affected shoots to healthy wood and burn prunings.

Elaeagnus pungens 'Maculata'

Which variety?

PLAIN-LEAVED
E. x ebbingei Grey-green foliage, silver underneath. Widely available.
E. macrophylla Silver foliage, ageing to grey-green.

VARIEGATED
E. x ebbingei **'Gilt Edge'** Green with yellow edges.
E. x ebbingei **'Limelight'** Green with gold splashes. Upright habit.
E. pungens **'Maculata'** ('Aureo-variegata') Large, irregular, yellow splashes on dark leaves. Widely available.
E. pungens **'Frederici'** Narrow green and creamy yellow leaves.
E. pungens **'Variegata'** Green with cream edges.

> **Buying tips** *Choose well-shaped bushy plants. Avoid grafted plants as these tend not to live as long as those on their own roots.*

Enkianthus campanulatus

Shape and size

3m
2m
1m

5 years 10 years At maturity

Position   Hardiness   Soil

ACID   MOIST

Uses

Features calendar

Jan	Feb	Mar	Apr	May	June
		✺	✺		
July	Aug	Sept	Oct	Nov	Dec
		🍃	🍃		

Growing guide

This acid-loving woodland plant will grow anywhere that camellias and rhododendrons thrive. It produces a cluster of bell-shaped flowers in March and April, generally lasting for around three weeks. The leaves colour up well in autumn, turning yellow and then scarlet.

It needs space and likes a deep, rich, open soil.

Pruning
No routine pruning is required, but take out any frost-damaged shoots in spring. Overgrown specimens can also be cut back at this time. Plants that are cut back quite severely, usually produce plenty of new growth.

Propagation
Propagate by naturally rooted or artificial layers. It can also be raised from seed collected in December and sown in a heated propagator.

Troubleshooting
Generally trouble-free if planted in acid, woodland conditions.

Which variety?

E. campanulatus is the most widely available but you may come across other species which vary in size.

The biggest is *E. chinensis* which is more like a tree at 5-6m (15-20ft). It has larger yellow-red flowers with darker veins through each petal. The leaves are also larger and autumn colour is good.

Much smaller (1.5-2.4m/5-8ft) are: *E. cernus* 'Rubens' deep red flowers, good autumn colour but not so hardy; and *E. perulatus* white flowers, good autumn colour.

Buying tips *Fairly slow-growing, so it is worth starting with a large plant. Widely available from specialist nurseries and larger garden centres*

Enkianthus campanulatus

Erica carnea

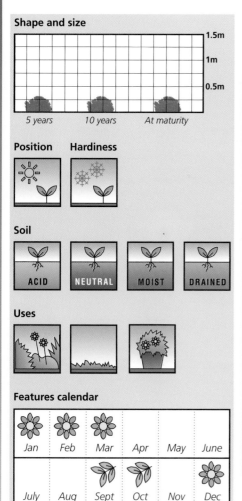

Shape and size

	1.5m
	1m
	0.5m

5 years   10 years   At maturity

Position   Hardiness

Soil

ACID   NEUTRAL   MOIST   DRAINED

Uses

Features calendar

Jan	Feb	Mar	Apr	May	June
July	Aug	Sept	Oct	Nov	Dec

Buying tips *Plants should be well-balanced with branches of roughly the same size, evenly spaced and compact. Avoid plants which are straggly or have stems that are not covered with leaves to the base.*

Winter-flowering heathers make attractive ground cover

Growing guide

There is a surprising variety of sizes, colours and flowering times. The most useful are the heathers that can tolerate alkaline soils up to pH7.8, the most important group being the winter-flowering heathers (*E. carnea and E. x darleyensis*).

For a good display of flowers, heathers need plenty of sun, although they can survive in shade. Open up compacted soils and improve dry soils with garden compost or composted bark before planting. Plant 30-40cm (12-15in) apart for cover within three years.

Pruning

Pruning is needed to keep a good shape and to encourage new shoots and flowers. Prune after flowering, but timing is not critical as long as the dead flowers are removed before spring growth starts. Summer-flowering ericas can be left over winter. Foliage varieties are best pruned in spring. Trim off the flowers with shears, then cut out any dead, straggly branches.

Propagation

Layering is the simplest method and can be done at any time of year. Cuttings from the root tips also root very easily during the summer.

Troubleshooting

The plants have fine fibrous roots which are very susceptible to dry conditions. It is worth improving soil before planting and mulching at least for the first year.

Erica carnea 'Springwood White' with Calluna 'Golden Feather'

Erica cinerea 'Pink Ice'

Which variety?

There are hundreds to choose from. First decide on the type, based on your soil and the height you want. Then select varieties on the basis of foliage or flowering interest.

E. carnea (was *E. herbacea*) Low-growing, 15x45cm (6x18in), lime-tolerant and winter-flowering.
FOR FOLIAGE
Golden with deeper tints e.g. red, orange tips in winter or spring:
'Ann Sparkes' red flowers, **'Aurea'** lilac-pink flowers, **'Foxhollow'** lilac-pink flowers, **'Westwood Yellow'** pink flowers.
Deep bronze tints: **'Adrienne Duncan'** red flowers, **'Vivellii'** red flowers.
FOR FLOWERS
'December Red' abundant lilac-pink flowers. **'King George'** pink flowers. **'Myretoun Ruby'** large, ruby-red flowers.
'Pink Spangles' large shell-pink flowers. **'Springwood White'** long, spikes of white flowers.

E. cinerea (bell heather). Grows on dry heaths in Britain, for acid soils only. It has fine foliage and oval flowers from June to autumn.
FOR FOLIAGE
'Alba Minor' bright green, white flowers. **'Golden Drop'** golden yellow, turning orange then copper-red in winter, mauve flowers.
'Velvet Night' dark green leaves, dark purple flowers.
FOR FLOWERS
'C D Eason' masses of magenta flowers on dark foliage, neat plants. **'Eden Valley'** free-flowering bicolor of lavender and white. **'Hookstone White'** long, flowering spikes of white flowers. **'Pink Ice'** compact with bright pink flowers, foliage is dark green, bronze in winter.

E. x darleyensis Lime-tolerant, usually flower from January to May. Quite sprawling. One of the neatest is **'Jack H Brummage'** with ruby-red flowers. Yellow foliage darkens in winter to reddish-gold. The new, spring growth is cream and pink.

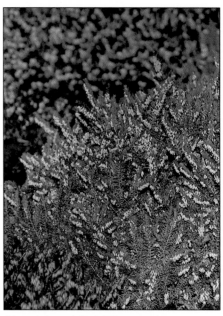

Erica x darleyensis 'Jack H Brummage'

Escallonia

Shape and size

		3m
		2m
		1m

5 years · 10 years · At maturity

Position

Hardiness

Soil

 ACID · NEUTRAL · DRAINED

Uses

Features calendar

Jan	Feb	Mar	Apr	May	June
					✿

July	Aug	Sept	Oct	Nov	Dec
✿					

Escallonia 'Donard Radiance'

Escallonia 'Apple Blossom'

Growing guide

The main virtue of escallonias is the masses of summer flowers on graceful, arching shoots. Flowering starts in June or July and lasts for six to eight weeks, although a few blooms will be produced until the autumn. In a shrub border, their flowers can follow on from berberis, rhododendrons and pyracanthas, while the dark, glossy foliage makes a good foil for other flowers.

Height and hardiness vary greatly. The small ones reach 1.5x1.5m (5x5ft), while a few can make 4x5m (13x17ft). The small-leaved types can be quite tough, but those with larger leaves may require a sheltered position. In cold areas, they can be grown against a south-facing wall or fence.

In mild areas, use cuttings of 'Crimson Spire' to make a cheap hedge. Plant 45-50cm (18-20in) apart. Escallonias are good seaside shrubs. Near the south and west coast they thrive in the sun and salt-laden winds, so here try 'Iveyi' and 'Macrantha' as screens.

Pruning

For the first two or three years, prune lightly in spring for a bushy habit. Thereafter, prune after the main flowering period.

Propagation

Take cuttings from July to September. Insert in a pot, cover with a polythene bag. Keep in a cold frame until April.

Troubleshooting

Generally trouble-free.

Which variety?

TOUGH
(i.e. will grow anywhere but may need protection from cold winds in the East).
'Donard Seedling' Pale pink flowers. 2.7x3m (9x10ft).
'Red Elf' Dark red flowers. 1.5x1.5m (5x5ft).

SLIGHTLY TENDER
(i.e. need shelter in cold areas).
'Apple Blossom' Pink and white flowers.1.5x1.8m (5x6ft).
'Crimson Spire' Crimson flowers. 2.7x2.7m (9x9ft).
'Donard Radiance' Red-pink flowers. 1.5x1.8m (5x6ft).
'Macrantha' Crimson flowers. 4x5m (13x17ft).

TENDER
(i.e. only grow by a south- or west-facing wall in cold areas).
'Iveyi' White flowers. 4x5m (13x17ft).
'Pride of Donard' Rose-pink flowers. 2.4x2.7m (8x9ft).

There are two new varieties with interesting foliage:
'Gold Brian' is compact at 0.6m (2ft) and has golden foliage and red flowers from August to September.
'Silver Anniversary' has a silver edge to the foliage and deep pink flowers.1.5x1.5m (5x5ft).

Buying tips *It's best to buy and plant escallonias in late spring or early summer.*

Eucryphia

Shape and size

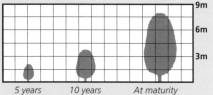

| 5 years | 10 years | At maturity |

Position

Hardiness

Soil

 ACID   NEUTRAL   MOIST

Uses

Features calendar

Jan	Feb	Mar	Apr	May	June
(flower)	(flower)	(leaf)	(leaf)		
July	Aug	Sept	Oct	Nov	Dec

Eucryphia glutinosa

Eucryphia x nymansensis

Growing guide

If grown under the right conditions, it can be a very showy shrub, smothered in bloom during much of the summer; though it is not a plant for the small garden.

Eucryphias prefer to grow in light shade or in a clearing among trees, or at the very least sheltered from cold winds. They can tolerate sun if their roots are shaded. The soil should be acid to neutral with plenty of organic matter to hold in the moisture.

The foliage is mostly evergreen. The attraction lies in the flowers which are white and saucer-shaped with prominent stamens. Size depends on variety but they are freely borne.

Pruning

Do not prune unless essential. Any damaged branches can be removed in early spring.

Propagation

Some species such as *E. glutinosa* can be layered from the parent. Otherwise, take cuttings in late summer.

Troubleshooting

Leaves can be damaged by cold winds and may drop. Usually no action is necessary and new growth will start the following spring.

Which variety?

There are about half a dozen species available from specialists. These vary in size, flower size and autumn colour.

E. glutinosa White flowers from July to August. Deciduous with good autumn colour.

E. x intermedia 'Rostrevor' Good display of fragrant flowers on a small shrub.

E. lucida Fragrant, hanging, white flowers from June to July. Very thick leaves. Less hardy than most.

E. milliganii Smaller shrub with smaller white flowers in July.

E. x nymansensis 'Nymansay' Large white flowers from August to September, on leathery evergreen leaves.

Buying tips *Widely sold by specialist nurseries, but may be hard to find at garden centres.*

Euonymus, deciduous
(e.g. Euonymus alatus)

Shape and size

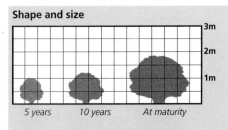

| 5 years | 10 years | At maturity |

Position

Hardiness

Soil

MOST

Uses

Features calendar

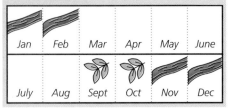

| Jan | Feb | Mar | Apr | May | June |
| July | Aug | Sept | Oct | Nov | Dec |

Buying tips *Slow-growing so buy the biggest plants that you can afford.*

Euonymus alatus in autumn colour

Growing guide

E. alatus is a deciduous relative of the well-known evergreen euonymus. It has outstanding autumn colour – the leaves turn an intense red. Another less usual feature is its corky winged stems, which become much more visible during the winter.

It prefers rich, moist sites but will grow reasonably well on most soils. In full sun or partial shade, it forms a rounded shrub. However, in shaded sites the growth is more open and the autumn colour is not as intense.

As it has little to offer during the summer, it is best sited where it can act as a foil for summer flowers, and where it can be seen as a prominent specimen in autumn and winter.

Pruning
None required other than to tidy up the shape or remove dead or damaged branches.

Propagation
Take cuttings from new shoots in June and root in a pot covered with a clear polythene bag. Plant out the following spring. If you want a lot of plants *E. europaeus* can be raised from fresh seed sown in autumn.

Troubleshooting
Generally trouble-free.

Which variety?

You are most likely to come across the species but there is a smaller form **'Compactus'**.

Another deciduous species is **E. europaeus** (spindle bush). It thrives on alkaline soils but will grow in most situations. The leaves turn red and scarlet in spring and the pinkish-red autumn fruits split to reveal the bright red seeds. It has several drawbacks: it is fairly large, reaching 3.5x4m (12x13ft) in ten years and can act as a host plant for aphids and caterpillars. There is a variety, **'Red Cascade'**, which is a more compact shrub. Both shrubs are poisonous.

Euonymus japonicus 'Ovatus Aureus'

Euonymus fortunei 'Sunspot'

Euonymus, evergreen
(e.g. Euonymus fortunei types)

Shape and size

3m
2m
1m

5 years | 10 years | At maturity

Position

Hardiness

Soil

MOST

Uses

Features calendar

Jan	Feb	Mar	Apr	May	June

July	Aug	Sept	Oct	Nov	Dec

Euonymus fortunei 'Emerald 'n' Gold'

Growing guide

These bright shrubs will grow anywhere and need little attention. Varieties of *Euonymus fortunei* have a low, spreading habit and make ideal fillers between other shrubs all around the garden.

They also make good ground cover as they are dense and bushy but not rampant. The versatile 'Emerald Gaiety' is good in sun or shade and once established will tolerate dry shade. The yellow variegated 'Emerald 'n' Gold' is also tough but may fade in deep shade. Both varieties make a neat edging if planted 30-38cm (12-15in) apart and clipped. Or use them as long-lasting foliage plants in tubs. Both develop attractive pink tinges after cold winter spells.

Given something to grow up, all start to produce long, upright shoots. On walls, the branching shoots become flattened and produce aerial roots at intervals, making them self-clinging. The best variety to cover a wall or fence is 'Silver Queen'. Alternatively, use it as a free-standing shrub towards the back of the border.

Pruning
The first spring after planting, cut back the previous year's growth by about one-third to encourage a bushy shape. After that no routine pruning is required. Old, neglected plants can have one stem in three cut out in early spring. If the plant is trained against a wall, simply prune back any stray shoots.

Propagation
All evergreen euonymus root easily from cuttings. Take cuttings from new shoots as they start to ripen in summer or hardwood cuttings in winter.

Troubleshooting
E. japonicus varieties can suffer from powdery mildew in dry weather or be attacked by small ermine moth caterpillars (signs are webbing or leaf rolling). Hard clipping can often solve both problems.

Which variety?

You can find varieties of *E. fortunei* at most garden centres. The following are all widely available and recommended:
'Emerald Gaiety' grey-green leaves with white margins. Very shade-tolerant, will climb to 2-3m (7-10ft) if trained against a wall or fence.
'Emerald 'n' Gold' green leaves with gold edges.
'Silver Queen' green with creamy white margin.1x1m (3x3ft) after five years but can reach 3x1.8m (10x6ft) if trained against a wall or fence. Adult shoots may produce orange fruits (poisonous).
'Sunspot' is very striking as it has bright yellow young stems as well as variegated foliage.

Two new varieties are **'Harlequin'** which has white and green foliage and **'Blondy'** which has very pronounced pale yellow blotches.

E. japonicus varieties are not as widely sold, though you are likely to come across the following:
E. japonicus makes a dense hedge up to 2m (7ft) tall. Being extremely tolerant of poor soils, pollution, heat and salt spray, it is ideal for city gardens near main roads.
The variegated varieties **'Aureus'** ('Aureopictus') and **'Ovatus Aureus'** ('Aureo-variegatus') are more tender, but will make good hedges for mild seaside gardens. They are often found on sale with houseplants. Tot plants bought in spring could be potted on and hardened off for use in window boxes and hanging baskets in their first year. When they get too big, they can be planted out into the garden or into tubs.

> **Buying tips** *Look for bushy plants with pronounced variegation. Avoid those with dull foliage or bare stems. Fairly quick growing so small plants are a good buy.*

Exochorda x macrantha 'The Bride'

Shape and size

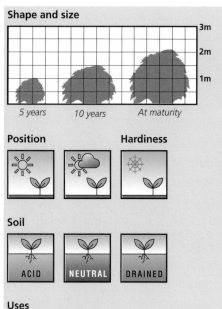

3m
2m
1m

5 years | 10 years | At maturity

Position

Hardiness

Soil

ACID | NEUTRAL | DRAINED

Uses

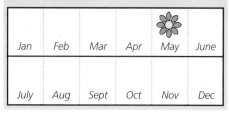

Features calendar

Jan	Feb	Mar	Apr	May	June
July	Aug	Sept	Oct	Nov	Dec

Buying tips *Plants at the garden centre often look very twiggy but will develop a better shape once planted out.*

The dazzling white flowers of 'The Bride'

Growing guide

This shrub has a graceful, arching habit and looks amazing in May when it becomes smothered in brilliant white flowers. After a brief flowering period, the shrub has little to offer in the way of interest. This should be taken into account when selecting and siting. It is perhaps best in a mixed border where its bluish-green foliage can act as a foil for other herbaceous flowers during the summer months.

Exochordas will flower in the shade if the soil is good, but have a tendency to sprawl and become leggy. Although exochordas can tolerate some alkalinity, they will show signs of chlorosis, such as yellowing of the leaves, on very alkaline soils. The variety 'The Bride' is more lime-tolerant than others.

Pruning

Their flowers are their main feature so it is worth pruning to keep them flowering well. Cut out one stem in three in early summer, after flowering. Young plants sometimes send up so many shoots from ground level, it is best to remove some of them to prevent over-crowding in future years.

Propagation

Take cuttings from new shoots in April, treat with a rooting hormone powder and root in a heated propagator. Difficult to root success-fully and slow-growing for the first few years.

Troubleshooting

On very alkaline soils leaves can become chlorotic. New foliage can be susceptible to late frosts in colder parts of the country.

Which variety?

E. x macrantha **'The Bride'** is the best choice as it produces more flowers on more compact plants than other species.

Fatsia japonica

Shape and size

		6m
		4m
		2m
5 years	10 years	At maturity

Position

Hardiness

Soil

 MOIST DRAINED

Uses

Features calendar

Jan	Feb	Mar	Apr	May	June
			✿	✿	✿
July	Aug	Sept	Oct	Nov	Dec

Buying tips *You may find this plant on sale more cheaply as a houseplant than in the shrub section of a garden centre. Only buy such plants for growing outdoors in late spring or early summer so that they will be thoroughly hardened off before the cold weather in the autumn.*

Fatsia japonica in flower

Growing guide

This evergreen bush can quickly make a fine specimen. The large, glossy leaves are palm-shaped and carried on long stalks. The cream flower spikes, which resemble the spokes of an umbrella, are produced in October and last for many weeks.

The ideal position for *F. japonica* is somewhere sheltered, by a south- or west-facing wall in cold areas. It is a good choice for town gardens as it likes shade and can withstand pollution. Also consider it for mild coastal areas.

The aim is to get the leaves as large as possible. Large clusters of black fruit are produced, removing these can increase leaf size. Growing in rich, moist soil will also produce the biggest leaves. Feed each spring with a general fertiliser such as growmore or balanced fish, blood and bone.

Pruning

Very little pruning is required if the shrub has plenty of room. Where it needs to be kept compact, cut out one stem in three each April.

Propagation

Take cuttings from shoot tips with a short section of stem and at least one leaf attached. Root in a heated propagator between June and August for best results.

Troubleshooting

Severe weather can damage the leaves and if the soil freezes for a long time the plant may be killed.

Which variety?

There is a variegated form (**'Variegata'**) although it is not widely available. This has white edges and blotches. It is more tender than the species and only worth considering in mild areas.

Fatsia brightened up in summer with pots of bedding pinks

97

Forsythia

Shape and size

6m
4m
2m

| 5 years | 10 years | At maturity |

Position

Hardiness Soil

MOST

Uses

Features calendar

Jan	Feb	Mar	Apr	May	June
		🌼			
July	Aug	Sept	Oct	Nov	Dec
		🍃	🍃		

Buying tips *Choose the plant with the most stems. If all the plants look rather gaunt, they are still worth buying but it is best to prune back the shoots by about half after planting. This may delay flowering by a year, however. Buying plants in flower is a good way to ensure that you get a good form.*

Grape hyacinths make good flowering companions

'Lynwood' is ablaze with flowers during May

Growing guide

Forsythias are well-known shrubs, but considering how easy they are to train as arches, standards or hedges it is surprising that they are not used more imaginatively. There are many lesser-known varieties that are worth considering for spring colour in different situations.

The long, pliable shoots of *F. suspensa* are the best for training over arches or against fences. *F. x intermedia* varieties can be easily trained as standards as they quickly form upright stems. For the same reason they make good hedges – plant 45cm (18in) apart for a good hedge within three years.

There are more modern varieties becoming available. These tend to be smaller, flower better and some even have variegated leaves. All varieties have yellow flowers, but they range from orange-yellow to pale yellow and many flower earlier than the more familiar ones.

Pruning

Pruning is not essential but can be done to keep them within bounds and it should also improve flowering in the long term. After flowering, prune out one-third of the branches and remove any low-growing shoots which have rooted in the surrounding soil.

Neglected plants tend to produce all their flowers at the top. You can prune hard back to renovate your plant but you will miss out on flowering in the following year.

Propagation

Take cuttings from soft shoots in June or July and root in a pot covered with a plastic bag.

The blooms of 'Spectabilis'

Forsythia viridissima 'Bronxensis'

Alternatively, take hardwood cuttings in October or November and root in open ground or a cold frame. Prune back rooted cuttings by about half during the winter to get bushy plants.

Troubleshooting

Many plants are affected by forsythia gall which causes rough, irregularly-shaped corky growths on the branches. This does no harm but can be pruned out if unsightly.

Which variety?

Within the **F. x intermedia** varieties are the familiar **'Lynwood'** and **'Spectabilis'**. Of the two, 'Lynwood' is the most floriferous. Also free-flowering is **'Spring Glory'**. For interesting foliage try **'Spectabilis Variegated'** with its cream variegated leaves turning purple in autumn.

New dwarf varieties you may come across include: **'Fiesta'** with gold and green leaves; and **'Golden Nugget'**. These will grow around 0.5-0.9x0.9m (1½-3x3ft) in five years. The smallest variety is still **F. viridissima 'Bronxensis'** at 30x30cm (12x12in) – which is ideal for a rock garden.

Large ones include: **'Beatrix Farrand'** with orange-yellow flowers and purple-red leaves in autumn, and **F. suspensa** with 3m (10ft) shoots. These are the best types for training against a wall or over an arch.

Fothergilla major

Shape and size

5 years	10 years	At maturity

3m
2m
1m

Position   Hardiness

Soil

ACID   NEUTRAL   MOIST

Uses

Features calendar

Jan	Feb	Mar	Apr	May	June
July	Aug	Sept	Oct	Nov	Dec

Buying tips *Slow-growing, so buy the biggest plant you can afford.*

The many shades of the autumn foliage

Fothergilla monticola on the turn in autumn

Growing guide

Fothergillas are grown for their colourful autumn foliage of orange, red and scarlet. They also produce flowers which have clusters of white stamens but no petals in March or April, opening before the leaves.

They are interesting shrubs to consider for a woodland setting, where they would thrive in moist, rich soil and receive the partial shade that they enjoy. However, they are not really shrubs for small gardens as they do little to earn their space for much of the year.

Pruning

No routine pruning is required other than to remove dead or damaged branches. Do not cut off the low shoots as these help to keep the plant covered with foliage close to the ground.

Propagation

Peg down low-growing stems in summer or autumn. Layers should root by the following autumn.

Troubleshooting

Can be slow-growing, so it may take several years before plants start to produce an impressive display of autumn leaf tints.

Which variety?

All have good autumn colours and spring flowers.

F. major is the most widely available species.
F. monticola is very similar but with less rounded leaves.
F. gardenii is smaller at 0.9x0.9m (3x3ft) and has fragrant flowers. It is worth considering for smaller gardens but is not very widely sold, even among shrub specialists.

Fuchsia magellanica

Shape and size

5 years	10 years	At maturity

3m
2m
1m

Position   Hardiness   Soil

DRAINED

Uses

Features calendar

Jan	Feb	Mar	Apr	May	June
					✿
July	Aug	Sept	Oct	Nov	Dec
✿	✿				

Buying tips *Avoid leggy plants with wilted leaves. Also inspect the undersides of leaves and growing tips for pests and diseases (see **Troubleshooting**).*

Fuchsia magellanica 'Versicolor'

Fuchsia magellanica gracilis

Growing guide

There are hundreds of varieties of fuchsias. Many are considered as tender and used for bedding out or greenhouses but *F. magellanica* varieties will grow like a deciduous shrub in mild areas.

They are not too fussy as long as the soil is well-drained. You can grow them in mixed borders or plant them as a hedge 0.6m (2ft) apart. Or grow them in containers, but choose a large one like a half barrel.

They are called 'hardy' fuchsias and although they can be left in the ground, it is still wise to protect their roots with a 15cm (6in) mulch of bark or bracken over winter in colder parts of the country.

Pruning

In most areas the top growth will be killed over winter. Cut back dead stems in mid- or late spring. Fuchsias shoot freely from old wood and flower on shoots produced in the current year so you can prune drastically with confidence. To keep a flowering hedge in good shape, prune back the side shoots in the spring as the new buds break.

Propagation

Take cuttings any time from spring through to autumn. Cuttings rooted from summer onwards should be overwintered in a greenhouse before planting out.

Troubleshooting

Leaves may discolour and bright orange spots appear on the lower surface, this is fuchsia rust. Remove and destroy affected leaves. Apply a systemic fungicide when the symptoms are first seen. Whitefly and aphids can also be a problem.

Which variety?

'Alba' One of the hardiest. White flowers tinged with pink, yellow autumn leaf tints.

F. m. gracilis **'Variegata'** Grey-green leaves with cream edge; red and violet flowers.

'Pumila' Very dwarf 0.5x0.5m (1½x1½ft); red and violet-blue flowers.

'Riccartonii' One of the hardiest. Good for hedging. Red and violet narrow flowers.

'Versicolor' ('Tricolor') silver-grey foliage with white and pink outer margin, scarlet and violet flowers.

Garrya elliptica

Shape and size

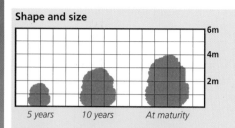

5 years	10 years	At maturity

Position

Hardiness

Soil

MOST

Uses

Features calendar

Jan	Feb	Mar	Apr	May	June
🌼	🌼				
July	Aug	Sept	Oct	Nov	Dec

Buying tips *Often featured at garden centres during the winter but best bought and planted in late spring or early autumn.*

Garrya elliptica in winter

The extra long tassels of 'James Roof'

Growing guide

Grown as a wall shrub supported by a trellis *Garrya elliptica* makes an elegant backdrop to seasonal flowers. In winter, the long silver tassels of the male plants make striking features in themselves and stand out particularly well against the dark green foliage.

A tough shrub that is not fussy about soil or position, it can cope with pollution and salt-laden winds but benefits from a sheltered spot.

Growing it as a wall shrub is recommended, not only to provide some shelter but also to keep the shrub looking neater.

Pruning

Cut out one stem in three in mid-spring each year to keep it from getting untidy.

Propagation

Take hardwood cuttings in the autumn. Root in a cold frame.

Troubleshooting

In early spring it can look a bit scruffy just before the old evergreen leaves are about to fall and the old tassels are still on the plant.

Which variety?

Look out for the variety **'James Roof'** which has longer tassels than the species, up to 35cm (14in) long.

Gaultheria procumbens

Shape and size

	3m
	2m
	1m

5 years   10 years   At maturity

Position   Hardiness

Soil   Uses

ACID   NEUTRAL

Features calendar

Jan	Feb	Mar	Apr	May	June
July	Aug	Sept	Oct	Nov	Dec

Gaultheria procumbens

Buying tips *Look for dense plants that fill their pots. In winter, choose ones with plenty of berries. Reddish tinges to the leaves are natural during cold weather but could be a sign of distress at other times of year.*

Gaultheria procumbens in winter

Growing guide

This creeping, evergreen shrub can be used to carpet the ground between rhododendrons and other acid-loving shrubs. It also makes a good edging plant. The white flowers look a bit like lily-of-the-valley, but it is the red berries that are the real feature. As well as the berries, the leaves develop reddish tinges during the winter.

It is a fairly tolerant shrub. However, it can only be grown in an acid soil.

Pruning

No pruning is necessary, but any branches that look straggly or are damaged can be cut back in early spring.

Propagation

Layer shoots in spring or lift and plant rooted suckers.

Troubleshooting

G. shallon can be invasive and it may be necessary to chop off pieces from the edge of the plant with a spade in spring to keep it within bounds. Even if cut to the ground in early spring, it will form new shoots.

Which variety?

You are most likely to come across **G. procumbens** with red berries, but you may also find forms with white or pink berries. **G. shallon** is a 1.5m (5ft) bush with dark purple berries in winter.

103

Genista
(e.g. Genista lydia)

Shape and size

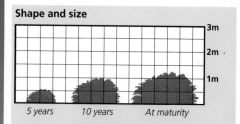

3m
2m
1m

5 years   10 years   At maturity

Position   Hardiness   Soil

MOST

Uses

Features calendar

Jan	Feb	Mar	Apr	May ✿	June ✿
July	Aug	Sept	Oct	Nov	Dec

__Buying tips__ Young plants are a good buy as brooms are quick-growing but make sure the roots are not pot-bound.

Genista lydia

Genista tinctoria 'Royal Gold'

Growing guide

G. lydia is the most widely planted species, giving year-round interest with its wiry, arching blue-green stems and a covering of yellow flowers between May and June. There are other brooms, all have yellow flowers mostly in May but their sizes and habits vary.

Genistas tolerate most soils provided they have reasonable drainage. They demand a sunny position.

G. lydia makes ideal cover for sunny banks but do not expect to suppress the weeds. When not in flower, the green stems and the arching habit of the plant provide interest. A single specimen could also be planted in a large rock garden or allowed to flow over the edge of a retaining wall or raised bed.

The Spanish broom, *G. hispanica,* makes an impenetrable hedge and animal deterrent thanks to its thorns. Within the garden, *G. tinctoria* 'Royal Gold' would make a long-flowering, informal hedge.

Genistas have a light framework of branches and delicate flowers so are easy to place in a border. Choose the plant according to the size and shape you want, aim for contrast of form with neighbouring plants. *G. pilosa* 'Vancouver Gold' or *G. tinctoria* 'Royal Gold' are good candidates for the front of a border. Further back, the Mount Etna broom, *G. aetnensis,* is useful as the wispy branches cast little shade on the ground below.

Pruning

To encourage a more bushy habit, pinch out the soft tips of the branches after flowering. Cutting into woody branches can kill plants.

Propagation

The seeds germinate very readily. Sow under glass in spring, plant out in June. Taking cuttings is more tricky. Take in October, root in a cold frame, plant out in spring. Softwood cuttings can be taken in June. Root in a pot covered with a polythene bag, overwinter in cold frame and plant out in spring.

Troubleshooting

Genistas are generally short-lived, becoming leggy and having fewer flowers after about ten years.

Which variety?

If you have room for only one genista, *G. tinctoria* **'Royal Gold'** is good as it flowers for up to ten weeks from July to September. Spreading with erect branches 0.8x1.5m (2½x5ft).

Other available varieties include:
G. lydia Spreading, arching at the tips, flowers May to June. 0.9x1.5m (3x5ft).
G. hispanica Spreading with erect branches, flowers June to July, spiny stems. 0.6x0.6m (2x2ft)
G. aetnensis Upright, arching at the tips, flowers in July. 4.5x4.5m (14x14ft).
G. pilosa 'Vancouver Gold' Very prostrate, flowers May to June. 0.3x0.9m (1x3ft).

Griselinia littoralis

Shape and size

	6m
	4m
	2m

5 years 10 years At maturity

Position

Hardiness

Soil

ACID

NEUTRAL

Uses

Features calendar

Jan	Feb	Mar	Apr	May	June
July	Aug	Sept	Oct	Nov	Dec

Griselinia littoralis 'Dixon's Cream'

Griselinia littoralis 'Variegata'

Growing guide

In mild, coastal areas griselinias can get very big when grown as free-standing shrubs. However, even in smaller seaside gardens they make very attractive hedges if planted 0.9m (3ft) apart. In colder, inland regions, growth tends to be more restricted and it makes a fresh-looking evergreen for a mixed bed. It will cope with most soils but may need some protection during the winter when the temperature dips below -5°C (23°F). Cover with a double layer of horticultural fleece.

Pruning

No routine pruning is required. The first spring after planting, shorten the previous year's growth by one-third to ensure the shrub develops a good bushy shape. Once established, any straggly shoots can be cut in mid-spring or late summer. It is best to use secateurs to trim hedges in order to avoid cutting through the leaves.

Propagation

Take hardwood cuttings in October and November and root in pots in a cold frame.

Troubleshooting

Some shoots may be damaged or killed over winter. These can be cut out in spring. On very alkaline soils, the leaves may become yellow. Treat with sequestered iron.

Which variety?

The variegated varieties look more eye-catching but are more tender and will not withstand more than light frosts over winter.

Buying tips *Buy in spring so plants can get established before winter. Look for plants with bright healthy foliage.*

Halesia

Shape and size

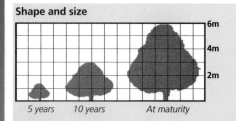

6m
4m
2m

5 years | 10 years | At maturity

Position

Hardiness

Soil

DRAINED

Uses

Features calendar

Jan	Feb	Mar	Apr	May	June
July	Aug	Sept	Oct	Nov	Dec

Halesia monticola

Buying tips *Consider buying an older plant as they can take three to five years to start flowering.*

The flowers of Halesia tetraptera

Growing guide

A large, spreading shrub with attractive, snowdrop-like flowers in the spring.

Halesias make attractive specimens if you have room for them and are prepared to wait a few years for flowers. They will grow on most soils, but an ideal soil is acid to neutral, moist but well-drained. They need a sunny, sheltered spot.

The white flowers hang down in clusters underneath the branches. In autumn there are small green-winged fruits. The grey-green foliage turns a rich yellow in the autumn.

Pruning

Halesias have low-spreading branches that come close to the ground. These should be left unpruned. Sometimes halesias are sold as small trees with a short single trunk. Branches that arise from the main trunk or are damaged can be pruned away in autumn.

Propagation

Layer shoots near to the ground in the spring or take cuttings from new shoots in June or July.

Troubleshooting

Generally trouble-free.

Which variety?

Only two species are usually grown: **H. monticola** has large flowers and fruit. There is a variety 'Vestita' with pink-tinged flowers.
H. tetraptera (also sold as *H. carolina*) is a smaller shrub around 2.4m (8ft) which becomes a small tree with age, with smaller flowers and fruit.

x Halimiocistus

Shape and size

5 years	10 years	At maturity

1.5m
1m
0.5m

Position   Hardiness

Soil   Uses

Features calendar

Jan	Feb	Mar	Apr	May	June
July	Aug	Sept	Oct	Nov	Dec

Buying tips *Not widely available, so you may have to buy from a specialist nursery. Avoid plants which have a lot of woody shoots that are bare at the base. This a sign that they have not been pruned properly at the nursery. Small plants are a good buy but larger specimens give you the opportunity to take plenty of cuttings.*

x Halimiocistus sahucii

x Halimiocistus sahucii is good for the front of a sunny border

Growing guide

These small shrubs are grown for their white summer flowers and dwarf bushy habits. They are not fully hardy, but are worth trying as they are very easy to propagate.

They thrive on hot, dry spots in poor soil. Heavy shade, clay soils, cold winds and constant wet are a greater danger than frost. Grow them at the front of a mixed border or on a sunny, dry bank.

Each delicate flower only lasts a day or two but they are produced in succession over several months.

Pruning

To encourage new flowering shoots, cut two-thirds off each shoot in late summer. Take care not to cut back into the old wood as severe pruning can kill the plants.

Propagation

In summer, take side shoots with a heel of old wood attached. Insert into an equal mixture of peat and sand and root in a cold frame. Pot up when they have rooted. Pinch out the growing tips to encourage bushy growth. Plant out in spring.

Troubleshooting

These are fairly short-lived shrubs. Take cuttings annually for replacements and as an insurance against winter losses.

Which variety?

The following three species are the most commonly grown in this country:

x **H. ingwersenii** Dwarf, spreading bush with white flowers from May to July.

x **H. sahucii** Dwarf, spreading bush with white flowers from May to September.

x **H. wintonensis** Hummock-shaped bush with grey-green foliage and white flowers from May to June. Each flower has a deep crimson band and yellow blotches at the base of the petals. The variety **'Merrist Wood Cream'** has dark-eyed, creamy-white flowers.

Hamamelis

Shape and size

5 years	10 years	At maturity

3m
2m
1m

Position

Hardiness

Soil

ACID NEUTRAL DRAINED

Uses

Features calendar

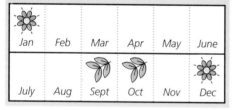

Jan	Feb	Mar	Apr	May	June
July	Aug	Sept	Oct	Nov	Dec

Buying tips *Be wary of very cheap H. mollis which are probably seed-raised and of uncertain quality. Most varieties are grafted on to one-year-old seedlings of H. virginiana. Young grafted plants can fail, so it is worth paying extra for a four-year-old plant. Look for a healthy plant with plump buds that is at least 45-60cm (18-24in) tall in a 3-litre pot. Larger plants are expensive but worth buying if you can afford them. Check the plant has a strong graft. If buying in spring after a bad winter, inspect the roots to make sure they are pale and firm. A brown or black colouration means that the roots are dead.*

Hamamelis mollis 'Pallida'

Growing guide

The witch hazel family contains some of the most reliable winter-flowering shrubs. The flowers can withstand wind and severe frost. Some varieties have a spicy fragrance, so make good cut flowers for the house. Another bonus is the autumn leaf colour.

The spidery flowers are borne on leafless stems, so it is essential to provide the right background to show them off. Dark evergreens work well as a foil for the yellow-flowered ones, or they could be underplanted with small evergreen shrubs like skimmias. The redder colours are best if positioned where the winter sun will shine through them, or against light-coloured foliage or walls.

Witch hazels grow well with dogwoods and together they make a colourful winter display. In summer they look dull, so underplant with long-flowering perennials such as hardy geraniums.

Witch hazels need a neutral to acid soil with reasonable drainage and a position in sun or light shade. Add plenty of bark or garden compost to the planting hole. When planting do not cover the graft as this can encourage suckers.

Pruning

Hard pruning can damage witch hazels as they are very slow-growing, so remove only diseased or dead wood. Prune lightly when necessary to maintain a balanced shape or to restrict branches growing where you do not want them.

Hamamelis x intermedia 'Jelena'

Hamamelis x intermedia 'Sunburst'

Hamamelis x intermedia 'Diane'

Hamamelis mollis 'Pallida'

Propagation

Difficult to propagate; most plants sold are grafted. Air layering, following the technique used for rubber plants, is worth a try. Prepare the layers in spring and check for rooting the following spring.

Troubleshooting

Plants sometimes do not establish well. This can be due to roots drying out when on sale, so inspect roots before buying. Another possibility is because the graft fails. Suckers may appear and should be pulled out when seen.

Which variety?

The Chinese witch hazel, *H. mollis* and its varieties are the finest group for winter flowers. **'Pallida'** has the largest flowers in the purest yellow.

'Brevipetala' has deep yellow flowers that appear orange from a distance. The leaves of both these varieties turn yellow in the autumn.

Many of the newer varieties of *H. x intermedia* like **'Moonlight'** (pale yellow flowers) and **'Sunburst'** (bright yellow flowers) are said to rival 'Pallida'. Also within this group are the red- and orange-flowered ones. Of these, **'Diane'** (red) and **'Jelena'** (coppery-red, appearing orange) are the best.

All these witch hazels have good autumn colour but if you want the richest autumn leaf tints, choose between **'Arnold Promise'**, **'Diane'** and **'Ruby Glow'**.

For their flowers alone, **'Pallida'**, **'Moonlight'** and **'Diane'** all come near the top of the list.

Hebes, low growing

(e.g. Hebe pinguifolia 'Pagei')

Shape and size

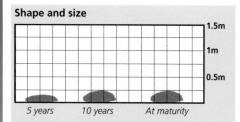

1.5m
1m
0.5m

5 years   10 years   At maturity

Position

Hardiness

Soil

DRAINED

MOIST

Uses

Features calendar

Jan	Feb	Mar	Apr	May	June
July	Aug	Sept	Oct	Nov	Dec

(flower symbol shown in May)

Buying tips *Certain varieties are heavily promoted in garden centres and you can pay a lot more for a plant in a coloured pot with a big glossy label. This can work out expensive if you want them for edging or ground cover. One of the unpromoted varieties would be better value. Watch out for aphids and mildew.*

Hebe rakaiensis

Growing guide

The smaller hebes are among the hardiest and easiest to grow. They form a supporting cast of useful, rather than spectacular, evergreens. They need well-drained, but not dry, soil and not too much shade. They can be used as fillers or edging in borders. *H. pinguifolia*, which has blue-grey foliage, looks effective with pinks, purples and yellows. Its prostrate habit can be utilised as ground cover or an edging. Single specimens can be planted in crevices in rock gardens.

Pruning

No regular pruning is required, but cutting out one stem in three in late summer will promote new growth and prevent plants from becoming bare in the middle.

Propagation

Take cuttings from the soft new shoots in May or June, or wait until the shoots ripen and take cuttings in September or October. Root in pots covered with polythene bags or direct into compost in a cold frame. Smaller-leaved types may take several months to root.

Troubleshooting

Hebes have shallow roots, so you may need to water in dry spells, but in winter the roots can rot if the soil is too wet. Established clumps can start to die off in the centre and become straggly and bare, particularly when grown in shade. Dig up the plants in autumn or spring and replant small clumps with roots. To prevent the problem in future years, prune to promote new growth.

Hebe 'Red Edge'

Which variety?

PROSTRATE TYPES

H. pinguifolia 'Pagei' Easy to find and one of the best with blue-grey foliage and white flowers in May. You may also come across:

H. albicans Grey-green leaves, white flowers in June and July.

H. youngii (more commonly sold as 'Carl Teschner'). Not as hardy as most small-leaved hebes but very low growing. Dark-green foliage and violet flowers in June and July.

H. 'Wingletye' Grey-leaved, small with amethyst flowers in June.

ROUNDED TYPES

'Baby Marie' Grows to about 30cm (12in), green leaves, pale lilac flowers.

H. buchananii Semi-erect, 20x60cm (2x3ft) with grey-green leaves, white flowers in June.

'Minor' is a dwarf form.

H. 'Pewter Dome' Grey-green foliage, white flowers in late May. 38cm (14in) high.

'Purple Pixie' Compact, green foliage, purple flowers summer to autumn. 0.6x0.5m (2x1½ft).

H. rakaiensis Can tolerate full shade, bright green foliage, dome-shaped 0.6x0.6m (2x2ft) with white and blue flowers in June and July.

H. 'Red Edge' Grey-green foliage edged with red. Otherwise similar to *H. albicans*.

H. 'Rosie' Neat mound of green foliage, pink flowers from May to September. 0.6x0.6m (2x2ft).

H. vernicosa Slow-growing but reaches 38cm (15in) high, leaves are dark green, pale lavender/white flowers in June.

Hebe 'Rosie'

Hebes, tall growing

Shape and size

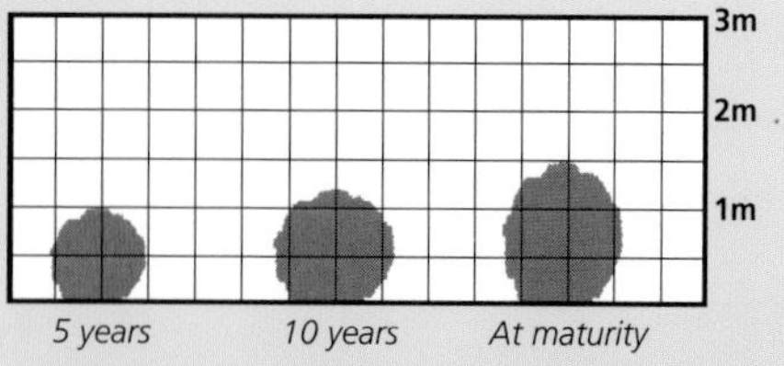
3m
2m
1m
5 years
10 years
At maturity

Position **Hardiness** **Soil**

DRAINED
MOIST

Uses

Features calendar

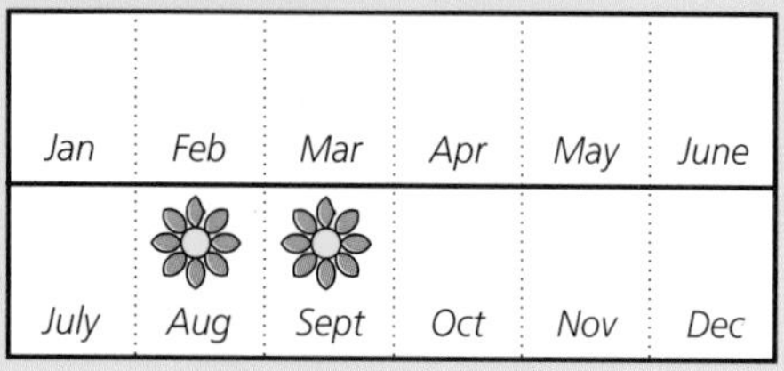
Jan
Feb
Mar
Apr
May
June
July
Aug
Sept
Oct
Nov
Dec

Buying tips *Buy and plant in spring rather than autumn. Downy mildew is a common disease on hebes in garden centres. Avoid any plants with yellow or purple tinges on the topside of the leaves and fluffy white growths underneath. Most are fairly quick-growing, so small plants are a good buy.*

Hebe 'Bowles's Hybrid' with the white-flowered Hebe 'Pewter Dome'

Growing guide

Among the taller hebes are some very spectacular flowering shrubs. Be warned, however, some of the most showy are tender and are only worth planting outdoors in sheltered, coastal areas. Two exceptions that offer showy flowers yet are moderately hardy are 'Great Orme' and 'Midsummer Beauty'. If you want to try the more tender ones, plant them in large tubs and keep them in a cold conservatory over winter. It is worth planting the taller hebes deep (i.e. so that four dormant buds are below ground). If frost subsequently kills off all the growth above ground, the shrub will then still be able to regrow in the following spring.

'Great Orme' can flower from July to September, although the display may be intermittent in very dry summers. As the flowers age, they become paler, giving a two-coloured effect. In mild areas it can make a good short hedge when planted 0.8m (1½ft) apart.

Those hebes with variegated or bronze foliage will have a better leaf colour in a sunny spot.

Pruning

Large-leaved varieties grown for their flowers can benefit from regular pruning. Cut back to the ground in mid-spring, annually or every other year. Variegated hebes may occasionally produce all-green shoots, cut these out.

Propagation

Take cuttings from the new shoots in May or in the autumn. Large-leaved types often root within a few weeks. Pot up individually once rooted and over winter in frost-free conditions.

Troubleshooting

They can be damaged by frosts, particularly when first planted. Look for bare stems and brown leaves. Large-leaved hebes may have leaves or branches torn off in strong winds.

Hebe 'Marjorie'

Which variety?

TALL TYPES

H. **'Autumn Beauty'** Green foliage, bright blue-mauve flowers from July into the autumn.

H. **x** *franciscana* **'Blue Gem'** Dark green, glossy leaves, pale violet-blue flowers from July to early autumn, widely grown in coastal areas.

H. **x** *franciscana* **'Variegata'** Leaves green with cream edge, pink-purple flowers in summer.

H. **'Great Orme'** Green leaves, bright pink flowers from July into the autumn.

H. **'La Seduisante'** Attractive but tender shrub. Reddish-green leaves and purple-crimson flowers.

H. **'Marjorie'** Compact shrub, green leaves, flowers blue-mauve fading to white in June and July.

H. **'Midsummer Beauty'** Green foliage with attractive, plum-coloured veins beneath. Mauve-blue flowers from July into the autumn. Moderately hardy.

MEDIUM SIZED

(i.e. 0.8x0.9m/1½x3ft after ten years). Most are moderately hardy.

H. armstrongii Whipcord hebe, greeny gold foliage, a few white flowers June to July. Useful gap filler.

H. cupressoides **'Boughton Dome'** A grey-green whipcord hebe that looks a bit like a conifer. Small blue flowers late May.

H. glaucophylla **'Variegata'** Semi-erect with grey-green, cream-edged foliage and pale lilac flowers from June to July. Prefers a sunny position. Not reliably hardy.

H. hulkeana Dark green, glossy leaves with reddish leaf margins, lavender blue flowers in May and June. More tender than most. Needs a warm, sunny, dry spot.

H. **'Mrs Winder'** Worth growing for its foliage, which is bronze-green with red edge, mauve-purple flowers in June to July.

H. ochracea **'James Stirling'** Whipcord hebe, erect, gold foliage with white flowers in June.

Hebe ochracea 'James Stirling'

Helianthemum

Shape and size

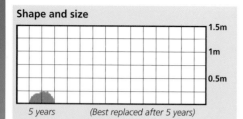

	1.5m
	1m
	0.5m

5 years   (Best replaced after 5 years)

Position   Hardiness

Soil

MOST   DRAINED

Uses

Features calendar

Jan	Feb	Mar	Apr	May	June
				✿	✿

July	Aug	Sept	Oct	Nov	Dec

Helianthemum 'Henfield Brilliant'

Helianthemum 'Wisley White'

Growing guide

Their low-growing habit makes helianthemums ideal for a wide range of uses, from edging paths to filling containers. One way to show them off to best advantage is to let them cascade over the edges of sunny, raised beds where they can be given good drainage and their petals can fall to the ground unhindered. The larger ones also add summer interest when planted between conifers. The smaller ones can be planted in troughs, raised beds or rock gardens.

Each flower only lasts a day or two, but the buds keep coming so they are in flower for about eight weeks.

Pruning

Cut hard back (almost to the base of the young growth) with shears immediately after flowering in June or July. This often encourages them to repeat flower in late summer and helps to keep the plants neat and compact.

Buying tips   You often find them in small pots in the alpine section of garden centres. These plants can be much cheaper than those in the shrub section. As helianthemums are quick-growing, small plants are good value. Buy in late spring or early summer, when they come into flower.

Propagation

In summer, pull off young side shoots with a heel of old wood attached. Insert into an equal mix of peat and sand in a cold frame. Pot up and overwinter in a cold frame. One month after rooting out pinch out the growing tips to promote bushy growth.

Troubleshooting

After about five years, plants start to go brown and straggly at their centres and it is best to replace them.

Which variety?

There are dozens of varieties in many colours. The **'Ben'** varieties have a neat habit. There are a few double ones available. The **'Wisley'** series is widely available and has silver-grey foliage.

SMALLER ones (i.e.10x30cm (4x12in)):
'Amy Baring' Apricot yellow.
'Alpestre' Golden yellow.

LARGER ones (i.e. 20x45cm (8x18in)):
'Ben Fhada' Golden yellow, orange centre.
'Ben More' Reddish-orange.
'Cerise Queen' Red, double.
'Fire Dragon' ('Mrs Clay') Orange-red.
'Fireball' ('Mrs C W Earle') Red, double.
'Henfield Brilliant' Bright red.
'Raspberry Ripple' White with red centre.
'The Bride' White, yellow blotch.
'Wisley' series in shades of pink, yellow or white.

Hibiscus syriacus

Shape and size

5 years | 10 years | At maturity

(3m, 2m, 1m)

Position

Hardiness

Soil

MOST | DRAINED

Uses

Features calendar

Jan	Feb	Mar	Apr	May	June
❀	❀	❀			
July	Aug	Sept	Oct	Nov	Dec

Growing guide

Hibiscus can make very spectacular late-summer flowering shrubs. However, incorrect growing conditions can be an obstacle to flowering.

To flourish they need plenty of sun and a well-drained soil. They don't get enough light to flower well in the North of England or Scotland and are not worth growing in these areas. Although hardier than they look, the flower buds can be damaged by late spring frosts, so there should be some shelter from cold winds. If you have such a site, hibiscus are worth growing as the large trumpet flowers come in a wide range of colours and add fresh interest late in the year. They come into leaf late, so take this into account when combining them with other plants.

Pruning

No routine pruning is needed, but you can cut out branches that are growing too big. Any shoots damaged in winter can be cut out in early spring.

Propagation

Take semi-ripe cuttings in summer and root in a cold frame, plant out in spring.

Troubleshooting

A plant that has no leaves early in the year is not necessarily dead, the plants are late into leaf. They can suffer from whitefly.

Which variety?

Single-flowered varieties tend to be more reliable in bloom as the double ones often get damaged in the rain. The following are the ones you are most likely to come across:
'Blue Bird' ('Oiseau Bleu') Violet-blue with a darker centre.
'Hamabo' White/pink with a dark red centre.
'Pink Giant' Large pink flowers.
'Red Heart' White with red centre.
'Woodbridge' Rosy-crimson with darker centre.

There are some newer varieties, such as **'Meehani'** with variegated leaves.

> **Buying tips** It is worth buying a three- or four-year-old specimen as young plants can take many years before they flower. Some named varieties are grafted so look for a strong union at the base of the stem.

Hibiscus syriacus 'Blue Bird'

Hibiscus syriacus 'Red Heart'

Hippophae rhamnoides

Shape and size

6m
4m
2m

5 years   10 years   At maturity

Position   Hardiness   Soil

MOST   DRAINED

Uses

Features calendar

Jan	Feb	Mar	Apr	May	June
July	Aug	Sept	Oct	Nov	Dec

Buying tips *Buy in berry so you know you have got a female plant.*

Detail of the berries

Growing guide

A strong-growing shrub suitable for large windy gardens, especially coastal ones. It will grow on most soils but is adapted to dry, sandy conditions.

Its quick growth and sharp spines mean it is usually grown as a screening plant where its ability to tolerate exposed conditions can be put to good use.

The foliage is silver grey and falls in autumn, revealing clusters of round orange-yellow berries. To ensure berries a female and male need to be planted. The berries are generally long-lasting. Birds do not eat them as the juice is poisonous.

To grow as a hedge, place young plants 45-60cm (18-24in) apart. After planting, encourage them to bush out by cutting off the top third of all shoots.

Pruning

No routine pruning is required. To control plants that have become too large, remove one stem in three in mid-spring. Wear gloves and eye protection to guard against the sharp thorns. Old or neglected plants can be cut back to 5-10cm (2-4in) above ground in early spring, although you will sacrifice berries on the female plants for a few years.

Propagation

Sow ripe berries in trays and leave out for the winter. Bring into a greenhouse or cold frame as soon as they start to germinate in spring.

Troubleshooting

Can be invasive due to self-sown seed and underground suckers.

Which variety?

Only the species *H. rhamnoides* is widely available.

Hippophae rhamnoides

Hydrangea, macrophylla varieties

Shape and size

5 years	10 years	At maturity

Position

Hardiness

Soil

MOIST

Uses

Features calendar

Jan	Feb	Mar	Apr	May	June
❀	❀	❀			
July	Aug	Sept	Oct	Nov	Dec

'Heinrich Seidel'

'Tricolor'

Growing guide

H. macrophylla varieties include the familiar mopheads (hortensias) and the less widely grown lacecaps. They are useful for late summer colour in light shade, so long as the soil is moist. They are hardy, but their tendency to grow late into the autumn and start early in the spring, exposes young growth to frost. To overcome this, choose a sheltered position and avoid frost pockets. On alkaline soils the leaves may yellow and the flowers will tend to pinky-mauve rather than blue.

As part of a shrub border, they will add colour from mid-summer to autumn. They also make good wall shrubs. It is possible to grow them in containers but they need plenty of water and regular feeding to look their best. Use a container at least 45cm (18in) in diameter and line the sides of terracotta pots with polythene to reduce water loss.

Pruning

If the plant is growing well, simply remove the dead flower heads in spring. They can also be pruned lightly to improve their shape e.g. by cutting back thin or old shoots near to ground level. Hard pruning will result in losing out on flowers the following year.

Propagation

Take cuttings from new shoots in July or August, root in a pot of compost covered with a plastic bag. Hortensias and lacecaps are easier to root than most hydrangeas.

Troubleshooting

In a dry soil, hydrangeas can look awful – the foliage droops and the bush does not grow – so it is worth mulching in spring and watering during dry spells.

'Lemmenhof'

Which variety?

Colours can vary with soil pH. Where this is likely to happen, the colour in an acid soil is given first. On alkaline soils, you'll get a more distinct colour by choosing a pink or white variety.

MOPHEADS

'Ayesha' Lilac, pink.
'Générale Vicomtesse de Vibraye' Blue, pink. Free-flowering, but tall stems can be weak.
'Madame Emile Mouillère' White with blue or pink eye. Flowers age to pink, especially in the sun. A good white variety for a north wall or in light shade.
'Pia' Red or violet flowers.

LACECAPS

'Lanarth White' Blue or pink, outer florets white. Very early-flowering, compact variety. Able to cope with full sun, more exposure and poorer soils than most.
'Mariesii' Pale blue, rose pink.
'Mariesii Perfecta' ('Blue Wave') Blue, pink.
'Tricolor' Pale blue, pink. Similar flowers to 'Mariesii' but more vigorous. Variegated green, grey and cream leaves.
'Veitchii' Blue, pink with white florets, one of the hardiest.

> **Buying tips** *Plants should have at least three main shoots arising near the base. The leaves should be a rich green - avoid those with yellowing leaves. Avoid plants in small containers i.e. less than 13cm (5in) diameter as they could be pot-bound. Plants can look leggy if they have not been pruned at the nursery to produce a bushy shape. They should be cut back when young to produce plenty of side shoots.*

Hydrangea paniculata varieties

Shape and size

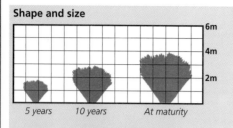

| 5 years | 10 years | At maturity |

Position

Hardiness

Soil

MOIST

Uses

Features calendar

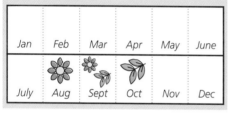

Jan	Feb	Mar	Apr	May	June
July	Aug	Sept	Oct	Nov	Dec

Hydrangea paniculata 'Floribunda'

Hydrangea paniculata 'Unique'

Hydrangea paniculata 'Praecox'

Growing guide

There are many other hydrangeas apart from the familiar mophead types. Some, such as *H. paniculata*, as well as being spectacular, are less fussy about their growing conditions. However, it does need a fair bit of space and regular pruning to get the best results.

In late summer, this arching bush has large, cone-shaped flower heads. It can be striking in a border with other hydrangeas or with blue agapanthus, for example. In a sheltered area, a trained standard would make a fine specimen, but in more exposed areas it would be better to grow it against a south- or west-facing wall or fence.

Pruning

The first spring after planting, cut back all the shoots to about 5cm (2in) of old wood to ensure a bushy shape. On established bushes, prune the main branches to within two buds of their bases in mid-spring.

Propagation

Take cuttings from new shoots in June and root in a cold frame.

Troubleshooting

Becomes woody with small flowers without regular pruning.

Which variety?

'Grandiflora' has massive blooms up to 45cm (18in) long. Flowers open white and age to pink. Often grown as a standard. **'Tardiva'** is a later-flowering variety.

There are other lesser-known hydrangeas worth growing. Most reach 1.8-2.4m (6-8ft) after ten years.
H. arborescens 'Annabelle' Does well in most conditions. No pruning needed. Very large white flowers.
H. aspera (*H. villosa*) Lacecap flowers, purplish-blue even on alkaline soils. Cream and brown stems are interesting in winter. No pruning needed. Needs protection from late spring frosts and a position in shade.
H. quercifolia Oak leaf-shaped foliage that turns crimson, orange, purple in autumn. White flowers that fade to pink. Needs some shelter for first few winters then hardy. Does well on most soils and in sun or shade.
H. sargentiana Good for shade. Tall upright shoots, lilac, pink flowers.
H. 'Preziosa' Rounded heads of blue, white or pink flowers and good autumn colour. Very hardy, best in acid soils. Forms a small rounded bush.

Buying tips *Avoid plants with dull foliage as these may have been watered erratically. The wood is quite brittle and easily damaged. Look for a specimen that has been handled carefully. .*

Hypericum calycinum

Shape and size

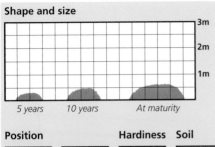

5 years   10 years   At maturity

Position   Hardiness   Soil

MOST

Uses

Features calendar

Jan	Feb	Mar	Apr	May	June
					✽
✽	✽	✽			
July	Aug	Sept	Oct	Nov	Dec

Hypericum x moserianum 'Tricolor'

Hypericum calycinum

Growing guide

Rose of Sharon is a very undemanding plant, but is best reserved for difficult sites where little else will grow. An ideal place for it would be a dry bank shaded by trees. In such a situation, a group planted 0.5m (1½ft) apart would quickly spread and provide year-round interest.

It can be very invasive, however, as it spreads by underground suckers. This should be considered when selecting a planting place.

There are other hypericums that are taller and grown either for their flowers or for their foliage. These can be used in mixed borders or as informal flowering hedges.

Pruning

The Rose of Sharon can be cut down to ground level each spring to remove the old foliage and stimulate plenty of flowers. It is tough, so use a powered grass trimmer. Other hypericums grown for their flowers benefit from having one stem in three removed in early spring. Hypericums grown for their foliage can be pruned down to the ground every other year or annually. Feed plants with a general fertiliser after pruning, then apply a mulch (e.g. a 5cm/ 2in layer of bark chippings).

Propagation

Use a spade to cut off a small division in spring. The tall shrubby types can be propagated by semi-ripe cuttings taken in summer or autumn and rooted in a cold frame.

Troubleshooting

Apart from being invasive, *Hypericum calycinum* is also prone to rust. Severe infections can be dealt with by cutting the plant back hard, burning the infected material and applying a systemic fungicide.

Which variety?

Hypericums vary greatly in height.
H. 'Hidcote' Semi-evergreen with large flowers. 0.9x0.9m (3x3ft).
H. x inodorum 'Elstead' Its elongated, red fruits are an eye-catching feature, but it is prone to mildew and rust. 0.9x0.9m (3x3ft).
H. x moserianum Attractive flowering shrub but avoid exposed locations. Flowers are yellow with red anthers. 0.6x0.6m (2x2ft).
H. x moserianum 'Tricolor', Variegated green and white foliage with red margins. Needs light shade or it can become scorched. Not suitable for dry conditions. 0.6x0.6m (2x2ft).

Buying tips *Inspect the plant for rust before buying. The signs to look for are yellow flecks on the upperside of leaves and bright orange spots underneath.*

Ilex

Shape and size

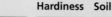

			6m
			4m
			2m

5 years   10 years   At maturity

Position

Hardiness

Soil

MOST

Uses

Features calendar

Jan	Feb	Mar	Apr	May	June
			⬤	⬤	⬤
July	Aug	Sept	Oct	Nov	Dec

Buying tips _Young plants are generally the quickest to establish as larger plants do not respond well to becoming pot-bound or having their roots disturbed._

The bright foliage of 'Silver Queen', a male variety with no berries

'Bacciflava' has yellow berries

A mature specimen of Ilex aquifolium 'Madame Briot'

Growing guide

There are many hundreds of hollies but among the most useful in the garden are the variegated ones. These are among the brightest shrubs for a border that is in shade or next to a north-facing fence. They will look best where there is indirect light. In heavy shade, the the growth habit tends to be more lax, and leaf and berry colour will become rather lacklustre.

Hollies will adapt well to most soils. They can cope with salt spray and, if protected with windbreak netting until established, can put up with exposed positions. They are slow to get going at first but many varieties can eventually reach tree-like proportions if not pruned.

Position them where you want year-round or winter colour. If planted 0.9m (3ft) apart as a hedge, they make a good backdrop to borders. In a small garden, they can be grown as standards or in containers – both methods limit their size.

Pruning

No routine pruning is required but they respond well to clipping in early spring. Variegated hollies sometimes produce shoots with all-green leaves. Cut these shoots out at their point of origin as soon as they are noticed, otherwise they can take over from the variegated growth.

Propagation

Take cuttings in early autumn and root in peaty compost in a cold frame. Holly cuttings are slow and difficult to root. Pot on any that do root in spring. It make take several years before they are big enough to plant out.

Troubleshooting

The first spring after planting, a holly may lose a lot of leaves. This does not mean there is a problem, it is likely that the old foliage has dropped and the new foliage has yet to be produced. You may see large yellow spots on the leaves with a grub inside. This is a leaf miner. Pick off and burn any affected leaves.

Berries of Ilex x altaclerensis 'Lawsoniana'. The variegated foliage can be prone to reversion

Which variety?

FOR BERRIES

Nearly all varieties are either male or female, so at least one male must be planted alongside females in order for them to produce a good display of berries. If you only want one plant, choose a self-fertile variety.

I. x altaclerensis **'Lawsoniana'** Gold-margined leaves. Female variety with red berries.

I. aquifolium **'Argentea Marginata'** Gold-margined leaves. Female variety with red berries.

I. aquifolium **'Handsworth New Silver'** Green leaves with creamy white margins. Female variety producing orange berries.

I. aquifolium **'Madame Briot'** Glossy, dark green leaves with yellow margins, purple stems. Female variety with orange-red berries.

I. aquifolium **'J. C. van Tol'** Green leaves with few prickles. Self-fertile variety with red berries. Prefers sun. **'Pyramidalis'** is similar.

I. x meserveae **'Blue Angel'** Blue-green foliage in spring, darkens to purple in winter. Female variety with dark red berries.

FOR FOLIAGE

I. aquifolium **'Ferox Argentea'** Compact, ultra-spiny with cream margins to the leaves and cream spines on the top of the leaves. Male variety with no berries.

I. aquifolium **'Golden Milkboy'** Green and gold variegated with large spines. Male variety with no berries.

I. aquifolium **'Golden Queen'** Very dark green leaves with golden margins. Male variety with no berries.

I. aquifolium **'Silver Queen'** Dark green leaves with creamy white edges, young shoots are purple-black. Male variety with no berries.

I. crenata **'Golden Gem'** Small-leaved, non-prickly, non-berrying holly with bright golden leaves in spring or summer, turning greenish yellow in autumn. Similar to *Lonicera nitida* 'Baggesen's Gold'.

'Golden Queen', a good foliage variety

Indigofera heterantha

Shape and size

3m
2m
1m

| 5 years | 10 years | At maturity |

Position

Hardiness

Soil

DRAINED

Uses

Features calendar

Jan	Feb	Mar	Apr	May	June
✿	✿	✿	✿		
July	Aug	Sept	Oct	Nov	Dec

Buying tips *Often looks very straggly as a young plant but this is nothing to worry about. Best bought and planted in late spring when it has come into leaf.*

Indigofera heterantha with Sedum spectabile in front

Growing guide

Also known as *I. gerardiana* or *I. heterantha gerardiana*, the indigo bush is a member of the legume family, valued for its long spray of purplish-pink, pea-like flowers in late summer. Its drawback is that it tends to be one of the last shrubs to come into leaf, sometimes not until late May or June, and so has a rather twiggy appearance for much of the year.

Against a wall or fence, it can make an attractive fan-trained shrub. Grown this way, it can reach up to a third or more taller than when grown as a free-standing shrub.

You can give it a bit of extra interest in spring by combining it with a not-too-vigorous climber such as *Clematis alpina* or *Clematis macropetala*.

Unless your soil is already very free-draining, improve the drainage by mixing in at least a 5cm (2in) layer of sharp grit prior to planting. Dig this in to a spade's depth.

Pruning

Cut old branches and any that have been damaged by frost back to near the base. If grown as a wall shrub, it is best to cut back all the long shoots by about two-thirds to keep it neat. Prune in April or May, when there is less risk of severe frosts.

Propagation

Take cuttings from new shoots in early summer and root in a pot covered with a polythene bag.

Troubleshooting

Shoots can be killed by frosts but the plants should throw up new shoots the following year. Waterlogged soils can kill the plant.

Which variety?

I. heterantha is the most common but you may find the following at specialist nurseries:
I. amblyantha Shrimp-pink flowers up to 20cm (8in) long from June to September.
I. potaninii Very similar to *I. amblyantha* and considered by some sources to be the same plant.

Itea ilicifolia

Shape and size

5 years 10 years At maturity

Position

Hardiness

Soil

MOST

Uses

Features calendar

Jan	Feb	Mar	Apr	May	June
July	Aug	Sept	Oct	Nov	Dec

Buying tips *Most likely to find it at large garden centres or specialist nurseries. Best bought in spring so can get established before the winter. Young plants can look a bit straggly for the first few years so get the biggest one you can afford.*

Iteas make good foils for other plants

Growing guide

The long catkin-like flowers, which often reach over 30cm (12in) in length, are a striking feature of this shrub. Its dark, evergreen, glossy foliage, similar to that of hollies, also make it a good foil for seasonal flowers – particularly pale colours or reds and oranges.

If growing in a container, choose one at least 45cm (18in) in diameter and depth, as it does not like having its roots restricted in its early years. Protect the top growth with a double layer of horticultural fleece and insulate the pot with bubble polythene for the coldest months of the winter.

Although it will withstand frosts, the leaves can be damaged by cold winds. Even for plants in the garden, unless in a very sheltered spot, it is best to protect the top growth with fleece (as for container-grown plants) or windbreak netting over the winter, especially for the first two or three years.

Pruning

Pruning is not essential other than to tidy up the shape or remove damaged branches. April or May is generally the best time.

Propagation

Cuttings taken from new shoots just as they start to ripen in late June or July should give the best chance of success. However, it is not an easy shrub to propagate.

Troubleshooting

Generally trouble-free if given winter protection.

Which variety?

You may come across *I. virginica* at specialist nurseries. This is a deciduous species with shorter, more upright flowers and is hardier than *I. ilicifolia*.

The catkin-like flowers of Itea ilicifolia

Jasminum nudiflorum

Shape and size

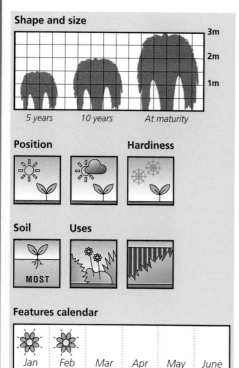

3m
2m
1m

5 years | 10 years | At maturity

Position

Hardiness

Soil

MOST

Uses

Features calendar

Jan	Feb	Mar	Apr	May	June
✿	✿				
July	Aug	Sept	Oct	Nov	Dec
				✿	✿

Jasminum humile 'Revolutum'

The cheery winter blooms of Jasminum nudiflorum

Buying tips *Look for plants with plenty of shoots so as to give a good flower display in the first winter.*

Growing guide

One of the most reliable winter-flowering shrubs which produces a mass of tiny, bright yellow blooms on its bare stems. Although deciduous, the stems remain green over winter giving it an evergreen appearance.

You can train it against a wall, as a free-standing weeping shrub, or let it cascade over a wall.

Pruning

Cut out one stem in three after flowering. Only prune established plants (i.e. three or more years old) and remove the oldest stems first.

Propagation

Easy to propagate either from new shoots in July, just as they start to ripen, or from 15cm (6in) lengths of stem after the leaves fall in autumn. The latter are best rooted in pots within a cold frame.

Troubleshooting

Trouble-free if regularly pruned. Neglected plants can be pruned hard back although there will not be any flowers the following winter.

Which variety?

There are several other shrubby jasmines, but the others all flower in the summer.
J. humile **'Revolutum'** is an evergreen with a bushy habit and has yellow flowers from June to August.
J. parkeri is a dwarf, prostrate species, growing up to 30cm (12in) tall and 60cm (24in) across, and is best suited to tubs or rock gardens. It too is evergreen with tiny yellow flowers in June.

Kalmia latifolia

Shape and size

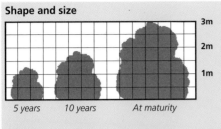

| 5 years | 10 years | At maturity |

3m
2m
1m

Position

Hardiness

Soil

MOIST

ACID

Uses

Features calendar

Jan	Feb	Mar	Apr	May	June
July	Aug	Sept	Oct	Nov	Dec

Kalmia latifolia

Flowering can take three or four years

Growing guide

Kalmias look beautiful in flower but they are fussy about their growing conditions so are rarely seen in gardens. They like an acidic soil that is moist but need more sun than other woodland acid-loving plants, as well as shelter from cold winds. However, if you have suitable conditions, they make attractive companions for rhododendrons.

Most people will have to grow them in large (minimum of 0.6m/2ft diameter) containers using an ericaceous compost. This will restrict their eventual size to about 1.2x1.2m (4x4ft).

Pruning

It is best not to prune this shrub as the flowers are produced on older stems. If it becomes too big, take out one stem in three in mid-summer after flowering.

Propagation

Peg down young shoots near the ground in spring. It can take up to two years for these layers to root.

Troubleshooting

The bushes can look weak and straggly if conditions are not ideal. Mulching with a 5cm (2in) layer of bark chippings each spring to keep the soil moist will help. It takes a long time for them to flower; at least three to four years after planting.

Which variety?

You may come across named varieties of **K. latifolia**, these can be more tender than the species but **'Ostbo Red'** with red flowers is one of the hardiest and most widely available.

Other kalmias include **K. angustifolia 'Rubra'**, the sheep laurel. This is a 0.9x0.9m (3x3ft) shrub with red flowers in May and June.

> **Buying tips** *Slow-growing, so larger plants are a better buy. Most likely to be available from nurseries specialising in acid-loving plants.*

Kerria japonica

Shape and size

| 5 years | 10 years | At maturity |

Position   Hardiness Soil

MOST

Uses

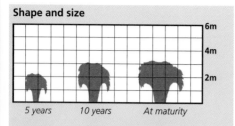

Features calendar

Jan	Feb	Mar	Apr	May	June
July	Aug	Sept	Oct	Nov	Dec

Kerria japonica 'Pleniflora'

Buying tips *A quick-growing shrub, so smaller and cheaper plants are better value for money.*

Kerria japonica 'Golden Guinea'

Growing guide

Kerria is a useful, cheap shrub for difficult conditions. It will grow almost anywhere, so concentrate on using it where little else will grow, such as north-facing walls, beneath trees and large shrubs, or fences and dry banks.

Its main feature is a display of yellow spring flowers which can be single or double. *K. japonica* 'Picta' provides a longer season of interest with its attractive variegated leaves, though all provide some autumn colour when the leaves yellow. One drawback is that it produces suckers which can emerge some way from the parent plant.

Pruning

To encourage vigorous new flowering shoots, cut out one stem in three in early summer after flowering. If the variegated variety produces all-green shoots, cut these out as soon as you notice them.

Propagation

The suckers can be detached in spring and replanted. Alternatively, hardwood cuttings can be taken in late autumn and inserted into open ground. Transplant the following autumn.

Troubleshooting

The plant can rapidly spread by suckering and outgrow its allotted space. Use a spade to chop off portions around the edge of the plant and keep it within limits.

Which variety?

It is worth going for a named variety as these often have an extra feature of interest.
'Golden Guinea' Larger flowers than the species.
'Picta' ('Variegata') Smaller (0.9x0.9m /3x3ft) and not so invasive with cream and green variegated foliage.
'Pleniflora' Double-flowered form, good for a wall shrub.

Kolkwitzia amabilis

Shape and size

			3m
			2m
			1m

5 years   10 years   At maturity

Position   Hardiness   Soil

MOST

Uses

Features calendar

Jan	Feb	Mar	Apr	May	June
July	Aug	Sept	Oct	Nov	Dec

Growing guide

The beauty bush is a pretty yet undemanding shrub, useful for late spring interest to the garden. The pink flowers are borne on arching stems and the foliage is grey-green, providing some extra colour in autumn when it turns yellow.

This shrub is particularly good if you want a quick filler shrub for the back of a border. For an informal hedge, plant 0.9m (3ft) apart.

Pruning

It needs regular pruning to keep the plant in good shape and producing plenty of flowers. Cut out one stem in three in mid-summer after flowering.

Propagation

Take semi-ripe cuttings in August and root in a cold frame. Pot on cuttings that have rooted in autumn and plant out the following spring.

Troubleshooting

Generally trouble-free.

Which variety?

There is only one species but you may find the variety **'Pink Cloud'** which has a darker pink flower.

The flowers of Kolkwitzia amabilis

Buying tips *A quick-growing shrub, so small plants are the best value. Choose ones with the most stems.*

The beauty bush in early summer

Lavandula angustifolia

Shape and size

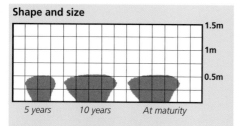

1.5m
1m
0.5m

5 years   10 years   At maturity

Position   Hardiness   Soil

DRAINED

Uses

Features calendar

Jan	Feb	Mar	Apr	May	June
❁					
July	Aug	Sept	Oct	Nov	Dec

Buying tips   *Avoid woody plants.*

The curious heads of French lavender

'Twickel Purple'

Growing guide

Most lavenders have grey-green foliage and, in July, scented purple flowers. However, height and hardiness vary so it is worth considering these factors when choosing. For the best scent look for the species *L. angustifolia* (also sold as *L. officinalis* or *L. spica*). Most garden varieties are hybrids, so the quality of their scent varies according to their parentage.

Lavenders need a free-draining soil, otherwise they can die after cold, wet winters. If your soil is heavy, grow them on top of a 0.8m (2½ft) trench half-filled with rubble and coarse sand, and topped up with garden soil mixed with grit.

For a low hedge or edging, alongside a path or herb garden, use a dwarf variety planted 30-45cm (12-18in) apart. For a low hedge, say 60cm (2ft) or so, choose 'Folgate' or 'Twickel Purple'.

Lavenders have a role in the border, where they can soften bright yellow flowers or foliage. The large varieties can be planted singly, but the smaller ones will have much greater impact if planted in groups of three or more.

The large lavenders can be planted by seats, steps or paths. All are suitable for planting in containers and this is a particularly good way to grow the more tender types, such as French lavender.

Pruning

After planting, when new shoots appear at the base in spring, cut back the previous year's growth to within 2.5-5cm (1-2in) of the ground. Most lavenders tend to sprawl with age and so benefit from regular trimming. Once flowering has finished, remove the flower stalks. In spring, just as growth begins, trim back most of the previous year's growth. Overgrown bushes can sometimes be rejuvenated by cutting back into the old wood, but there is a risk that such hard pruning can kill the plant. As a rule, prune above live shoots.

Propagation

It is worth taking cuttings regularly so bushes can be replaced every five to six years with two-year-old plants.

A mass planting of 'Hidcote'

Lavandula angustifolia

'Hidcote' with hypericums

If your garden suffers from bad frosts, it is wise to take cuttings each year. Cuttings of semi-ripe shoots root easily in the cold frame in early autumn and can be planted out in spring.

Troubleshooting

Lavender can get infested with cuckoo spit (frog hoppers). Though serious damage is unlikely, they can be picked off or blasted off with a jet of water. Lavender scab is a rare but fatal disease. Shoots wilt suddenly from May onwards and the young flower heads curl up like a corkscrew. The plant then dies. Dig up and burn.

Which variety?

TALL VARIETIES (0.6m/2ft or over) you are most likely to come across:
L. angustifolia is the most widely grown. Good for hedging and one of the most strongly scented.
'Alba' is a vigorous variety reaching 0.9-1.2m (3-4ft) with white flowers.
'Folgate' Vigorous purple variety very free-flowering.
'Grappenhall' has large leaves and purple flowers.

'Twickel Purple' is a compact grower.
L. lanata has woolly leaves but is not very hardy.

DWARF VARIETIES (30-50cm/12-20in) you are likely to come across:
'Hidcote' ('Hidcote Blue') A good variety with narrow, silver leaves and dark purple flowers. Some resistance to lavender scab.
'Hidcote Pink' is a pink version.
'Nana Atropurpurea' is similar.
'Munstead' Good purple-flowered variety, but susceptible to scab.
'Nana Alba' has white, strongly scented flowers.
L. stoechas **(French lavender)** has distinctive purple bracts which stick up above the flower heads. The foliage is downy with a pine scent. Many varieties are available including **'Papillon'** (*L. stoechas pedunculata*) with larger bracts, and **'Alba'** with white bracts.
L. dentata has green cut-edged leaves and purple flowers. ***L. dentata candicans*** ('Silver Form') has cut-edged silver leaves.
L. viridis has green leaves and cream-coloured flowers.

Lavatera

Shape and size

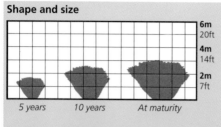

5 years	10 years	At maturity

6m 20ft
4m 14ft
2m 7ft

Position   Hardiness   Soil

MOST   DRAINED

Uses

Features calendar

Jan	Feb	Mar	Apr	May	June
					✿

July	Aug	Sept	Oct	Nov	Dec
✿	✿				

Lavatera 'Barnsley'

Buying tips *Avoid plants which are yellowing as these take longer to establish and flower. It is a good idea to buy 'Barnsley' in flower to check that it is the right variety. Small plants are a good buy.*

The flowers of 'Rosea'

Lavatera 'Rosea' with pampas grass

Growing guide

Lavateras are fast-growers and they start flowering in their first year, so they are ideal as a quick filler in borders where an injection of summer colour is needed.

The original 'Rosea' is still widely-grown but the paler-coloured 'Barnsley' is becoming popular. There are also new varieties which offer more flowering impact on smaller shrubs and a wider range of colours. There are regional differences in habit and hardiness, although, as they are inexpensive to buy, it is worth experimenting.

Lavateras like a free-draining soil in full sun. Avoid very rich soils as too much fertiliser encourages leaf growth at the expense of flowers. The large ones can put on a huge amount of growth in summer, which can make them susceptible to wind rock. In windy gardens, try to find them a sheltered spot and cut them back by a third in autumn. Vigorous types such as 'Rosea' can be trained as standards, which if kept well-pruned and staked, will be less likely to suffer wind damage.

Pruning

Cut back all the stems to within a few centimetres from the base in spring. Plants which appear to have died back over winter will often sprout again from the base as late as May or June. Cut out reverted shoots on 'Barnsley' and 'Wembdon Variegated'.

Propagation

Most lavateras ('Ice Cool' is an exception) are easy to propagate. Take cuttings from the shoot tips as they start to ripen in July or August, or take hardwood cuttings in autumn. Root in a cold frame using multipurpose compost.

Lavatera 'Burgundy Wine'

Lavatera 'Candy Floss'

Troubleshooting

Physical damage can trigger off reversion of 'Barnsley' back to 'Rosea', so take care when cultivating around these plants. If your whole bush reverts to producing pink flowers there is nothing that you can do about it. Odd shoots can be pruned out at the base.

Which variety?

COMPACT VARIETIES

Of the more compact forms (i.e. 1.2m/4ft after five years), choose between the following:

'Candy Floss' has pale-pink flowers with a white eye from August to September. It is not totally hardy in colder areas.

'Burgundy Wine' is a small variety with purple-red flowers and darker foliage than usual. It should do well in colder areas.

'Ice Cool' ('Peppermint Ice') has white flowers with a green eye. It is not totally hardy in colder areas.

'Lara Rose' is a semi-evergreen with green and gold foliage. The variegation fades once the rose-pink flowers appear. It is claimed to be compact enough to grow as a container plant.

'Pink Frills' has small flowers and large shrivelled leaves.

LARGER VARIETIES

'Rosea' is the established variety but it is very vigorous and can reach over 2m (7ft) after five years. **'Kew Rose'** is similar but with slightly frillier flowers.

'Barnsley' is one of the best of the larger varieties with its lovely white, blush pink flowers with a deep pinkish-red eye.

'Wembdon Variegated' has cream variegated leaves but is very prone to reversion to plain green.

Lavateras on trial in the Gardening Which? Demonstration Gardens at Capel Manor, near Enfield in Middlesex

131

Lespedeza thunbergii

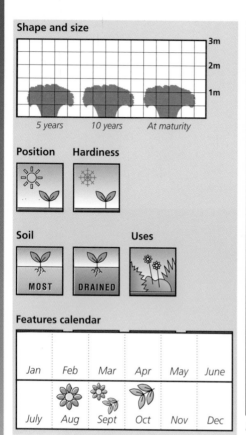

Shape and size

		3m
		2m
		1m

5 years   10 years   At maturity

Position   **Hardiness**

Soil   **Uses**

MOST   DRAINED

Features calendar

Jan	Feb	Mar	Apr	May	June
July	Aug	Sept	Oct	Nov	Dec

Lespedeza thunbergii with Hebe ochracea 'James Stirling' in the foreground

Growing guide

The long trails of pinkish-purple, pea-like flowers are an attractive feature in late summer. The silver-grey leaves turn yellow in autumn, giving added interest. It needs to be cut back hard every year, which can leave a gap in the border until early summer, when it comes into leaf. However, it grows very quickly and can easily swamp neighbouring plants unless carefully situated. A corner of a border where it can tumble over a low wall would be an ideal spot. It will grow on all but waterlogged soils, tolerating extremes of acidity and alkalinity.

Buying tips *Young plants establish quickly, but even straggly specimens can be pruned back to form good plants. Most likely to be stocked by specialist nurseries.*

Pruning
Cut back all stems to just above ground level in March or April.

Propagation
Take cuttings from side shoots just as they start to ripen in early July. Alternatively, take 15cm (6in) lengths of the woody stems in October or November and root in pots in a cold frame over winter.

Troubleshooting
Generally trouble-free, though can be killed if it gets waterlogged.

Which variety?

L. thunbergii (sometimes sold as *L. sieboldii*) is the most widely sold. There is also a white-flowered form.

L. bicolor has purple and pink flowers in July and August. The flowers are less showy but its more upright habit may make it easier to place in the border.

Leucothoe fontanesiana

Shape and size

5 years	10 years	At maturity

Position

Hardiness

Soil

ACID NEUTRAL

Uses

Features calendar

Jan	Feb	Mar	Apr	May	June
July	Aug	Sept	Oct	Nov	Dec

Cold weather causes the leaves to develop red tints

The new leaves are red on some forms

Growing guide

Grown mainly as a foliage shrub, with attractive arching stems. The leaves develop a red or purple tinge as the weather gets cold in winter. Even in summer, the contrast between the green uppersides of the leaves and the purplish undersides has a pleasing effect. White, pendulous, pitcher-shaped flowers in spring are a bonus. Although it will tolerate quite heavy shade, it does not like dry soil, so incorporate plenty of organic matter when planting and mulch annually. It quickly forms a dense canopy of foliage and is an effective weed smotherer. It slowly spreads by means of underground suckers but is not invasive and can easily be kept within bounds with a spade.

Pruning

Cut back one-third of the shoots to ground level each April on established plants to encourage new foliage, which is the most attractive.

Propagation

Peg down shoots in spring. Layers should root in 12 to 18 months.

Troubleshooting

Generally trouble-free provided you avoid planting on alkaline soils.

Which variety?

'Rainbow', also called 'Multicolor', has cream and pink splashes on the leaves and is the most widely available at garden centres. This variety does best in light shade as the variegation will be far less pronounced in heavy shade.

Buying tips Look for bushy specimens with healthy unmarked leaves. Large plants provide instant effect.

Leycesteria formosa

Shape and size

6m
4m
2m

5 years   10 years   At maturity

Position

Hardiness

Soil

MOST

Uses

Features calendar

Jan	Feb	Mar	Apr	May	June
🌼	🌼		🔵		

July	Aug	Sept	Oct	Nov	Dec
🌼	🌼				

Large coloured bracts surround the flowers

Growing guide

The main attraction of this shrub is the hanging bunches of long-lasting purple-red bracts which are tipped with pale pink flowers from late July or early August. Later they are followed by purple berries. Despite these exotic blooms, the shrub is hardy and is ideal for filling a small space at the back of a border.

It will thrive on almost any soil, including heavy, waterlogged clay, and forms a dense thicket of green stems that are attractive in winter.

Leycesteria is very quick-growing

Pruning

After planting, cut all the stems to within 5cm (2in) of ground level in early spring. This will help to produce a bushy shrub. Once established, remove a third of the oldest shoots each year to ensure plenty of flowers.

Propagation

Fresh seed can be collected in August and sown in trays in a cold frame. Prick out in spring and plant when they reach a reasonable size. Hardwood cuttings can also be taken in winter and inserted into a sand-lined trench. They should root by the following spring.

Troubleshooting

The fruits may attract insects, so take this into account when choosing a site. If the shrub is growing in ideal conditions, it may self-seed and this can become a nuisance.

Which variety?

Only the species is widely available.

Buying tips *Tough and quick-growing, so small plants are the best value.*

Berries just starting to ripen

Ligustrum

(e.g. Ligustrum ovalifolium 'Aureum')

Shape and size

	6m
	4m
	2m

5 years   10 years   At maturity

Position

Hardiness

Soil

MOST

Uses

Features calendar

Jan	Feb	Mar	Apr	May	June

July	Aug	Sept	Oct	Nov	Dec

Ligustrum lucidum 'Excelsum Superbum' with skimmia in the foreground

Growing guide

The ordinary privet makes a useful but rather dull hedge. However, it does have some more interesting relatives of which the golden privet is the most widely available. The golden privet has larger leaves and branches more freely. Left unpruned in a shrub border it makes a bright evergreen, which can provide plenty of material for flower arranging. Alternatively, it can be planted 0.5m (1½ft) apart and clipped to produce a good hedge.

In mild areas, the leaves may be retained over winter but you cannot rely on this in most parts of the country.

Pruning

After planting, shorten all the shoots by one-third in spring. This will encourage the formation of a well-shaped bush. Do not do this to slow-growing, compact varieties like *L. japonicum* 'Rotundifolium'.

In future years, you can leave privet unpruned or clip it into a shape. If it becomes too large and bare at the base, cut back all branches to 5-10cm (2-4in) above the ground.

Buying tips *Bare-rooted plants are sold more cheaply in bundles for hedging in autumn*

Variegated varieties may throw up all-green shoots and these should be cut back to their point of origin as soon as noticed.

Propagation

Take cuttings as the new shoots start to ripen in July. Root in peaty compost in a well-shaded cold frame. Alternatively, take hardwood cuttings in October. Bury up to two-thirds deep in open ground and transplant the following autumn.

Troubleshooting

Privet roots rob neighbouring plants of nutrients. Feeding with a general fertiliser such as growmore would benefit adjacent plants.

Which variety?

***L. japonicum* 'Rotundifolium'** Evergreen 1.8x1.8m (6x6ft), compact, slow-growing habit, glossy leaves, white flowers July to August.

***L. lucidum* 'Excelsum Superbum'** Evergreen 5.5x3m (18x10ft), leaves edged with creamy-yellow, white flowers August to September.

***L. lucidum* 'Tricolor'** Leaves are tinged with pink when young.

L. quihoui Deciduous, 2.4x2.4m (8x8ft). Large flower spikes September to October.

***L. sinense* 'Variegatum'** A semi-evergreen 4.5x4.5m (14x14ft) grey-green leaves with white variegation, white flowers in July.

Ligustrum ovalifolium 'Aureum'

Lonicera
(e.g. Lonicera nitida 'Baggesen's Gold')

Shape and size

5 years	10 years	At maturity

3m
2m
1m

Position   Hardiness   Soil

MOIST

Uses

Features calendar

Jan	Feb	Mar	Apr	May	June
July	Aug	Sept	Oct	Nov	Dec

Buying tips *Look for bushy plants with good leaf colour. Small plants are a good buy as they are fairly quick to get established.*

Lonicera nitida 'Baggesen's Gold'

A five-year-old hedge of Lonicera nitida

Growing guide

L. nitida is a plant much used as a low hedge (plant 30cm/12in apart) in suburban front gardens. It is not fussy about soil or site and responds well to clipping. There are two varieties which look good in sunny shrub borders if left unpruned. 'Baggesen's Gold', the most well-known, has golden-yellow leaves. A newer variety to look out for is the silver-variegated 'Silver Beauty'. Both have tiny leaves which make them ideal for creating a contrast in texture next to larger-leaved shrubs.

There are also several other shrubby loniceras. *L. pileata* (privet honeysuckle) is another foliage type, while others produce fragrant flowers in late winter, spring or summer, depending on the species.

Pruning

After planting, shorten the previous year's growth on *L. nitida* and *L. pileata* by one-third in spring. Allow other species to grow without pruning until established.

L. nitida must be clipped hard in mid-spring if you want to maintain a formal outline. To control the size of a free-standing bush, prune out one stem in three each year. *L. pileata* needs no regular pruning, but if it grows too large, reduce the new shoots by two-thirds in mid-spring.

Flowering shrubby honeysuckles need no regular pruning. But to control a large specimen, cut out one stem in three in mid-spring (winter-flowering ones) or after flowering (early and mid-summer flowering ones).

Close-up of the tiny flowers of Lonicera fragrantissima

Propagation

Take cuttings in June or July just as the new shoots start to ripen. Root in a pot covered with a polythene bag. Pot on or plant out in autumn if they are well-rooted.

Alternatively, take hardwood cuttings in late autumn and root in sandy compost in a cold frame. Pot on or plant out the rooted cuttings in spring.

Troubleshooting

L. nitida 'Baggesen's Gold' may lose its colour if there is too much shade, becoming pale-green rather than golden. With age the plants can become woody and outgrow their space in a mixed border. Hard pruning can correct this. Prune all the main branches to within a few centimetres of the base.

Which variety?

FOR FOLIAGE

***L. nitida* Baggesen's Gold'** and **'Silver Beauty'** are the best for mixed borders, providing attractively coloured foliage and a contrast in texture to most other shrubs.
L. pileata is a useful ground cover plant with green foliage. It grows around 0.8x1.8m (2x6ft) after ten years. It is often used as a low hedge to divide areas of the garden.

FOR FLOWERS

L. fragrantissima has fragrant, cream flowers in late winter or early spring and grows 1.8x3m (6x10ft) after ten years. **L. x purpusii** is similar but has fewer flowers.
L. rupicola syringantha has fragrant, pale-lilac flowers in May and June.

Lonicera x purpusii

Magnolia x soulangeana

Shape and size

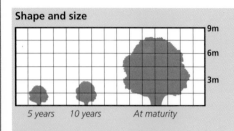

| 9m |
| 6m |
| 3m |

5 years   10 years   At maturity

Position

Hardiness

Soil

ACID   MOIST

Uses

Features calendar

Jan	Feb	Mar	Apr	May	June
July	Aug	Sept	Oct	Nov	Dec

The dark flowers of 'Nigra'

Growing guide

M. x *soulangeana,* along with the smaller *M. stellata,* are the most suitable for small gardens. Other species, though magnificent in flower, tend to grow into trees.

For all magnolias, the soil needs to be moist but well-drained and the greater the depth of topsoil the better. Avoid positions that get the early morning sun as this could encourage premature growth in spring, which can subsequently be damaged by frosts. In cold, exposed gardens, some protection is needed as the wind can tear and bruise the leaves and flowers. However, once established, magnolias are surprisingly hardy and they will tolerate atmospheric pollution, which can be a serious problem in front gardens which face on to busy roads.

The open-branched structure is ideal for underplanting. However, the roots are quite delicate and near the surface so avoid too much digging or forking around the root area.

Pruning

No pruning is required, but small branches which cross can be removed in winter to create a more attractive shape. They can withstand severe pruning if they get too big, though this may cause the plant to stop flowering for a few years.

Propagation

Layers from one-year-old shoots taken in spring can root by the autumn. You can also layer in August using current year's shoots, but rooting may take two years.

Troubleshooting

They can take up to five years or more to flower well. Blooms may fall prematurely during a spell of warm weather, so avoid planting in very sunny parts of the garden.

Which variety?

There are named varieties of **M. x soulangeana**. These are worth looking out for:

'Alexandrina' Fragrant flowers, white sometimes flushed with purple.

'Brozzonii' Vigorous, late-flowering, white flowers.

'Lennei' Fast-growing, free-flowering, large pink flowers.

'Nigra' (*M.* x *liliiflora* 'Nigra') Long-flowering with purple flowers.

'Rustica Rubra' Vigorous, spreading plant with rose-purple flowers.

Buying tips *Buy container-grown plants, ideally when they are in flower; do not be tempted by cheap, bare-rooted plants. It is worth paying more for a grafted plant or one raised from cuttings to avoid having to wait years for the plant to flower.*

A mature specimen of 'Rustica Rubra'

Magnolia stellata

Shape and size

5 years	10 years	At maturity

Position

Hardiness

Soil

ACID   DRAINED   MOIST

Uses

Features calendar

Jan	Feb	Mar	Apr	May	June
July	Aug	Sept	Oct	Nov	Dec

Magnolia stellata

Magnolia stellata 'Royal Star'

Growing guide

Magnolia stellata is the smallest of the magnolias, slowly making a round, compact bush of 1.5m (5ft) or so; though ancient specimens can get much larger. They are ideal feature shrubs for a small garden and there is plenty of seasonal interest. The beautiful, slightly scented, spring flowers come about two years or less after planting. The green leaves turn yellow in autumn and, in winter, the hairy leaf buds are an extra feature.

To ensure the flowers give a good display, plant where the shrub will not get the early morning sun. Frozen flowers heated up by the early morning sun will turn brown. Flowers allowed to thaw out slowly should escape frost damage.

Pruning

No pruning required, but small branches that cross can be removed in winter to improve the shape.

Propagation

Layers from one-year-old shoots taken in spring can root by the autumn. You can also layer in August using the current year's shoots but rooting can take a couple of years.

Troubleshooting

Generally untroubled by pests and diseases. Cold winds and hot weather when they are in flower are the main problems.

Which variety?

The species is the most widely available and is a good garden plant. Varieties you may come across are:
'Rosea' is similar to species but with rosy-pink flowers.
'Royal Star' is hardier than the species, with larger white flowers in April and May.
'Water Lily' is similar in size to the species but with pink or white flowers in April and May that look a bit like water lilies in outline.

Buying tips *Always buy container-grown plants but avoid any which are the slightest bit pot-bound. Grafted plants grow faster than those produced by cuttings. It is worth paying more for an older plant if you want it to be a feature in the garden straight away.*

Mahonia
(e.g. Mahonia x media 'Charity')

Shape and size

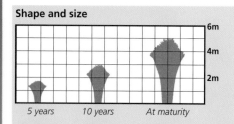

5 years	10 years	At maturity

6m
4m
2m

Position ## Hardiness

Soil

 ACID **NEUTRAL** **MOIST**

Uses

Features calendar

Jan	Feb	Mar	Apr	May	June
❋	❋	●●			
July	Aug	Sept	Oct	Nov	Dec
				❋	❋

Buying tips *Choose plants with bright, unblemished leaves. Older plants should have several stems.*

Mahonia aquifolium 'Atropurpurea'

Growing guide

Mahonias are invaluable as architectural evergreens and for their winter flowers. Their size, hardiness and flowering times vary depending on the species.

Mahonias will succeed in a wide range of conditions. They can tolerate alkalinity provided there is plenty of humus and topsoil; thin, chalky soils will not do. The hardiest are *M. aquifolium* and its varieties, these will also succeed in coastal areas if sheltered from salt-laden winds. *M. japonica* and the *M. x media* hybrids are relatively hardy but need some shelter to come through the winter unscathed. More unusual mahonias might be tender.

As specimen shrubs, *M. japonica* and the *M.* x *media* hybrids are hard to beat. But for ground cover under trees and shrubs, choose *M. aquifolium* or *M.* 'Undulata'.

Pruning
To encourage bushy growth in the early years on *M.* x *media* 'Charity' or *M. japonica*, cut off the flower heads to below the new leaf joints beneath them as soon as flowering is over. Even if a stem has not flowered, remove the top rosette of leaves. *M. aquifolium* is a strong grower and will need to be controlled. Cut out one stem in three in early summer. Mahonias grown as ground cover need to be pruned back hard every other year.

Propagation
Take cuttings in early autumn or early spring. Cut just above a leaf with a bud in the axil and a few centimetres below it. Root in a heated propagator or a pot covered with a polythene bag indoors.

Troubleshooting
Rust can be a problem. Spray with a systemic fungicide when seen and repeat at fortnightly intervals. Cut back severely affected plants and destroy infected leaves. You may need to control the sideways spread of *M. aquifolium*. Chop off the suckers with a spade or edging tool.

Which variety?

You are most likely to come across *M. x media* 'Charity', a good variety for flowers. Most of the other *M. x media* varieties are similar, although flowering times may vary and they are slightly more tender:

'Buckland' has long sprays of flowers from January to April.
'Lionel Fortescue' has very long sprays of flowers from November to February.
'Winter Sun' flowers from January to March.

Other species that are a similar size:
M. japonica has highly scented, pendulous flowers of lemon-yellow from January to March.
M. japonica **'Bealei'** has upright sprays of flowers from December to February.
M. lomariifolia is tender so needs a sheltered, sunny site. It has long sprays of flowers from November to December.
M. pinnata is a vigorous plant with blue-green foliage and lots of lemon yellow flowers from March to May, but they are not highly scented.

The following mahonias are smaller (i.e. around 0.9x0.9m/3x3ft):
M. aquifolium has a reddish tinge to the leaves in winter. Very hardy but a suckering shrub. Flowers appear February to April but have little scent. Varieties worth looking out for include:
'Apollo' is a good compact shrub with more scented and larger flowers than most *M. aquifolium* varieties.
'Atropurpurea' has wine-purple leaves in winter.
'Moseri' has bronze-red foliage in the spring.
M. nervosa is a low-growing, suckering form, rather tender. Flowers are produced late (May to June) and are not highly scented.
M. x wagneri **'Undulata'** is a very hardy shrub with glossy foliage and scented flowers from February to April. It has a spreading habit, reaching around 0.9x1.2m (3x4ft) after five years.

Mahonia x media 'Charity'

Myrtus communis

Shape and size

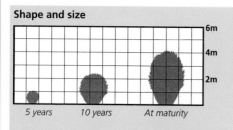

		6m
		4m
		2m

5 years   10 years   At maturity

Position   Hardiness   Soil

   DRAINED

Uses

Features calendar

Jan	Feb	Mar	Apr	May	June
✿	✿		● ●		
July	Aug	Sept	Oct	Nov	Dec

Myrtus communis 'Variegata' is more tender than the species

Close-up of myrtle flower

Buying tips *Buy in late spring so plants can get well established before the winter. Most likely to be stocked by specialist nurseries.*

Growing guide

Common myrtle has sweet-scented flowers in July and August, sometimes followed by purple-black berries in October. Its glossy evergreen foliage is aromatic too.

Myrtle is most reliable in mild areas, but it can be grown elsewhere if given a hot sunny spot. A south-facing wall or fence where there is plenty of shelter would be suitable.

If this is not possible, grow it in a container so that you can move it indoors over winter. Choose a pot that is at least 45cm (18in) in both depth and diameter and fill with a John Innes No 2 potting compost.

Pruning

To create a formal outline, clip or cut back hard in early summer. Any frost-damaged shoots should be removed in early or mid-spring.

Propagation

Take cuttings in November, root in a cold frame or a heated propagator and plant out in spring.

Troubleshooting

Plants may be severely damaged or cut down to ground level by the cold. Leave until late spring for signs of new shoots from the old wood at the base before dismissing them as dead.

To avoid problems insulate plants with a 15cm (6in) layer of bracken in winter and cover with a double layer of horticultural fleece.

Which variety?

There are variegated varieties but these are more tender than the species. *M. communis* **'Tarentina'** is a smaller version, reaching 0.9x0.6m (3x2ft). Could be useful for small gardens or a conservatory.

Nandina domestica

Shape and size

5 years	10 years	At maturity

3m
2m
1m

Position

Hardiness

Soil

DRAINED

Uses

Features calendar

Jan	Feb	Mar	Apr	May	June
July	Aug	Sept	Oct	Nov	Dec

Growing guide

This is a member of the berberis family, but it looks more like a bamboo. It is useful for adding colour to small spaces. The leaves turn orange-red and purple in autumn and, being evergreen, retain their fiery colouration through much of the winter. In spring the new leaves are tinged with red.

Give it a sheltered position if possible as cold, winter winds can scorch the leaves. Although the plant will recover, this can ruin its appearance during the main season of interest. A sunny position is essential for good leaf colour.

Other features of this shrub are white flowers in July and, during a hot summer, red berries in August. When formed , the berries often remain throughout the winter.

Pruning

No routine pruning is required, but you may need to deal with an old congested plant. Cut out one stem in three in mid-spring. Make the cut as far down to soil level as possible, to avoid a clump of dead stumps. New growth will then be produced from the base. Neglected plants can be renovated by cutting them back to ground level in spring.

Propagation

Lift and divide in spring, like you would a herbaceous perennial.

Troubleshooting

In cold areas, the plant may look very ragged over winter or the top growth may be killed right back. Leave the plant in place as new growth will usually start to resprout from the base by late spring or early summer. Pests and diseases are rarely a problem.

Which variety?

The variety **'Firepower'** is worth seeking out as it forms a neat, compact plant, less than 0.6m (2ft) tall, and has even brighter autumn leaf colours.

> **Buying tips** Look for a well-shaped plant with bright green leaves (or good leaf tints if buying during the autumn). Avoid specimens with spindly shoots and limp, pale leaves.

Autumn foliage of Nandina domestica 'Firepower'

Nandina domestica in flower

Olearia macrodonta

Shape and size

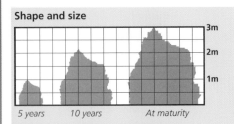

3m
2m
1m

5 years   10 years   At maturity

Position

Hardiness

Soil

MOST

DRAINED

Uses

Features calendar

Jan	Feb	Mar	Apr	May	June
					🌼
🌼					
July	Aug	Sept	Oct	Nov	Dec

Olearia x scilloniensis

Olearia macrodonta

Growing guide

Daisy bushes are shrubs for a mild climate where they can play a useful role sheltering smaller plants in seaside gardens. In cold areas they may not survive unless you site them in a warm sunny spot, such as against a south-facing wall. They do well in urban gardens, where they are favoured by the milder conditions and will tolerate high levels of atmospheric pollution.

The main feature of this shrub is its clusters of daisy-like flowers that appear in great profusion during the summer. The leaves are mid-green on top and white below, creating a shimmering effect in the breeze.

Pruning

To encourage a regular supply of new shoots, cut out one stem in three in mid-summer after flowering has finished. Also remove any dead shoots in April.

Propagation

Take cuttings from the sideshoots in early to mid-summer and root in a cold frame. Alternatively, take hardwood cuttings in October and root in pots in a cold frame. Transplant or pot on in early summer the following year.

Troubleshooting

Shoots may be killed or damaged over winter. However, new shoots should sprout freely from the old wood in spring.

Which variety?

O. x haastii is one of the hardiest, with masses of white daisy flowers in July and August.
O. ilicifolia has the added attraction of serrated, holly-like leaves. It flowers in June.
O. macrodonta grows up to 3.6m (12ft) tall with large clusters of small daisy-like flowers during June and July. It too has serrated leaves.
O. x scilloniensis is smaller than average, growing no more than 1.5m (5ft) and is smothered with flowers from May to July.

> **Buying tips** Don't worry if plants look a bit straggly when you buy them as they can easily be pruned back to form bushy specimens.

Osmanthus x burkwoodii

Shape and size

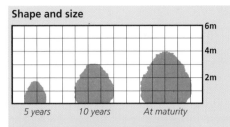

| 5 years | 10 years | At maturity |

Position

Hardiness

Soil

MOST

Uses

Features calendar

Jan	Feb	Mar	Apr	May	June
			✿	✿	
July	Aug	Sept	Oct	Nov	Dec

Osmanthus heterophyllus in bloom

Osmanthus x burkwoodii with bergenias

Growing guide

Osmanthus is a useful group of evergreens with the bonus of fragrant flowers. The flowers are white or cream trumpets and these may be produced either in late autumn or early spring, depending on the species.

They can be used as part of a mixed planting in a large border or, if planted 0.6m (2ft) apart, as a hedging plant.

O. x burkwoodii has leathery, glossy dark leaves, which make a good foil for flowers. It is often used for hedging and is a good choice for dry, chalky soils.

Pruning

No routine pruning is required. However, they grow freely from old wood so can be cut back hard if they become overgrown. Cut back two-thirds off each new shoot in early summer to restrict their size. Remove any dead or winter-damaged wood in early spring.

Propagation

Layer branches in the autumn; they should root the next autumn or spring. Or take hardwood cuttings in October and root in a cold frame. Pot up or plant out in late spring.

Troubleshooting

The leaves can be scorched by cold winds. In exposed gardens, it is best to site them where they will get some shelter from north-east winds, which do the most damage.

Which variety?

O. delavayi Dark, grey-green, serrated foliage. Scented, white flowers in early to mid-spring.

O. heterophyllus The dark green, holly-shaped leaves often vary on the same plant; some being covered in prickles, others with spined tips. Scented, white flowers in autumn. Slow-growing.

O. heterophyllus 'Rotundifolius' Very dark, toothed but spineless leaves and scented, white flowers in spring. Slow-growing.

Ozothamnus

Shape and size

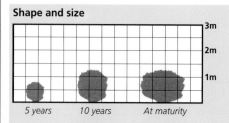

5 years	10 years	At maturity

(chart markings: 3m, 2m, 1m)

Position

Hardiness

Soil

DRAINED

Uses

Features calendar

Jan	Feb	Mar	Apr	May	June
July	Aug	Sept	Oct	Nov	Dec

(flower symbols in July and August)

Ozothamnus ledifolius

Growing guide

An attractive shrub for a tub on a sunny patio. The foliage resembles that of rosemary. The dense heads of white flowers emerge from red buds and provide a pleasant summer scent. The dried flower heads remain on the plant all winter and also make an attractive feature. Although it can withstand frost, it will die in very cold weather or wet winter conditions. For this reason, it is best grown in a container and brought into a conservatory, greenhouse or well-lit room over the winter.

Put it in a tub at least 45cm (18in) in depth and diameter, filled with a John Innes No 2 compost. If you use a terracotta pot, line it with polythene to reduce water loss from the compost. Feed regularly with a liquid fertiliser through the spring and summer, or use slow-release Osmocote granules.

Pruning

Remove one or two of the oldest branches each year on established plants to encourage new growth from the base and maintain a bushy habit. The best time for pruning is May or when the risk of heavy frosts is past.

Propagation

Take cuttings from the tips of new shoots in June. Root in a pot covered with a clear polythene bag or in a heated propagator.

Troubleshooting

Give winter protection and prune plants if they start to get leggy or bare at the base.

Which variety?

You may also come across **O. ledifolius**, which forms a very neat, rounded bush.

Buying tips Most likely to find it at specialist nurseries. As it is slow-growing, larger plants are a better buy.

Pachysandra terminalis

Shape and size

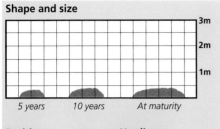

5 years	10 years	At maturity

3m
2m
1m

Position

Hardiness

Soil

ACID NEUTRAL MOIST

Uses

Features calendar

Jan	Feb	Mar	Apr	May	June
July	Aug	Sept	Oct	Nov	Dec

Buying tips *Large clumps are often a better buy than small plants as they can be split up prior to planting.*

The variegated pachysandra is a good plant for brightening up dry shady areas of a garden, where little else will grow

Pachysandra terminalis 'Variegata'

Growing guide

A useful ground cover plant if you have an acidic soil. It will tolerate full sun through to full shade so long as the soil is moist.

Pruning

Annual pruning is not needed. If old plants need to be rejuvenated, cut back the previous year's growth to about 5cm (2in) above the ground in early spring to stimulate new shoots. Pruning to control the spread is best done with a spade.

Propagation

Split up clumps and replant 20cm (8in) apart in spring.

Troubleshooting

Japanese spurge spreads by underground suckers, but as long as it is used for ground cover this should not be a problem.

Which variety?

There is a variegated variety with white edges. It is not quite so vigorous and is more tender.

147

Paeonia suffruticosa

Shape and size

	3m
	2m
	1m

5 years   10 years   At maturity

Position

Hardiness

Soil

MOST

Uses

Features calendar

Jan	Feb	Mar	Apr	May	June
July	Aug	Sept	Oct	Nov	Dec

Buying tips *Resents disturbance so avoid pot-bound plants as they may take several years to establish and flower.*

Paeonia suffruticosa

Paeonia suffruticosa 'Rock's Variety'

Growing guide

Unlike herbaceous peonies, *P. suffruticosa* sprouts from a woody clump each year. They are all spectacular in flower and have attractive divided foliage which contrasts well with other shrubs. Improve the soil to a depth of 90cm (3ft) and plant 10cm (4in) deeper than they were planted before to encourage new shoots from the base. Feed each spring with 70g a sq m (2oz a sq yd) of growmore, or the equivalent, and mulch with bark chippings.

Pruning

Not essential, but if plants in shade become a bit leggy, prune out one in three stems, starting with the oldest.

Propagation

Difficult, but air layering is worth a try if you want to multiply a prized specimen.

Troubleshooting

Young foliage may be damaged by spring frosts. Protect with horticultural fleece if your garden is in a frost pocket.

Even when not in flower, the stems and leaves of tree peonies are attractive features

Which variety?

Varieties are available in white and shades of red and pink. Widely available ones include:
'Cardinal Vaughn' Ruby-purple, double flowers.
'Duchess of Kent' Scarlet, semi-double flowers.
'Mrs William Kelway' White, double flowers.

Parahebe catarractae

Shape and size

1.5m
1m
0.5m

5 years   10 years   At maturity

Position

Hardiness

Soil

DRAINED

Uses

Features calendar

Jan	Feb	Mar	Apr	May	June
✿	✿				
July	Aug	Sept	Oct	Nov	Dec

Growing guide

An attractive, late-flowering dwarf shrub. Although tender, it makes an interesting addition to the patio garden. You could even grow it in a pot and place it in a rock garden for the summer.

The flowers vary from white to purplish-pink with a red ring in the centre. It should do well in an ordinary multipurpose compost but it will resent drying out in the summer. To make watering easier, plunge its container into a larger tub or trough with other suitable plants.

Pruning

Cut back older branches by about one-third in spring if it starts to look a bit straggly.

Propagation

Take cuttings from new shoots in June. Root in a propagator or a pot covered in a polythene bag.

Troubleshooting

Needs to be kept in well-lit, frost-free conditions over the winter.

Which variety?

Blue-flowered forms are sold occasionally.

Buying tips   *Buy in spring or early summer and look for compact plants with dense foliage. Most likely to be available from nurseries specialising in plants from New Zealand.*

Parahebe catarractae at Probus Gardens in Cornwall

Parrotia persica

Shape and size

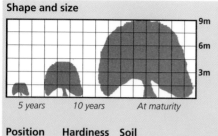

5 years	10 years	At maturity

9m
6m
3m

Position   Hardiness   Soil

ACID   NEUTRAL

Uses

Features calendar

Jan	Feb	Mar	Apr	May	June
July	Aug	Sept	Oct	Nov	Dec

Parrotia persica as the leaves are on the turn in autumn

Buying tips Widely available at garden centres. Slow-growing, so look for a reasonable sized plant.

Mature specimen in the summer

Growing guide

This shrub is grown primarily for its fiery orange, yellow and red autumn foliage. On older plants, more than ten years old, it is also of value for its curious red winter flowers that are surrounded by rings of hairy bracts. Although it will grow in soils that are slightly alkaline, the autumn displays are generally reported to be disappointing if the soil pH is above neutral (although there are exceptions to this rule). It does eventually grow very large and so is only really suitable for large gardens.

Pruning

Pruning is not essential other than to control size or remove damaged branches.

Propagation

Mature plants can be propagated from seed. Otherwise try layering one of the lower branches in spring or autumn.

Troubleshooting

Generally trouble-free.

Which variety?

P. persica 'Pendula' is often sold at specialist nurseries. It has more weeping branches than the species.

Pernettya mucronata

Shape and size

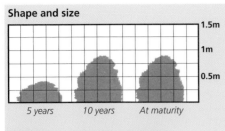

5 years   10 years   At maturity

1.5m
1m
0.5m

Position

Hardiness

Soil

ACID

Uses

Features calendar

Jan	Feb	Mar	Apr	May	June
🫐	🫐			🌼	🌼

July	Aug	Sept	Oct	Nov	Dec
				🫐	🫐

Pernettya mucronata 'Mulberry Wine' in early winter

Growing guide

The marble-like, winter berries are the main feature of this plant but the masses of small white flowers in early summer are also attractive. The species generally has purple berries, though the colour can vary considerably from seed-raised plants. A neutral to acid soil is essential. If you want to grow them in containers a peat-based, multipurpose compost should be sufficiently acidic – you do not need a special ericaceous compost. Plants in a sunny position will have the best display of berries. Although shade-tolerant, plants grown in the shade tend to become taller and more straggly. Male, female and hermaphrodite forms of the plants exist and it is best to plant them in groups of at least three, ideally five, to ensure cross-pollination for good crops of berries. Including a male form such as 'Thymifolia' should ensure plenty of berries on the other plants.

> **Buying tips** Buy plants in berry so that you can choose the colours you like. Buy at least three plants to ensure good pollination and try to include a plant of the male form 'Thymifolia'.

Pruning

Cut back long, straggly shoots on old plants in March.

Propagation

Take cuttings from current year's shoots in September or October. Treat with rooting hormone, insert into a lime-free compost and keep in a cold frame over winter. The species is easy to grow from seed and may even self-seed in favourable conditions.

Troubleshooting

Generally trouble-free provided that the soil remains acidic.

Which variety?

There are many varieties, the main difference between them being the colour of the berries. Those you are most likely to come across include:
'Alba' White berries with pink shading.
'Bell's Seedling' Larger than average, dark-red berries. Hermaphrodite form.
'Mother of Pearl' Large, white berries.
'Mulberry Wine' Magenta berries, ripening to deep purple.
'Sea Shell' Shell-pink, ripening to a deeper pink.
'Thymifolia' A non-berrying male form which grows only 30cm (1ft) in height.

Pernettya mucronata 'Alba'

Perovskia atriplicifolia 'Blue Spire'

Shape and size

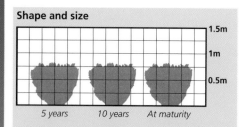

5 years   10 years   At maturity

Position   Hardiness   Soil   Uses

DRAINED

Features calendar

Jan	Feb	Mar	Apr	May	June
July	Aug	Sept	Oct	Nov	Dec

Growing guide

This grey-leaved shrub has erect stems with sprays of pale blue flowers. Russian sage looks more like a herbaceous perennial than a shrub and its main use is to provide late summer colour in a mixed border. When the leaves are crushed they smell of sage.

A well-drained sunny site is needed. Perovskia reaches about 0.8m (2½ft), including the flower spikes, so it is possible to see through the blue haze of flowers. This feature can be used to make a border appear bigger than it really is.

In winter, the bare stems are not an unattractive feature, especially if there are a group of plants.

Pruning

In mid-spring, cut back the previous year's shoots to within about two buds of the base. Do not remove old stems before the spring, as they provide the plant with a bit of protection during the winter.

Propagation

Take semi-ripe cuttings in summer and root in a pot covered with a polythene bag. Pot on and overwinter in a cold frame.

Troubleshooting

It comes into leaf very late, leaving a gap in the border until early summer, so take this into account when selecting a site for it.

Which variety?

'Blue Spire' has larger flower heads and makes a more impressive plant.

Buying tips *Quick-growing, so young plants are a good buy.*

Perovskia stems in winter

Philadelphus, low-growing

Shape and size

3m
2m
1m

5 years   10 years   At maturity

Position   Hardiness   Soil

MOST

Uses

Features calendar

Jan	Feb	Mar	Apr	May	June
				🌸	🌸
July	Aug	Sept	Oct	Nov	Dec
		🍃	🍃		

Buying tips *Avoid any with leaf spotting on the foliage as this can be disfiguring, especially on the yellow-leaved varieties.*

Philadelphus coronarius 'Variegatus' likes some shade

The pineapple-scented Philadelphus microphyllus

Growing guide

The smaller philadelphus varieties make good specimen plants for small gardens or they can be used towards the front of large borders.

The advantage of the smaller varieties is that they are easy to place amongst other flowers, which will carry on the show after the relatively short flowering season of philadelphus.

You are most likely to come across 'Manteau d'Hermine'. It has a powerful orange scent to match its larger cousins. To show it off in flower, try growing it in front of a dark evergreen, such as a camellia or a *Garrya elliptica*. Do not plant anything underneath as the branches will trail right down to the ground.

All most philadelphus demand is a sunny position to give their best display of flowers. They will grow on any soil from heavy clay to chalk. However, while they might not mind an exposed situation, it would mean that you would not be able to appreciate the scent fully.

Pruning

Once flowering is over, cut out one in three of the branches which have flowered. Cut down to a vigorous side branch or to ground level, choosing the oldest and weakest branches first.

Propagation

Take semi-ripe cuttings in early summer, root in a pot covered with a polythene bag. Pot on and overwinter in a cold frame. Or take hardwood cuttings in winter and bury the bottom two-thirds in the ground.

Troubleshooting

They can become infested with blackfly but this is more of a problem with the larger varieties.

Which variety?

P. coronarius **'Variegatus'** ('Bowles' Variety') has grey-green leaves with a broad, creamy-white margin. Plant in dappled shade as the foliage can scorch in full sun.

P. **'Manteau d'Hermine'** forms a compact mound, rarely exceeding 0.9x0.9m (3x3ft). It becomes smothered with creamy-white, double flowers which are heavily scented.

P. microphyllus has small, dark green leaves which are silvery-grey underneath. The flowers are small with a pineapple scent. It needs a sheltered, sunny position to flower well, though it is completely hardy.

Philadelphus, medium and tall types

MEDIUM-SIZED TYPES: Shape and size

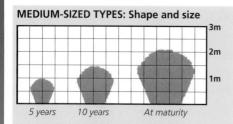

5 years   10 years   At maturity

TALL TYPES: Shape and size

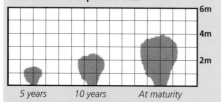

5 years   10 years   At maturity

Position   Hardiness   Soil

MOST

Uses

Features calendar

Jan	Feb	Mar	Apr	May	June
July	Aug	Sept	Oct	Nov	Dec

Growing guide

The major reason for growing these shrubs is for their rich fragrance that fills the air in summer. However, not all are strongly scented. For example, 'Boule d'Argent' and 'Enchantment' have a very subtle orange fragrance.

They are tolerant of most soils and positions, but need careful siting. Flowering aside, the larger varieties can look rather dull for all but their three weeks of flowering splendour. Also, you cannot prune them back drastically without spoiling their shape or losing the flowers.

Pruning

Once flowering is over, cut out one in three of the branches which have flowered. Cut down to a vigorous side branch or to ground level, choosing the oldest and weakest branches first.

Propagation

Take semi-ripe cuttings in early summer, root in a pot covered with a polythene bag. Pot on and overwinter in a cold frame. Alternatively, take hardwood cuttings in winter and bury the bottom two-thirds in the ground.

Troubleshooting

They can become infested with blackfly which is disfiguring and may spread to other plants. Treat serious infestations with an insecticide.

Which variety?

MEDIUM-SIZED TYPES

P. 'Belle Etoile' has a more upright habit than most philadelphus. The dark green leaves provide a good foil for the flowers, which are creamy white with a purple base. There is some winter interest in the stems; from a rich mahogany they peel with age to show a fawn colouring.

P. coronarius 'Aureus' has yellow-green foliage. To protect the leaves from damage by late frosts or sun scorch, choose a semi-shaded, sheltered spot or a north-facing border.

TALL TYPES need plenty of space; in time they can reach 4m (13ft).

'Virginal' is one of the more upright philadelphus. It has large, pure white double flowers and dark green leaves.

'Beauclerk' has large, single flowers up to 8cm (3in) across, which are often flushed with pink in the centre and very fragrant.

P. coronarius is the species from which many garden hybrids were derived. It is less attractive than either 'Beauclerk' or 'Virginal', with small flowers and a scent that is too overpowering for many people.

> **Buying tips** *Avoid any with leaf spotting on the foliage as this can be disfiguring, especially on the yellow-leaved varieties.*

Philadelphus coronarius 'Aureus'

Philadelphus 'Belle Etoile'

Philadelphus 'Beauclerk'

Phlomis fruticosa

Shape and size

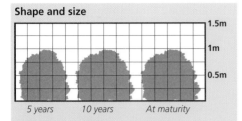

				1.5m
5 years	10 years	At maturity		1m
				0.5m

Position Hardiness Soil

DRAINED

Uses

Features calendar

Jan	Feb	Mar	Apr	May	June
July	Aug	Sept	Oct	Nov	Dec

Buying tips *Buy young plants as they will be cheaper, quicker to establish and should live for longer.*

A well-established clump

Phlomis fruticosa makes a good contrast to purple flowers

Growing guide

This is an interesting looking grey-leaved shrub that can be used in borders or planted in groups. Give it a sunny, well-drained position, it can tolerate drought but dislikes shade and waterlogged soil.

Yellow whorls of flowers appear in summer and are held high above the foliage. This shrub is best considered as a short-lived plant, as it looks less attractive as it gets older.

Pruning

The first spring after planting, cut back the previous year's growth to within 2.5-5cm (1-2in) of the ground once new shoots emerge from the base. Repeat this each year but only cut back to 5-10cm (2-4in).

Propagation

Take semi-ripe cuttings in September, root in a cold frame and plant out in spring.

Troubleshooting

The soft tips of the plant are prone to winter damage, although new shoots come up freely from the old wood.

Which variety?

P. fruticosa is the most widely-available and the hardiest. You may come across ***P. italica*** which is more tender with an upright habit and has pale lilac flowers on terminal spikes.

Phormium tenax

Shape and size

					3m
					2m
					1m

5 years   10 years   At maturity

Position   Hardiness   Soil

DRAINED

Uses

Features calendar

Jan	Feb	Mar	Apr	May	June
July	Aug	Sept	Oct	Nov	Dec

Buying tips *Buy and plant in spring so the plants can get established before the winter.*

'Dark Delight'

'Maori Sunrise'

Growing guide

Phormiums look striking all year round thanks to their sword-like leaves which come in a range of colours. Use their strong shape to add a tropical air to sunny patios or borders.

Young plants do best in a sunny position and settle in quickly if the soil is not too dry. Not much growth will take place the first year after planting but once established they become more tolerant of drought, cold and partial shade.

They are reasonably hardy, but in cold areas protect them in winter with straw or leaves. Phormiums are good container plants but can be killed if the compost freezes, so move them to a sheltered position and insulate the tub if heavy frosts are expected.

Pruning
Remove any dead or winter-damaged foliage in spring.

Propagation
Divide the plants in spring. Cut up into sections, each with a leaf and root, and pot up into compost. Plant out once new roots form.

Troubleshooting
Scale insects can be a problem. Small numbers can be squashed with a thumbnail; if there are a lot wipe down the leaves with a sponge to dislodge them.

'Cream Delight'

Which variety?

There are two species **P. cookianum** and **P. tenax** and their varieties, plus hybrids between the two species.

P. cookianum has small leaves 0.5-0.9m (1½x3ft) that bend over. Their small size makes them ideal for containers. Yellow flowers held on long spikes on established plants. Varieties include:

'Cream Delight' Green leaves with broad, cream bands in the centre.
'Dark Delight' Dark bronze leaves.
'Tricolor' Green leaves with band of white and red margins.
'Maori Chief' Bronze leaves with red and yellow vertical stripes.
'Maori Sunrise' Bronze leaves with with broad red and yellow banding.

P. tenax has stiff, upright leaves 1.8-3m (6-10ft) long. These make good focal points in borders or in gravel. Maroon flowers may be held above the leaves on long spikes in summer. Varieties include:

'Sundowner' Copper-coloured leaves with pink and salmon bands.
'Veitchii' Dark green leaves with bold yellow stripes along the centre.

Hybrids tend to have some features of each species – the leaves are slightly curving and sometimes twisted. Varieties include:

'Bronze Baby' Grows to about 0.6m (2ft) and has coppery-bronze leaves.
'Purpureum' A big plant, up to 3m (10ft), with purple-black leaves.

'Maori Chief'

Photina x fraseri 'Red Robin'

Shape and size

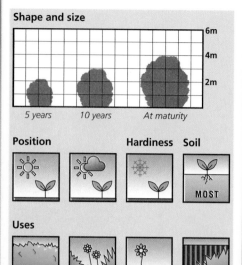

5 years	10 years	At maturity

Position

Hardiness Soil

MOST

Uses

Features calendar

Jan	Feb	Mar	Apr	May	June
July	Aug	Sept	Oct	Nov	Dec

Buying tips *Plants on sale often have single stems and will take several years to form bushy plants. Choose one with several stems if possible.*

Photina x fraseri 'Red Robin' with Philadelphus coronarius 'Aureus'

The new leaves of 'Red Robin' will turn bronze by summer

Growing guide

The striking feature of this evergreen shrub is the bright red new foliage, which is most prominent in spring. The leaves turn bronze and then green but there are generally some red leaves all through the year. In very mild areas it may produce small white flowers in spring, but it is mainly grown for its foliage.

Although fairly hardy, new foliage can be damaged by frosts and cold winds, so provide a sheltered position, such as a south- or west-facing wall. In mild areas it can be planted 0.9m (3ft) apart to make a tall, informal hedge.

Pruning

The first spring after planting, shorten all the previous year's growth by one-third. This will encourage a good shape. They do not need annual pruning but they can be cut back by up to a third in early spring if they get tall and leggy. This will not only control the size but encourage more young, red shoots.

Propagation

Take semi-ripe cuttings in summer and root in a pot covered with a polythene bag. Pot up and overwinter in a cold frame.

Troubleshooting

Generally trouble-free.

Which variety?

P. x *fraseri* **'Red Robin'** is very common (**'Robusta'** is similar) and is the best for its bright red spring growth. There is also **'Birmingham'** with dark red shoots.

Physocarpus

Shape and size

5 years   10 years   At maturity

3m
2m
1m

Position   Hardiness   Soil   Uses

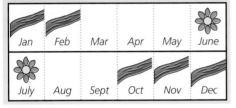

MOST

Features calendar

| Jan | Feb | Mar | Apr | May | June |
| July | Aug | Sept | Oct | Nov | Dec |

Buying tips *Quick-growing, so small plants are a good buy if you can find them. Most likely to be on sale at garden centres during the summer months.*

Growing guide

A tall foliage shrub with golden-yellow foliage that combines well with purple-leaved shrubs, such as the purple varieties of cotinus and berberis.

It needs light shade as the foliage scorches in full sun, while too much shade will cause the leaves to lose their golden colouration and turn green.

The flowers are off-white and do not show up very well against the foliage. However, with regular pruning, the mahogany colour of the newer stems provides an interesting winter feature.

It is easy to grow and does well on nearly all soils, though it may struggle a bit in extreme alkaline conditions.

Pruning

Cut back one-third of the shoots to ground level every year as soon as it finishes flowering. This is essential to maintain a good supply of new stems for winter interest. The older stems become a greyish-brown and look dull by comparison.

Propagation

Very easy to propagate from tips of the new shoots in July or August, or from hardwood cuttings. Root the latter in a cold frame for plants ready to move in early summer. Hardwood cuttings rooted in the ground will not be ready for moving until the following autumn.

Troubleshooting

Keep an eye out for aphids in late spring and early summer. If not controlled at this time, they can ruin the foliage for the rest of the year. The only other problem is leaf scorch in direct sunlight.

Which variety?

P. opulifolius **'Dart's Gold'** has lusher and brighter foliage and never grows more than to about 1.8m (6ft).

Physocarpus opulifolius with the purple foliage of Corylus maxima 'Purpurea' in the background

Pieris

Shape and size

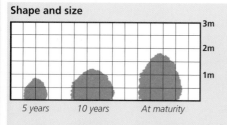

3m
2m
1m

5 years | 10 years | At maturity

Position   Hardiness   Soil

ACID   MOIST

Uses

Features calendar

Jan	Feb	Mar	Apr	May	June
July	Aug	Sept	Oct	Nov	Dec

Buying tips *March or April is a good time to buy as you can check the spring colour. Look for plants that are established in their pots with good, glossy foliage. Steer clear of plants with lots of new soft growth in spring, as these are likely to have been grown in polythene tunnels over winter and may not have been properly hardened off. Avoid any plants with notching around the edge of young leaves – this is a sign of vine weevil.*

Pieris japonica

Pieris japonica 'Blush'

Growing guide

Pieris are among the most spectacular spring evergreens if grown in acidic woodland conditions. If you cannot provide those conditions, they can be grown in tubs.

In spring, the new leaf growth takes on red, pink or white hues, depending on the variety. The flowers look like lily-of-the-valley; usually they are white, but some have pink or red flowers. Some varieties have flowers that lie draped over the foliage, others are upright. The flower buds are produced the previous summer and in some varieties they make an attractive winter feature. The contrast between brown or bronze buds and paler petals is striking.

Pruning

Very little pruning is needed except to remove any frost-damaged shoots in early summer.

Propagation

Take basal cuttings in summer and root in a heated propagator. Pot up rooted cuttings and overwinter in the cold frame. Alternatively, layer shoots in autumn; rooting should take about a year.

Troubleshooting

Spring foliage can be damaged by late spring frosts, so choose a sheltered position.

Which variety?

Varieties differ, sizes given are after ten years.
'Forest Flame' Red, pink and

Pieris japonica 'Variegata'

cream spring foliage, good for flowers but **'Firecrest'** is better if you can find it. 2.4m (8ft).

P. formosa forrestii 'Wakehurst' Outstanding, bright red spring foliage and white flowers, but only for mild areas. 3.5m (12ft).

P. formosa forrestii 'Jermyns' Similar to 'Wakehurst' but with slightly deeper red spring foliage.

P. japonica 'Blush' Smothered with pink flowers in April.

P. japonica 'Purity' Very free-flowering. White flowers in April, spring foliage is green. 1.2m (4ft).

P. japonica 'Little Heath Green' Rarely flowers but makes a neat dwarf shrub with pink spring foliage in April to June. 0.9m (3ft).

P. japonica 'Variegata' Mature leaves are green and white turning cream-yellow with age.

Pieris japonica 'Geisha' (similar to 'Purity')
– good for flowers but spring foliage is green

Piptanthus laburnifolius

Shape and size

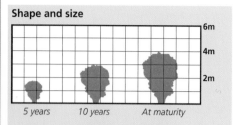

			6m
			4m
			2m
5 years	10 years	At maturity	

Position

Hardiness

Soil

DRAINED

Uses

Features calendar

Jan	Feb	Mar	Apr ✿	May ✿	June
July	Aug	Sept	Oct	Nov	Dec

Buying tips *Widely available from shrub nurseries although may be harder to find in garden centres. Buy in spring in order to get plants well-established by the winter.*

The pea-like blooms of Piptanthus laburnifolius

Growing guide

The bright yellow, pea-like flowers are similar to those of the laburnum except that they are in short, upright clusters rather than long trails. Although reasonably hardy on well-drained soils, it can lose its leaves during a severe winter, though this is not a cause for concern. In colder areas, it is best trained against a south- or west-facing wall, where it will form a good foil for seasonal flowers. Wall-trained plants tend to grow quicker and larger than free-standing ones.

Pruning

Cut out any shoots damaged by the cold weather in spring.

Propagation

Layer shoots near the ground in spring or autumn, take cuttings from the young lateral shoots in July or August as they start to ripen, or sow seeds in spring.

Troubleshooting

Shoots may tend to die back if the shrub is subject to drought or if the roots get damaged. In some gardens, piptanthus have been known to die out after five to ten years for no obvious reason.

Which variety?

You may see plants labelled **P. nepalensis**. This an alternative name for the same species.

Pittosporum tenuifolium

Shape and size

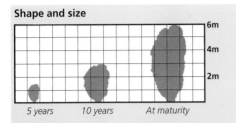

		6m
		4m
		2m

5 years   10 years   At maturity

Position

Hardiness   Soil

DRAINED

Uses

Features calendar

Jan	Feb	Mar	Apr	May	June
July	Aug	Sept	Oct	Nov	Dec

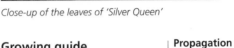

Close-up of the leaves of 'Silver Queen'

Pittosporum tenuifolium 'Silver Queen'

Growing guide

A neat evergreen shrub for mild areas, or other parts of the country if protected. In mild areas, it can be used as a hedge if planted 0.9m (3ft) apart. Otherwise, grow in sheltered positions, perhaps as a wall shrub or in a container, or grow as a conservatory plant.

On mature plants there may be scented, brown flowers, but the main attraction is the foliage, which is good for flower arranging.

Pruning

The first spring after planting, shorten all the previous year's growth by one-third to get a well-shaped plant. Established plants do not need regular pruning, but you can clip with shears in late spring.

P. tenuifolium and its varieties will usually grow readily from old wood, so any winter damage can be cut out in late spring.

Buying tips Buy in late spring or early summer and look for a well-branched plant with unblemished foliage.

Propagation

Take semi-ripe cuttings in October. Insert cuttings into a cold frame and cover with thin, clear polythene (like that from dry cleaners). Check cuttings regularly from early spring onwards. Harden off and pot on as soon as they have rooted.

Troubleshooting

Generally trouble-free if planted in a suitable location.

Which variety?

P. 'Garnettii' White variegated leaves with pink spots. One of the hardiest variegated ones. Slightly smaller than most.
P. tenuifolium One of the hardiest. Grey-green leaves show up well against dark stems.
P. tenuifolium 'Silver Queen' Variegated silver-grey foliage shows up well against dark stems, very neat appearance.
P. tenuifolium 'Warnham Gold' A small variety with yellow-green foliage.
P. tobira Glossy, green leaves and white, scented flowers. Can be used as hedging in mild areas; otherwise grow as a wall shrub or as a patio or conservatory plant.

Potentilla fruticosa

Shape and size

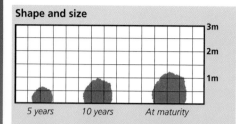

			3m
5 years	10 years	At maturity	2m
			1m

Position   Hardiness   Soil

MOST

Uses

Features calendar

Jan	Feb	Mar	Apr	May	June
					✿
July	Aug	Sept	Oct	Nov	Dec
✿	✿	✿			

Buying tips *Look for young, bushy plants with foliage right down to the base of the stems. Avoid old plants with bare woody stems as these will have to be pruned right back to the ground to renovate them.*

The best time to buy is when they are in flower. This allows you to choose one with plenty of buds. Check the foliage for signs of mildew, not to be confused with hard water stains caused by overhead irrigation.Mildew is generally seen as a dense, white powdery covering and is usually accompanied by some dieback on the new shoots.

Pale spots on the leaves, distorted growth and fine webbing are signs of red spider plants. Any plants showing these symptoms should be avoided.

'Goldfinger' – one of the best bright yellow varieties

Growing guide

Shrubby potentillas are some of the easiest and most reliable deciduous shrubs for summer colour. Many flower on and off from May until October, but the peak is in July and August. Some flower much better than others (see 'Which variety?' for details). For the maximum impact, plant a group of three shrubs in a triangle 45cm (18in) apart and prune regularly.

There is a wide range of colours, so a variety can be chosen to fit into any established colour scheme.

Flowering is generally best in full sun, but they tolerate partial shade. The pink, red and orange varieties do better in light shade. The more sunshine the plant gets, the paler and more bleached its flowers.

Low, bushy, compact types are ideal for narrow beds around the patio. Single specimens could add height to a rock garden. For flowering ground cover, look for the low or prostrate ones. The taller ones can be grown further back in the border.

Pruning
Trim back by about one-third with shears each spring. They will then develop an attractive dome shape. After three to six years their vigour and flowering will start to decline. To rejuvenate them, cut all the stems to the ground in spring; in a few years the dome shape will have re-formed.

Propagation
In September, take semi-ripe cuttings and root in a cold frame, plant out the following summer. Established plants with many stems can be lifted and divided in the autumn.

Troubleshooting
Powdery mildew and red spider mite can be a problem in hot, dry spells. They can become woody if not pruned regularly.

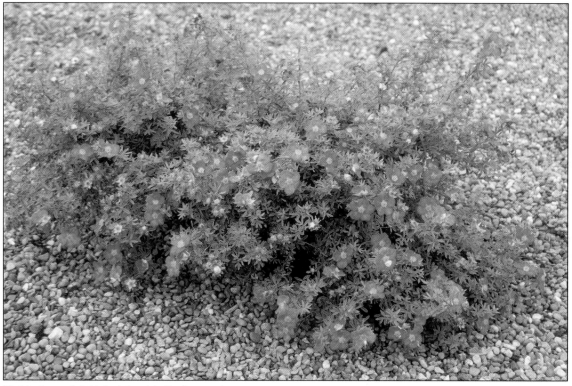

'Red Ace' – needs light shade to retain the flower colour

Which variety?

Listed below are the most widely available by flower colour.

WHITE

'Abbotswood' Tall, bushy, long-flowering and very reliable.
'Manchu' Low, almost prostrate.
'Mount Everest' Tall, vigorous with poor flower display.

PALE YELLOW

'Primrose Beauty' Tall, spreading and very reliable.
'Maanelys' ('Moonlight') Tall, bushy. Worth considering.
'Tilford Cream' Low, broad, bushy. Poor in flower.

BRIGHTER YELLOW

'Goldfinger' Tall, bushy. Reliable.
'Longacre Variety' Low, almost prostrate. Reliable.
'Beesii' Low, spreading. Reliable.
'Dart's Golddigger' Low, spreading. Poor in flower.
'Klondike' Low, compact. Poor in flower.

'Elizabeth' ('Arbuscula') Spreading, dome-shaped, mildew-prone.
'Goldstar' Bushy, compact.
'Jackman's Variety' Erect.
'Katherine Dykes' Upright, bushy.

ORANGE

'Daydawn' Pinky-orange flowers fade in full sun. Recommended for light shade only. Spreading, bushy.
'Sunset' Low, spreading. Reliable.
'Tangerine' Tall, bushy. Reliable.

PINK

'Royal Flush' Low, bushy. Reliable.
'Pretty Polly' Low, compact. Fairly reliable.
'Princess' ('Blink', 'Pink Panther') Low, spreading. Can look untidy, even when pruned regularly.

RED

'Marian' ('Red Robin') Low bushy. Generally reliable.
'Red Ace' Low, bushy. Worth considering for light shade because the flowers fade to a dull orange in full sun.

'Abbotswood ' – recommended for its long and abundant display of flowers

Prunus laurocerasus

Shape and size

| 5 years | 10 years | At maturity |

Position

Hardiness

Soil

MOST

Uses

Features calendar

Jan	Feb	Mar	Apr	May	June
			🌸		
July	Aug	Sept	Oct	Nov	Dec

Buying tips *Check for bacterial canker (see 'Troubleshooting').*

The berries of Prunus laurocerasus

Growing guide

Cherry laurels are an ideal choice if you want to plant a large screen or hedge. There are also several low-growing varieties that make excellent ground cover.

Apart from their glossy leaves, there are white flowers in spring and red berries in late summer. The berries slowly turn black and may remain until winter. The leaves and stems are poisonous and they give off cyanide when crushed. It is best not to shred the prunings or to use them as a mulch for this reason.

Cherry laurels will grow almost anywhere provided the soil is not extremely alkaline (i.e. above pH 8). For a hedge or screen, plant 0.9m (3ft) apart. Ground cover varieties can be planted 0.6m (2ft) apart for quick cover or 0.9m (3ft) apart to save money.

Pruning

The first spring after planting, the previous year's growth can be shortened by one-third to encourage a bushy shape. On established shrubs, no routine pruning is required, though, if necessary, they will tolerate hard pruning to keep the plant within bounds. Late winter is the best time for this. Hedges are usually trimmed in late summer. Hedgetrimmers can damage the leaves; use shears where feasible.

Propagation

Take cuttings from the side shoots in September and root in a cold frame. Pot on or plant out in late spring.

Troubleshooting

Laurels are prone to bacterial canker. This is a serious disease which is difficult to control. Open wounds on stems or branches exude an amber-coloured gum. The leaves may have a 'shothole' appearance caused by spots of dead tissue falling out. Remove affected branches promptly and spray with a copper fungicide, repeating as necessary. As a preventive measure, spray three weeks after flowering has finished and again two weeks later.

Which variety?

Many of the varieties have more to offer in terms of garden interest than the species.

P. laurocerasus **'Marbled White'** Grey-green leaves with white marbling. Does not flower or fruit prolifically. Good for hedging or large borders. 2.4m (8ft) after ten years.

P. laurocerasus **'Otto Luyken'** Attractive white flowers. Good for ground cover or shady borders. 1.2x1.2m (4x4ft) after ten years.

P. laurocerasus **'Rotundiflora'** Rounded leaves. The best one for hedging.

P. laurocerasus **'Zabeliana'** Spreading, good for ground cover.

P. lusitanica (Portugal laurel) Neat foliage, looks good when clipped into formal shapes. 2.4x2.4m (8x8ft) after ten years.

Prunus lusitanica

Prunus laurocerasus 'Marbled White'

Prunus triloba

Shape and size

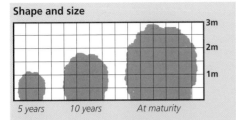

5 years   10 years   At maturity

3m
2m
1m

Position

Hardiness   Soil

MOST

Uses

Features calendar

Jan	Feb	Mar	Apr	May	June
July	Aug	Sept	Oct	Nov	Dec

Prunus triloba

Growing guide

This spring-flowering shrub is worth planting on its own as a specimen plant, or siting near the front of a border. Its main feature is the display of large, double, peach-pink flowers borne on dark, bare stems. There is also some autumn colour when the leaves turn yellow.

It will grow in any soil or situation. Attractive ways to grow it are as a small mophead tree or trained as a fan against a wall.

Buying tips   *Plants do not start to flower well until three or four years old, so older plants are a better buy. Sometimes sold as a standard, grafted on top of a stem of Prunus avium.*

Pruning

It will flower more reliably if pruned annually. Cut out one stem in three in early summer. With wall-trained plants, prune back any branches growing out from the wall to one or two buds after flowering.

Propagation

Difficult. Most plants are budded or grafted. Try layering in spring or autumn, or taking cuttings from side shoots in late summer.

Troubleshooting

Generally trouble-free.

Which variety?

Prunus tenella **'Fire Hill'** (dwarf Russian almond) is also covered with pink flowers in spring and the leaves develop red autumn tints. 1.5x0.9m (5x3ft) after five years.

Pyracantha

Shape and size

5 years	10 years	At maturity

6m
4m
2m

Position

Hardiness   Soil

MOST

Uses

Features calendar

Jan	Feb	Mar	Apr	May	June

July	Aug	Sept	Oct	Nov	Dec

Buying tips *Check for signs of scab, particularly on 'Mohave' which is susceptible. An infected plant will be slow to establish and may die or act as a source of infection.*

'Orange Charmer'

Pyracanthas are good for brightening up north- and east-facing walls

Growing guide

Pyracanthas brighten up the garden in mid-autumn with brilliant berries. They are very tough plants, tolerating most sites and weather, even roadside pollution.

They are often grown as wall shrubs on cold north- or east-facing walls. Being densely branched, evergreen and thorny, they make a good hedge when planted 0.6m (2ft) apart. They can be grown as free-standing shrubs and the lower-growing ones can be used as ground cover. If you are prepared to train them, there are even more options – an espalier up a wall or a mophead standard, for example.

Pruning

Pyracanthas grown as free-standing shrubs do not need to be pruned, but they can be cut back hard to control their size. In winter, cut back the shoots to points close to the centre of the plant.

Wall-trained plants must be pruned annually. To keep it tidy, a clip with shears in late winter will suffice, but it needs more formal training for the best show of berries. This involves cutting back all the new shoots after flowering to expose the berries, regularly tying the branches into the desired shape while they are still flexible, and removing any wayward branches.

Propagation

Take semi-ripe cuttings in September and root in a cold frame. Pot on or plant out in late spring.

Troubleshooting

Scab can be a major problem, particularly in coastal areas or after a wet summer. The foliage and fruit are peppered with small brown spots and the twigs develop small rough lesions. No variety is thought to be completely resistant but some are less susceptible. Remove and burn infected parts. It can be controlled by spraying a systemic fungicide in spring and early summer.

Fireblight is rare but can be fatal. An infected plant looks as if it has been burnt and should be dug up and destroyed.

'Mohave'

Hedge of 'Orange Glow' and 'Golden Charmer'

You may come across blotches on the leaves caused by the firethorn leaf miner – this causes no serious harm.

Which variety?

YELLOW BERRIES

'Golden Charmer' One of the best, some resistance to scab.

'Soleil d'Or' One of the best, resistance to scab.

You may come across variegated varieties – these are weaker-growing and do not produce as much fruit as the green-leaved ones.

ORANGE BERRIES

'Orange Charmer' Small leaves give a dainty appearance. Has some resistance to scab.

'Orange Glow' Vigorous and free-fruiting. Susceptible to scab.

'Teton' Larger but slower-growing than most. Orange-yellow berries. Susceptible to scab.

RED BERRIES

P. coccinea 'Red Column' Has an upright habit, which makes it ideal for training by doors and windows.

'Mohave' Orange red berries. Prone to scab.

Rhamnus alaternus 'Argenteovariegata'

Shape and size

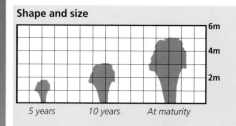

| 5 years | 10 years | At maturity |

Position   Hardiness

Soil   Uses

MOST

Features calendar

Jan	Feb	Mar	Apr	May	June
July	Aug	Sept	Oct	Nov	Dec

Buying tips *Look for symmetrical bushy plants with bright, healthy leaves.*

Close-up of the foliage

Mature specimen of Rhamnus alaternus 'Argenteovariegata'

Growing guide

An attractive shrub with grey marbling and white edges to the leaves. In mild areas or following a good summer, it produces a good crop of red berries in the autumn. Its neat pyramidal habit makes it a good choice for containers. Standing up well to pollution and salt, it is an ideal shrub for city gardens and coastal areas, but it fares less well in colder, inland gardens. It will withstand some frost, but protect it with a double layer of horticultural fleece whenever temperatures are likely to dip below -5°C (23°F). It will tolerate most soils, except those prone to severe waterlogging.

Pruning

None required but can be clipped into different shapes.

Propagation

Take cuttings from shoot tips in July or August.

Troubleshooting

Generally trouble-free providing given winter protection where needed.

Which variety?

The green-leaved species may be occasionally found. This is much hardier and is good for hedging in seaside gardens.

Other buckthorns are deciduous and grow quite large. These include the **common buckthorn (*R. cathartica*)** and the **alder buckthorn (*R. frangula*),** which are generally grown as windbreaks or shelter belts in large gardens.

The ripening berries of Rhamnus alaternus 'Argenteovariegata'

Rhododendron, dwarf

Shape and size

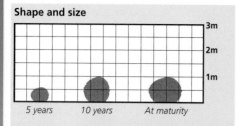

5 years	10 years	At maturity

3m
2m
1m

Position

Hardiness

Soil

ACID

NEUTRAL

Uses

Features calendar

Jan	Feb	Mar	Apr	May	June
	✿	✿	✿	✿	
July	Aug	Sept	Oct	Nov	Dec

Rhododendron yakushimanum hybrids become completely covered in flowers

Buying tips *Usually flower about three years after planting. If you want flowers sooner, you can pay extra for larger plants (20-30cm/10-12in). Avoid any that exhibit yellowing of the leaves or look stunted, lop-sided or leggy.*

Avoid any plants with notches cut out of the young foliage as this could be due to vine weevil. Also look out for powdery mildew, particularly in hot, dry spells. The signs are yellow blotches on the upper surfaces of leaves, felty patches underneath.

Growing guide

There are thousands of different rhododendrons: some grow over 4.5m (15ft) tall; others are prostrate and are only a few centimetres tall. The dwarf ones – i.e. 0.3-1.2m (1-4ft) high – tend to be the most useful in the majority of gardens.

Their needs are precise: no lime, no waterlogging and no drying out. If your soil is naturally like that, then they are fairly trouble-free. Otherwise, grow a few favourites in tubs such as half-barrels.

Rhododendrons have fibrous roots and a compact root sytem, so dig a planting hole at least 0.6m (2ft) in diameter and mix in garden compost, leafmould or composted bark. As they are shallow-rooting, they are prone to drought until established. Mulch annually with a 5cm (2in) layer of bark chippings to conserve moisture in the soil.

They are hardy but the flowers can sometimes be damaged by frost, as well as scorched by sun. Grow them in a sheltered, lightly shaded position.

Pruning

No pruning is required, but you can cut back any long, ungainly branches in winter.

To encourage new shoot growth, deadhead young plants by removing the seed pods before they swell. Hold the bottom of the seed head between finger and thumb, twist sharply and pull. Do this carefully or else you may remove the embryonic buds of the following year's flowers.

Propagation

Layer in spring or autumn. Make a slit in the stem of a young shoot about 15cm (6in) from the tip to make a tongue. Add peat and sand to the soil and peg down. Lift after two years.

'Elizabeth'

'Hydon Dawn'

Troubleshooting

Yellowing leaves are more likely to be due to a limy soil, too much wind or waterlogging rather than pests or diseases. Curled or deformed leaves are due to cold, frost or drought. Blackened, hairy buds are caused by a fungus which gets in through holes made by leaf hoppers laying their eggs in summer. Pick off and burn any affected buds.

Which variety?

There are hundreds of varieties to choose from. The following are a selection of the most widely available at garden centres.

R. yakushimanum Hybrids are outstanding plants. Look out for the following:
'Dopey' Rich red.
'Golden Torch' Salmon-pink buds, vivid yellow inside.
'Hydon Dawn' Warm pink.

'Percy Wiseman' Cream and pink.
'Sleepy' Pale-mauve, brown speckles.
'Sneezy' Rose-purple, deeper at the edges.
'Starshine' Clear, soft pink.
'Surrey Heath' Rose-pink.
'Vintage Rose' Pink, deeper in throat.

Other dwarf varieties you are likely to come across include:
'Blue Diamond' Violet-blue flowers April to early May. Aromatic leaves.
'Elizabeth' Large, blood-red flowers in large clusters April to early May; sometimes flowers again later.
'Pink Drift' Profuse, small, pinky-mauve flowers mid-May to early June. Aromatic leaves.
'Scarlet Wonder' Compact but spreading, bright-red flowers with a frilly edge mid-May to early June.

'Sneezy'

Rhus typhina

Shape and size

5 years	10 years	At maturity

6m
4m
2m

Position

Hardiness

Soil

 MOST

Uses

Features calendar

Jan	Feb	Mar	Apr	May	June
July	Aug	Sept	Oct	Nov	Dec

Buying tips *If you have a choice, pick the one with the best shape. Avoid plants that show any signs of dieback on the stems.*

Rhus typhina in autumn

The autumn tints of Rhus typhina 'Laciniata'

Growing guide

This is one of the most spectacular shrubs for autumn foliage tints, taking on shades of orange, red, yellow and purple. The flowers are quite dazzling too. Though each one is minute, they are formed in dense cones up to 20cm (8in) long, giving the shrub a candelabra effect. These are followed by clusters of red fruits. In winter, the gaunt, hairy branches take on an extraterrestrial appearance.

It is a very easy shrub to grow, though it tends to produce a lot of suckers. These can appear in the lawn or even grow through paving and can be a nuisance. One way round this is to plant it in a large tub. Otherwise, plant the variety 'Laciniata', which is much less troublesome in this respect.

Pruning

None essential but can be cut back to ground level in February, which will result in larger leaves at the expense of flowers and fruit.

Propagation

Take cuttings from new shoots with a sliver or heel of the old wood attached in July or August.

Troubleshooting

Generally trouble-free but suckering can be a problem with the species, especially near paving or buildings.

Which variety?

R. typhina 'Laciniata' has deeply-cut leaves and tends to colour up slightly later in the autumn, turning mainly yellow and orange. It has the advantage that it is less prone to suckering.

Ribes sanguineum

Shape and size

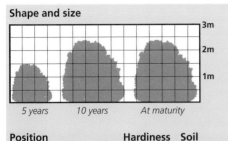

5 years	10 years	At maturity

3m
2m
1m

Position   Hardiness Soil

MOST

Uses

Features calendar

Jan	Feb	Mar	Apr	May	June
			✸		

July	Aug	Sept	Oct	Nov	Dec

Ribes sanguineum 'Pulborough Scarlet'

Golden foliage of Ribes 'Brocklebankii'

Growing guide

These quick-growing, cheap shrubs are often used as fillers in a border. After a brief moment of glory in April when in flower, they tend to look dull for much of the year. However, there are some interesting varieties with bolder flowers and many have yellow foliage too.

Ribes will thrive in most gardens, but, as they have shallow roots, they are vulnerable in very wet or very dry conditions. The yellow-leaved varieties can become scorched by the sun.

Pruning

Prune deciduous ribes annually to keep them compact with plenty of flowers. Cut out one stem in three as soon as possible after flowering. The evergreen ribes (e.g. *R. laurifolium* and *R. viburnifolium*) need no routine pruning.

Buying tips *The species is commonly sold as bare-rooted plants in garden centres. Container-grown varieties are a better buy.*

Propagation

Take hardwood cuttings in October and bury the bottom two-thirds in the ground. Root in final position or transplant in spring or autumn. Trim back in the second spring to encourage branching.

Troubleshooting

Mature plants can die suddenly in summer due to drought or root damage. Mulch well in spring and do not cultivate the ground near their roots.

Which variety?

A variety of *R. sanguineum* is a better choice for the garden than the species. They are generally smaller – 0.9-1.2m (3-4ft) – and have more colourful flowers. The evergreen species is tender and not widely sold.

'Brocklebankii' Compact habit. Pink flowers. Golden foliage.
'King Edward VII' Crimson flowers.
'Pulborough Scarlet' Red flowers.
R. odoratum (*R. aureum*) Yellow, scented flowers, purple fruits and good autumn colour.
R. speciosum Small, red flowers. Grow by a sheltered wall.

Romneya coulteri

Shape and size

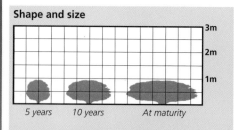

5 years	10 years	At maturity

3m / 2m / 1m

Position Hardiness Soil

DRAINED

Uses

Features calendar

Jan	Feb	Mar	Apr	May	June
July	Aug	Sept	Oct	Nov	Dec

Buying tips Resents root disturbance so avoid pot-bound plants as they may fail to establish. Small plants are often the most successful.

Close-up of flower

Romneya coulteri

Growing guide

This is one of the most spectacular summer-flowering shrubs with white, poppy-like flowers up to 13cm (5in) across. It tends to be a quite fickle plant, failing to establish in some gardens while becoming invasive in others, spreading quickly by means of its underground runners. It rarely survives in Scotland or the North-East of England as it takes several years to get established and gain its hardiness. The top growth is killed off in the winter and, for the first two or three years, it is advisable to protect the crown with a 15cm (6in) layer of bark chippings or bracken held in place with wire netting. It resents root disturbance so avoid cultivating near the plant.

Pruning

Cut back all the top growth to near ground level in autumn or early spring.

Propagation

Difficult but can be propagated from root cuttings in early spring. Insert 7.5cm (3in) long, pencil-thick portions of root the right way into pots of sandy compost. Keep at 13°C (55°F). You should see signs of growth within eight weeks if they are going to take. An easier method is to dig up suckers that arise at some distance from the plant.

Troubleshooting

Give up if it will not get established in your garden. Can become a nuisance if grown with herbaceous plants due to its invasive nature in good growing conditions. Not reliably hardy for the first few years after planting.

Which variety?

'White Cloud' (sometimes sold as *R.* x *hybrida*) has even larger flowers and is said to be easier to get established.

Rosa rugosa

Shape and size

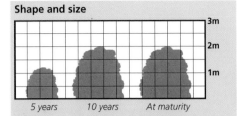

| 5 years | 10 years | At maturity |

Position

Hardiness

Soil

MOST

Uses

Features calendar

Jan	Feb	Mar	Apr	May	June
July	Aug	Sept	Oct	Nov	Dec

Buying tips *Bare-rooted plants are often sold in bundles of five or ten for hedging during the dormant season and this is a cheap way to buy them. For a good choice of varieties, go to a rose specialist. Garden centres generally stock one or two types.*

Rosa rugosa 'Roseraie de la Hay'

Rosa rugosa 'Alba'

The giant hips of the single-flowered varieties

Growing guide

Rosa rugosa varieties are a good choice for a border because they put on a good flush of flowers in early summer and continue flowering intermittently until the autumn. The single varieties, like 'Alba', produce hips the size of small tomatoes in late summer and early autumn while the plants are still flowering. The double-flowered varieties do not produce hips, but they have scented flowers instead. Single specimens make attractive plants for mixed borders. If you want to grow them as an informal hedge, plant around 45cm (18in) apart.

Pruning

Pruning is not necessary other than to control size or remove damaged or dead wood. However, plants can be pruned hard back or pruned to shape in March, though this may delay flowering.

Propagation

Take hardwood cuttings in October. These should be 23-30cm (9-12in) long and of pencil thickness. Treat with rooting hormone and bury to two-thirds their length in a trench lined with sharp sand. Cuttings should have rooted and be ready for moving by the following autumn.

Troubleshooting

Watch out for aphids in early summer and spray with an insecticide if infestations build up. Less prone to blackspot than other roses, but spray with a fungicide if this is a problem in your area. Watch out for suckers with different foliage and remove if seen, as these will develop into briars.

Which variety?

'Blanc Double de Coubert' White, double, scented.
'Frau Dagmar Hartopp' Pale, rose-pink, single.
'Roseraie de la Hay' Reddish-mauve, double, scented.
'Rubra' Magenta, single
'Scabrosa' Wine red.

Rosmarinus officinalis

Shape and size

Rosmarinus officinalis in flower

			3m
			2m
			1m
5 years	10 years	At maturity	

Position   Hardiness   Soil

DRAINED

Uses

Features calendar

Jan	Feb	Mar	Apr ✿	May ✿	June
July	Aug	Sept	Oct	Nov	Dec

Rosmarinus x lavandulaceus

Growing guide

Rosemary is ideal for planting around doorways, sunny patios and alongside paths where you can brush against it to release its aroma.

There are many types, ranging from 'Miss Jessopp's Upright', which makes a good centre-piece for a herb garden or a good hedge planted at 0.6m (2ft) intervals, to prostrate types which are ideal for raised beds or sunny slopes. Rosemary foliage blends well with silver-leaved shrubs, so cistus or helianthemums would make good partners.

Rosemaries do well in patio containers. This is an excellent way to grow them in colder areas, or to try the more tender varieties, as the pots can be moved to an unheated greenhouse or porch for the winter.

Waterlogging is more likely to kill them than the cold. It is worth digging in plenty of pea shringle or sharp grit before planting.

Pruning

Most need regular pruning so that they do not become woody and unattractive; the exception being the ground-hugging types. To encourage compact plants with plenty of foliage, cut back the previous year's growth to within 5-10cm (2-4in) of the ground as new growth begins in the spring. For a large plant, cut back to within 5-10cm (2-4in) of a taller framework of old woody stems.

With upright varieties, cut back the new shoots by half after flowering.

Propagation

Rosemary roots very easily from cuttings taken during the summer and early autumn. Take 13cm (5in) basal or heeled cuttings and insert in a cold frame in pots.

Troubleshooting

Can become very woody if not regularly pruned.

Which variety?

R. officinalis is among the largest and hardiest with strongly aromatic leaves.
'Benenden Blue' Smaller with an arching habit. Needs a warm, sheltered position.
'Miss Jessopp's Upright' ('Fastigatus') has an upright habit, Good for hedges or as a focal point.
'Severn Sea' Small variety with arching stems. Free-flowering and looks good in pots, but tender.
R. x lavandulaceus Prostrate, 7.5cm (3in) tall. Tender.

Rosemary does well in raised beds

Rubus, flowering and ground cover types

FLOWERING TYPES: shape and size

3m
2m
1m

5 years   10 years   At maturity

Position

Hardiness   Soil   Uses

MOST

Features calendar

Jan	Feb	Mar	Apr	May	June
July	Aug	Sept	Oct	Nov	Dec

GROUND COVER TYPES: shape and size

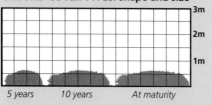

3m
2m
1m

5 years   10 years   At maturity

Position, hardiness and soil – as above

Uses

Features calendar

Jan	Feb	Mar	Apr	May	June
July	Aug	Sept	Oct	Nov	Dec

FLOWERING TYPES

Growing guide

A group of tough, flowering shrubs that are useful for providing colour where other plants may struggle to grow. The flowers are white or in shades of pink, depending on the species, and up to 5cm (2in) across. Although related to the blackberry, fruits are not reliably produced and not worth eating. They do produce suckers, but are not particularly invasive.

Pruning

Cut back one-third of the shoots to near ground level in March.

Propagation

Dig up and replant suckers or layer shoots in the spring.

Troubleshooting

Generally trouble-free, but may suffer if the soil becomes very dry in summer.

Which variety?

R. odoratus has scented, rose-pink flowers from June to September and thornless stems with peeling bark. *R. spectabilis* has magenta-pink flowers in April and May and stems covered with fine prickles. *R. tridel* has large, white flowers with golden stamens in May and thornless stems with peeling bark. **'Benenden'** is an improved form of *R. tridel* with larger flowers.

Buying tips   Not often seen at garden centres so you will probably need to go to a specialist nursery.

GROUND COVER TYPES

Growing guide

These shrubs are ideal for ground cover, especially on banks, where they are good at preventing soil erosion. They are also good for filling in between established shrubs and keeping down the weeds. For quick cover you can plant as close as 45cm (18in) apart. However, to save money, more vigorous ones, such as *R. tricolor* can be planted 90cm (3ft) apart. To get them established quickly, peg the shoots down to the ground, where they will take root.

Pruning

Not essential other than to control spread, although can be pruned hard back in the spring.

Propagation

Dig up and replant rooted suckers.

Troubleshooting

Can become invasive in small areas unless regularly trimmed back to within bounds.

Which variety?

R. calycinoides (sometimes sold as *R. fockeanus*). Forms dense mats of glossy green, lobed leaves. Best type for restricted space as it spreads only to about 0.9m (3ft). The flowers are generally hidden by the leaves. *R. microphyllus* **'Variegatus'** Foliage has cream and pink mottling. Attractive ground cover, but arching branches which root wherever they touch the ground can make it very invasive. *R. tricolor* Creeping type with red stems and leaves which are green on top and white underneath. Good for covering large areas, but easy to control where space is more limited. Can also be trained as a climber to grow against a fence.

Buying tips   Quick-growing so small plants are a good buy. R. tricolor is the most widely found at garden centres. You may need to go to specialist nurseries for the others.

Rubus, white-stemmed types

Shape and size

3m
2m
1m

5 years   10 years   At maturity

Position

Hardiness

Soil

MOST

Uses

Features calendar

Jan	Feb	Mar	Apr	May	June
July	Aug	Sept	Oct	Nov	Dec

Rubus biflorus

Growing guide

The main period of interest for these shrubs is in winter once they have lost their leaves. Although shade-tolerant, they look most spectacular when the stems are back-lit by the low, winter sun. During the growing season, the leaves are quite attractive, particularly the fern-like foliage of *R. cockburnianus* which is grey-green on top and white below, giving a two-tone effect in a breeze. In smaller gardens, it is important to control their spread. Sink a large drainpipe or other physical barrier into the ground before planting.

Pruning
Cut back all stems to ground level in March.

Propagation
Dig up and replant rooted suckers.

> **Buying tips** *Choose a plant with plenty of stems for quickest effect. More likely to be on sale in winter at garden centres.*

Rubus cockburnianus

Troubleshooting
Can become invasive due to its suckering habit.

Which variety?

R. biflorus has brilliant white, hairy stems and forms yellow, edible fruits in the autumn.
R. cockburnianus (also sold as *R. giraldianus*) has purple stems covered with a brilliant white bloom and can grow up to 4m (13ft) tall.
R. thibetanus has brownish-purple stems covered in a white bloom.

Rubus crataegifolius – a rare form

Salix, low-growing shrubby types

Shape and size

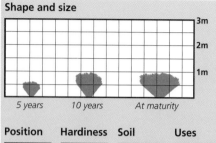

			3m
			2m
			1m

5 years   10 years   At maturity

Position   Hardiness   Soil   Uses

MOST

Features calendar

Jan	Feb	Mar	Apr	May	June
July	Aug	Sept	Oct	Nov	Dec

Buying tips *Check the alpine section of the garden centre as these willows are often on sale here because of their small size. As they are slow-growing, choose the largest one.*

Salix helvetica in the border

The silver leaves of Salix helvetica

Growing guide

Salix is a large group which includes species of all shapes and sizes. Besides the ones that form large spreading trees and those that are only a few centimetres high, there are the shrubby willows.

Shrubby willows are slow-growing shrubs, grown mainly for their display of catkins, although many have silver-grey foliage. They are very tolerant of different soils and will even grow in waterlogged ground. They are good plants for a bog garden next to a pond, where they will provide invaluable cover for wildlife.

Pruning

With shrubby willows such as *S. helvetica* and *S. lanata*, it is best if you cut back all the shoots by one-third in the first spring after planting, as this will improve their shape in future years. Once established, they can be clipped to shape or tidied up as necessary in mid-spring.

Propagation

Take hardwood cuttings in late winter (January to February) and root them in pots in a cold frame.

Troubleshooting

They may suffer from leaf spots from various fungi, but these are not usually serious. Slug damage or heavy rain can spoil the downy foliage of *S. lanata*.

Which variety?

There are three widely available ones.

S. hastata 'Wehrhahnii' has large catkins on purple-red stems, dark green leaves, turning yellow in autumn. May be found as a standard tree grafted on to the stem of another willow.

S. helvetica Small, twiggy bush with catkins and silver-grey foliage. May be found as a standard grafted on to the stem of another willow.

S. lanata (woolly willow) has silver-grey foliage covered with down, small catkins. Very slow-growing.

Salix lanata and leaf detail

Salix alba 'Chermesina'

Willows for winter interest

Many of the larger *Salix* varieties that would normally grow into trees can make attractive winter-interest shrubs on account of their coloured stems. To control their size and encourage plenty of colourful new stems, simply cut them back to near ground level every year in late March or April. These willows are extremely tough plants, withstanding the heaviest clay soils and waterlogging. They do not like to go dry at the roots, however. Varieties include:

S.alba'Chermesina' ('Britzensis') Red stems.
S. alba 'Vitellina' (*S. vitellina*) Yellow stems.
S. daphnoides Purple stems with a white bloom.
S. irrorata Purple stems with a white bloom.

Salix alba 'Vitellina'

Salvia officinalis

Shape and size

		3m
		2m
		1m

5 years   10 years   At maturity

Position

Hardiness

Soil

DRAINED

Uses

Features calendar

| Jan | Feb | Mar | Apr | May | June |
| July | Aug | Sept | Oct | Nov | Dec |

Buying tips *Buy small plants as these establish quickly. Often found in the herb section at garden centres, where they may be cheaper than plants sold as ornamentals.*

Salvia officinalis 'Icterina'

Salvia officinalis 'Purpurascens'

Growing guide

True sage (*S. officinalis*) is a familiar culinary herb, with its grey-green leaves and purple flowers. There are also a number of attractive varieties with variegated leaves which, although just as good for culinary purposes, are more commonly grown as ornamental shrubs. All are easy to grow in sunny, well-drained spots, although the variegated varieties are slightly more tender and can often be killed by wet soils over the winter.

They can be used to edge herb gardens and borders if planted 0.6m (2ft) apart. In large mixed borders, they will create more of an impact if planted in clumps of three or more.

Pruning

The first spring after planting, cut back all previous year's growth to within 2.5-5cm (1-2in) of the ground once new shoots can be seen growing from near the base. To prevent them becoming straggly, prune them near to ground level in late spring. Sprinkle a handful of general fertiliser around each plant after pruning.

Old plants may be killed by severe cutting back if they have not been pruned regularly. If they have reached this stage, it is better to start again with new plants from cuttings.

Propagation

Take cuttings from the shoot tips in

New leaves of Salvia officinalis 'Purpurascens'

Salvia microphylla 'Wislizeni'

Salvia officinalis 'Tricolor'

Salvia guaranitica

Salvia microphylla

summer or early autumn and root in a cold frame or in a pot covered in a polythene bag.

Troubleshooting

The shrubs can become woody with age if not pruned. The foliage of the variegated ones can look very tatty over winter, but they can soon be rejuvenated by spring pruning.

Which variety?

'Icterina' Green leaves with a butter-yellow margin. The hardiest of the variegated forms.
'Purpurascens' Greyish-purple leaves.
'Tricolor' Green leaves splashed with red and white.

Other shrubby salvias

There are also a number of semi-tender, shrubby salvias which could be planted against a sunny wall or near a patio. All need full sun, a deep mulch to protect them in winter, and a sheltered position and a well-drained soil.

S. microphylla (*S. grahamii*) has pink or red flowers which stand above semi-evergreen foliage. It grows up to 1.2m (4ft) tall.

***S. guaranitica* 'Black and Blue'** can grow up to 1.8m (6ft) in height. It has rough, hairy leaves and black bracts from which blue flowers emerge in late summer.

***S. guaranitica* 'Blue Enigma'** is smaller than 'Black and Blue' and has shiny leaves and paler blue flowers.

Sambucus racemosa 'Plumosa Aurea'

Shape and size

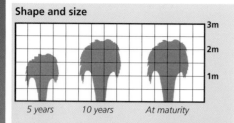

5 years   10 years   At maturity

Position

Hardiness

Soil

MOST

Uses

Features calendar

Jan	Feb	Mar	Apr	May	June
			✿	✿	
July	Aug	Sept	Oct	Nov	Dec

Buying tips *Small plants are a good buy for the quicker-growing varieties. With the slower ones, choose larger plants for instant effect.*

Growing guide

Elders are among the best shrubs for filling out borders with attractive foliage. They will grow in almost any soil, including heavy, waterlogged sites.

The golden-leaved elders are among the most popular, providing colour from early spring to late autumn at the back of the border. Also look out for others with different coloured foliage and growth rates. For example, for the front of the border, the slow-growing *S. racemosa* 'Tenuifolia' is ideal. It has beautiful green-lace foliage and looks like a Japanese maple only it is more tolerant of heavy clay soils.

The darkest leaf of all is produced by *S. nigra* 'Guincho Purple' with its deep purple-bronze foliage. Variegated elders like *S. nigra* 'Aureo-marginata' are larger shrubs with leaves edged with yellow, fading to white. In autumn, the purple suffusions in the leaves show clearly in the pale margins.

Pruning

For foliage, hard prune in March each year, starting the second spring after planting. For flowers and berries, cut out just one in three stems (starting with the oldest) in spring. Slow-growing varieties need no pruning.

Propagation

Take hardwood cuttings in late winter (January to February) and bury the bottom two-thirds in the ground. Root in final position or transplant the following autumn.

Troubleshooting

Golden-leaved varieties can suffer from leaf-scorch if grown in full sun. They will become woody if not pruned.

Which variety?

FOR YELLOW FOLIAGE
***S. racemosa* 'Plumosa Aurea'** Widely available ('**Sutherland Gold**' is similar).
'**Goldenlocks**' Slower-growing and smaller. The best choice for a small garden.

OTHER COLOURS
***S. racemosa* 'Tenuifolia'** Green foliage. Slow-growing.
S. nigra* 'Aureo-marginata'** (S. nigra* 'Marginata'** is similar) Variegated foliage. Spreading habit.
***S. nigra* 'Guincho Purple'** ('Purpurea') Purple foliage. Spreading habit.

Sambucus nigra 'Guincho Purple'

Sambucus nigra 'Aureo-marginata'

Sambucus racemosa 'Plumosa Aurea'

Santolina chamaecyparissus

(S. incana)

Shape and size

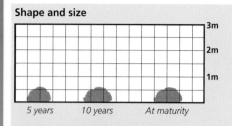

	3m
	2m
	1m

5 years   10 years   At maturity

Position   Hardiness   Soil

DRAINED

Uses

Features calendar

Jan	Feb	Mar	Apr	May	June
❀					
July	Aug	Sept	Oct	Nov	Dec

Santolina virens

Santolina chamaecyparissus

Growing guide

S. chamaecyparissus with silver-grey foliage is the species most often grown, but there are green forms too.

It can be used to create a Mediterranean look to the garden, along with other plants that thrive in sunny, well-drained spots.

Although it has flowers, it is the silvery foliage that is of most value in the garden. It makes a neat edging if planted 40cm (16in) apart. Or it can be used as a foliage contrast to bedding.

Pruning

The first spring after planting, prune all the shoots back to within 2.5-5cm (1-2in) of the ground as soon as you see new growth near the base. It needs to be pruned every year in this way to keep it dense. The flower stems can be clipped off for the best shape.

If it is grown as an edging, clip with shears in early spring and again in summer when the flowers appear.

Propagation

Take semi-ripe cuttings in September and root in a cold frame. Pot on or plant out in spring.

Troubleshooting

Plants can become tall and straggly, and the shape can be spoilt by wind or snow opening up the plant. Regular pruning will prevent this. Cold, wet conditions can kill the plant, so incorporate plenty of sharp grit before planting on clay soils.

Which variety?

The species **S. chamaecyparissus** is a good one that is easy to find. **'Lambrook Silver'** is more silvery. **'Nana'** ('Corsica') is a dwarf form. **S. neapolitana** is a compact species with lemon-yellow flowers. **S. virens** (S. viridis) has vivid green foliage and bright yellow flowers.

> **Buying tips**   Buy young, bushy plants. Avoid woody plants with stems that are bare at the base.

Sarcococca hookeriana 'Digyna'

Shape and size

			3m
			2m
			1m
5 years	10 years	At maturity	

Position

Hardiness

Soil

MOST

Uses

Features calendar

Jan	Feb	Mar	Apr	May	June
❀	❀	🍇			
July	Aug	Sept	Oct	Nov	Dec

Buying tips *Most likely to be found at garden centres in winter, which may not be an ideal time for planting evergreens.*

Growing guide

This is a compact, winter-flowering shrub. The flowers are quite tiny, almost insignificant, but they are very strongly scented.

It is quite tolerant of most soils, but do not expect it to do well on a poor soil which is low in nutrients. To overcome this problem add plenty of well-rotted organic matter and a handful of fish, blood and bone when planting.

It can be useful as part of a mixed border, but is best sited near a door or window so that you can appreciate the scent. Planted 30cm (12in) apart, it makes an attractive low hedge.

Pruning

This is a naturally dense shrub so little pruning is needed. Leave it alone, apart from removing any dead or damaged growth in late spring.

Propagation

Lift divided clumps just as they are showing signs of growth, divide with a sharp knife and replant at once. Or take hardwood cuttings of one-year-old wood in October. Root in a cold frame, then pot on or plant out in late spring.

Sarcococca hookeriana 'Humilis'

Troubleshooting

Generally trouble-free.

Which variety?

S. hookeriana 'Digyna' is widely available. You may also come across **S. hookeriana 'Humilis'** which is similar, but 30cm (12in) high and forms a thicket 0.9m (3ft) across.

The tiny flowers of Sarcococca hookeriana 'Digyna'

Sarcococca hookeriana 'Digyna' in January

Senecio 'Sunshine'

Shape and size

3m
2m
1m

5 years   10 years   At maturity

Position

Hardiness   Soil

DRAINED

Uses

Features calendar

Jan	Feb	Mar	Apr	May	June
✿	✿				
July	Aug	Sept	Oct	Nov	Dec

Buying tips *Avoid old plants that have become woody and bare at the base. Small specimens are a good buy.*

The brightly coloured summer flowers

Growing guide

Senecio makes an attractive, silver foliage shrub that is easy to grow, except in wet, shady spots. Although it does have daisy-yellow flowers in early summer, these can be removed if grown for foliage.

It is very useful near the front of a mixed border, but can also be used as a low hedge or as ground cover; plant 0.6m (2ft) apart.

Pruning

The first spring after planting, cut back all shoots to within 2.5-5cm (1-2in) of the ground. Thereafter prune regularly, but not necessarily annually, to stimulate foliage instead of flowers. Cut back the stems to within 5-10cm (2-4in) of the ground in spring as soon as shoots can be seen from the base.

Propagation

Take semi-ripe or hardwood cuttings from late summer to early autumn and root in a cold frame using a sandy compost. Plant out in spring.

Troubleshooting

Unless regularly pruned, can become woody and bare in the middle.

Which variety?

S. 'Sunshine' is the common name, it has been renamed *Brachyglottis* Dunedin Hybrid Group 'Sunshine' but is most likely to be found under its old name.

The silver foliage of Senecio 'Sunshine'

Senecio 'Sunshine' can look a bit untidy when in flower

Skimmia

Shape and size

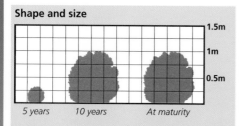

1.5m
1m
0.5m

5 years | 10 years | At maturity

Position | Hardiness | Soil

ACID | NEUTRAL

Uses

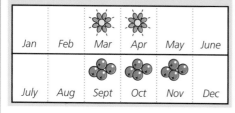

Features calendar

Jan	Feb	Mar	Apr	May	June
July	Aug	Sept	Oct	Nov	Dec

Skimmia reevesiana produces berries without a pollinator

Buying tips *There is some confusion about the accurate naming of some skimmias. Many have now been found to be varieties of* S. japonica *but you may see them on sale as* S. x foremanii *or* S. x rogersii.

Look for plants with deep green leaves. Avoid plants where the leaves look dull or faded, or are turning yellow at the edges. These are all signs that the plants have not been looked after properly.

Growing guide

Evergreen foliage, scented flowers and long-lasting berries make skimmias ideal shrubs for winter and spring interest. They are tolerant of pollution and many are compact growers, making them good choices for front gardens or patios.

The male varieties have larger, more fragrant flowers, while the female varieties have brightly coloured berries in autumn and winter. For the females to produce berries, there must be a male variety nearby. One male should pollinate at least three females.

The dark foliage of skimmias combine well with golden, variegated or grey-leaved shrubs. For a winter display, combine with hellebores.

They can be grown in containers. If you live in a hard-water area, water with a weak solution of ammonium sulphate (one teaspoon in a gallon of water) once a month. Protect plants in containers from frost, which can kill the roots. Either move the pots to a more sheltered position or lag them with insulating material.

Pruning
No routine pruning is required, but if a bush becomes too large, try cutting it back close to the ground in spring. If you are certain which is the male variety, then remove the dead flower heads. If in doubt leave them, as if you remove the female you will remove the berries.

Propagation
Either take cuttings from whole side shoots in September and root them in a cold frame or under polythene over winter, or use the young shoot tips in early summer.

Troubleshooting
Generally trouble-free if planted in the right soil.

Skimmia x confusa 'Kew Green'

Which variety?

Most garden skimmias are varieties of **S. japonica**, but there are many sizes and forms. The most widely available is **'Rubella'** (male). Its leaves, stems and flower buds are flushed with dark red and it is noted for its flowers. You may also come across the following **S. japonica** varieties:

'Bowles' Dwarf' Both sexes are available. It is one of the smallest at 0.5x0.9m (1½x3ft) after ten years.

'Fragrans' (male) Sweetly-scented flowers on large plant, 1.2x1.2m (4x4ft) after ten years.

'Fructu Albo' (female) Slow-growing variety with white berries. Needs ideal conditions to do well.

S. japonica reevesiana 'Robert Fortune' Has both male and female flowers on the same plant, so it will produce berries on its own, though does better with a pollinator.

S. x confusa 'Kew Green' (male) Very sweetly-scented, green-tinted flowers on large plant. 3x2m (10x7ft) after ten years.

The male flowers of Skimmia japonica 'Rubella'

Sophora tetraptera

Shape and size

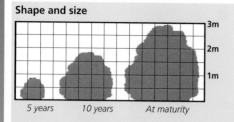

5 years   10 years   At maturity

3m
2m
1m

Position

Hardiness

Soil

DRAINED

Uses

Features calendar

Jan	Feb	Mar	Apr	May	June
			✿	✿	
July	Aug	Sept	Oct	Nov	Dec
	🫐	🫐			

Buying tips *Slow-growing so buy the biggest plant that you can afford. Most likely to be available in mild areas and from nurseries specialising in conservatory plants.*

Growing guide

A very attractive shrub. Its wiry stems are covered for their entire length with small, oval, light-green leaves. In spring, it is smothered with drooping clusters of yellow, pea-like flowers. The winged seed pods in late summer and early autumn are an additional feature. It makes a good conservatory plant or a container plant to put out on the patio for the summer. Start it off in a 30cm (12in) pot and move it on into a 45cm (18in) pot when it outgrows this. Use a John Innes No 2 compost. If you choose a terracotta pot, line the sides with polythene to prevent the compost from drying out too quickly in summer. Keep watering to a minimum in winter.

Pruning

None required other than to tidy up the shape of older plants or to remove any damaged ones.

Propagation

Easiest to propagate from seed, which can be sown fresh in autumn or stored for spring sowing.

Troubleshooting

Generally trouble-free if it is protected from frosts and not overwatered during the winter.

Which variety?

S. microphylla is very similar but has smaller foliage.

The blooms of Sophora tetraptera

Sophora microphylla

Sorbaria

Shape and size

Sorbaria in bloom

			3m
			2m
			1m
5 years	10 years	At maturity	

Position

Hardiness

Soil

 MOST

Uses

Features calendar

Jan	Feb	Mar	Apr	May	June
✿	✿				
July	Aug	Sept	Oct	Nov	Dec

Buying tips *Not widely available from garden centres, so try specialist nurseries.*

Sorbaria arborea

Growing guide

A very attractive shrub with large frothy flowers up to 20cm (8in) long. The long, unbranching stems and elegant pinnate leaves also make it an excellent foliage shrub, rivalling bamboos for their architectural effect. It's very easy to grow. The one drawback is that it can spread by underground suckers to form dense thickets. To prevent this from becoming a problem in smaller gardens, sink a large drainpipe into the ground before planting.

Pruning

Cut back the stems that have flowered in February to encourage bigger leaves and flowers. Apply a general fertiliser after pruning.

Propagation

Divide the shrub during the dormant season. Remove a small section from the outside of the shrub without disturbing the roots too much.

Troubleshooting

Can become invasive in good growing conditions, so take steps to control its spread if this is likely to be a problem.

Which variety?

S. aitchisonii Similar but with toothed edges to the leaflets.
S. arborea Slightly larger shrub.
S. sorbifolia Grows to about two-thirds the size of other species and has smaller flowers, though can still be invasive.

Spartium junceum

Shape and size

6m
4m
2m

5 years   10 years   At maturity

Position   Hardiness   Soil

MOST

Uses

Features calendar

Jan	Feb	Mar	Apr	May	June
					✿
✿	✿				
July	Aug	Sept	Oct	Nov	Dec

Buying tips *Quick-growing so young plants are a good buy. Avoid older plants that are woody and bare at the base.*

Spartium tends to become straggly with age

Flowers of Spartium junceum

Growing guide

This is like a giant broom, bearing its characteristic bright yellow flowers for much of the summer. It is easy to grow providing the soil does not get waterlogged in winter. Like all brooms, however, it can get rather woody and may suddenly die after five to ten years. It is a good shrub for windy, coastal gardens. In sheltered town gardens, it often grows tall and straggly and tends to be shorter-lived.

Pruning

Cutting back into the old wood can kill this shrub. To keep it under control, you can trim back the new green shoots while they are still soft. Do this during or just after flowering.

Propagation

Easiest to propagate from seed though you may get cuttings from the soft green shoots to root in early summer. Sow seed in March or April and grow on in pots for autumn planting.

Troubleshooting

May be short-lived and tends to get straggly if too shaded or grown in a very sheltered position.

Which variety?

S. junceum is the only species.

Spiraea, dwarf varieties

Shape and size

5 years	10 years	At maturity

1.5m
1m
0.5m

Position   Hardiness

Soil   Uses

ACID   NEUTRAL

Features calendar

Jan	Feb	Mar	Apr	May	June
July	Aug	Sept	Oct	Nov	Dec

Buying tips *Avoid any plants that are dry in the pots and check for signs of powdery mildew.*

Spiraea japonica 'Goldflame' in spring

Spiraea japonica 'Anthony Waterer'

Growing guide

The smaller spiraeas are summer-flowering shrubs, but some are worth growing for their foliage too. Their neat habit means they can be grown in mixed borders without swamping other plants. Some of the smallest can be grown in rock gardens.

Spiraeas grow best in full sun. They will tolerate partial shade but will produce fewer flowers. Yellow-leaved varieties need careful siting; too much shade and they lose their attractive colour, too much sun and they can scorch.

Pruning

How you prune the summer-flowering spiraeas depends whether they flower on old wood or on the current year's growth. In the first case, routine pruning is not essential, but one stem in three can be cut out if need be. In the second group, one-third of the stems can be removed. Very compact varieties can be cut to the ground in spring with shears.

Propagation

Take nodal cuttings mid-summer and put in a pot covered with a plastic bag. Pot up once rooted and plant out in autumn or spring. Alternatively, take hardwood cuttings in autumn and plant out into their final positions or move the following autumn.

Troubleshooting

They can get powdery mildew when grown in dry conditions.

Which variety?

There are many **S. japonica** varieties to choose from, you may see them prefixed with their old name, *S.* x *bumalda*.

S. japonica varieties:
'Anthony Waterer' Variegated leaves of green, cream and pink. Long-flowering. Prone to reversion.
'Shirobana' Pretty white and pink flowers on the same plant. 0.5x0.5m (1½x1½ft) after five years

GOLDEN-LEAVED VARIETIES
'Goldflame' Orange in spring, fading to lime-green through yellow.
'Gold Mound' and **'Golden Princess'** have yellower foliage.
'Candle Light' has soft yellow foliage in spring, becoming deeper in summer and reddish in autumn.
'Fire Light' is a red-orange when it comes into leaf, golden yellow in summer then red in autumn.

SMALL VARIETIES
(i.e. 0.5m (1½ft) high)
S. japonica **'Little Princess'** and **'Nana'**, both form low, neat domes of light green leaves with deep pink flowers in July.
S. japonica **'Bullata'** is even smaller with dark green leaves and dark pink flowers which fade to light pink.

Spiraea, medium and large varieties

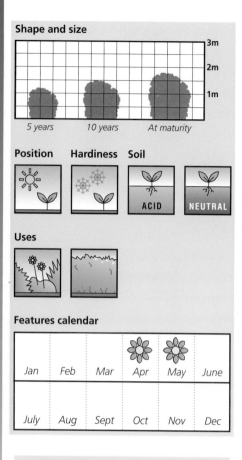

Shape and size

5 years	10 years	At maturity	

3m
2m
1m

Position Hardiness Soil

ACID   NEUTRAL

Uses

Features calendar

Jan	Feb	Mar	Apr	May	June
July	Aug	Sept	Oct	Nov	Dec

Buying tips *Avoid any plants that are dry in the pots and check for signs of powdery mildew.*

Spiraea 'Arguta'

Growing guide

Most of these are white spiraeas that flower mainly in the spring and grow quite large. They are useful at the back of borders or for hedging.

The most familiar is the bridal wreath, *S. arguta,* which bears clusters of pure white flowers on graceful, arching branches. However, it is one of the tallest at 2x2m (7x7ft) after ten years and has little to offer the rest of the year.

The tall spiraeas have a dense, twiggy, suckering habit and respond very readily to pruning. This can be utilised to make an informal hedge that will not go bare at the base. Plant 0.6m (2ft) apart.

Pruning

Spring-flowering spiraeas should be pruned after flowering. Cut right out about a third of the oldest shoots each year. Spiraea hedges should be lightly pruned after flowering.

Propagation

Take nodal cuttings in mid-summer and put in a pot covered with a plastic bag. Pot up once rooted and plant out in autumn or spring. Alternatively, take hardwood cuttings in autumn and plant out into their final positions or move the following autumn.

Troubleshooting

They can become infected with powdery mildew when dry.

Spiraea x cinerea 'Grefsheim'

Which variety?

S. 'Arguta' (**S. x arguta 'Bridal Wreath'**) is widely available and popular, but it does grow quite large. For something smaller look out for **S. x cinerea 'Grefsheim'**.
S. nipponica 'Snowmound' is upright when young and arching later. It flowers in late June to July in clusters along the tops of branches.
S. prunifolia is a similar size to **S.** 'Arguta' but has double flowers and good orange-red autumn colour.
S. thunbergii has a graceful arching habit and is very early to flower (March to April), with yellow autumn colour.
S. x vanhouttei is similar to **S. 'Arguta'** but flowers later (May-June). Leaves turn purple in autumn.

Spiraea thunbergii

Stephanandra incisa

Shape and size

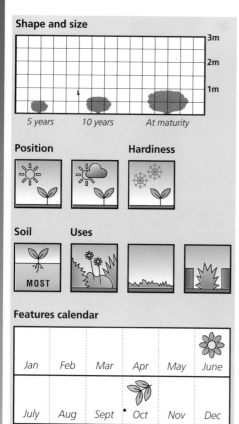

| 5 years | 10 years | At maturity |

3m
2m
1m

Position

Hardiness

Soil

MOST

Uses

Features calendar

Jan	Feb	Mar	Apr	May	June
July	Aug	Sept	Oct	Nov	Dec

Stephanandra incisa

The autumn foliage of Stephanandra tanakae

Growing guide

The attractive cut leaves and low-growing habit make this a good shrub for edging a border, filling gaps in front of other shrubs, or for mass planting as ground cover. In June, it becomes smothered with clusters of tiny, white flowers. In October, the leaves turn to shades of yellow and pale orange before they fall for the winter. If growing as edging or ground cover, plant 45cm (18in) apart.

Pruning

You can just thin out any old, woody shoots in spring or cut back a third of the branches every year. Old neglected plants can be cut right back but they will not flower again until the following year.

Buying tips *Look for dense bushy plants. Widely available at garden centres.*

Propagation

Take cuttings from the new shoots just as they start to ripen in July or August or take hardwood cuttings once the leaves have fallen.

Troubleshooting

May be attacked by scale insects, especially if there are maples nearby. Difficult to control so it is best to prune out infected shoots and carefully inspect those that are left, squashing any hemispherical lumps with your thumbnails or scrubbing them off with a toothbrush soaked in methylated spirit.

Which variety?

***S. incisa* 'Crispa'** has more crinkly and deeper cut leaves and grows only two-thirds the size of the species.
S. tanakae, on the other hand, forms a 2m (7ft) bush. It has bright greenish-brown stems which make an attractive winter feature.

Stranvaesia davidiana

Shape and size

5 years	10 years	At maturity

Position

Hardiness

Soil

MOST

Uses

Features calendar

Jan	Feb	Mar	Apr	May	June
July	Aug	Sept	Oct	Nov	Dec

Buying tips *Plants are sometimes raised from seed and these can be very variable. Buy plants in berry to make sure that you get a good form.*

The old leaves remain red all winter

Stranvaesia davidiana and 'Fructolutea' in berry

Growing guide

A good shrub for the back of a border, or for creating an informal hedge or screen. It has white, hawthorn-like flowers in June, followed by prolific clusters of red berries in late summer. On established plants, the older leaves may turn red in autumn and remain so all winter, while the younger leaves remain bright green. In severe winters, it may lose its leaves but this is not a cause for concern. If you are planting it as a screen, space plants 90cm (3ft) apart; otherwise put it where it has plenty of space to develop.

Pruning

None required, although cutting back one or two of the oldest branches every three or four years will improve the overall shape.

Propagation

Take cuttings from new shoots in July or layer branches near the ground in spring.

Troubleshooting

Susceptible to fireblight, a fungal disease that causes the leaves and stems to die, giving the shrub a scorched appearance as the withered leaves do not fall. There is no cure and infected plants should be destroyed. Older branches can also become infected with stem cankers which should be cut out.

Which variety?

'Fructolutea' is similar to the species, but with yellow berries. **'Prostrata'** is a low-growing prostrate form.

Stuartia pseudocamellia

(Stewartia pseudocamellia)

Shape and size

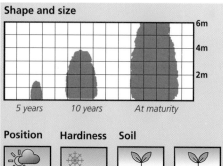

6m
4m
2m

5 years   10 years   At maturity

Position   Hardiness   Soil

ACID   MOIST

Uses

Features calendar

Jan	Feb	Mar	Apr	May	June
July	Aug	Sept	Oct	Nov	Dec

Stuartia pseudocamellia in autumn colours

Buying tips *Slow-growing, so buy as large a plant as you can afford. Widely sold by shrub specialists, but rarely found at garden centres.*

The peeling bark of a mature Stuartia sinensis

Growing guide

Stuartia pseudocamellia is very slow-growing, but eventually forms a large, pyramid-shaped shrub or small tree. It needs a lightly shaded position as the leaves scorch in full sun and it will only grow on acid soils.

The main feature is the pure white flowers with yellow stamens, which look very much like those of a camellia but are produced in summer. You need to be patient though, as it can take anything from five to ten years for it to come into full flower. While you wait, however, you can enjoy the vibrant colours of the autumn foliage. The brownish-grey stems look attractive as the brownish-grey bark peels to reveal patches of green. In spring, the new bark often takes on a shiny, reddish sheen. Like the flowers, this feature improves with age and is less prominent on young plants. Stuartias are not really suited to smaller gardens, where every plant needs to earn its space quickly, but make excellent specimen plants for woodland conditions where you have the room to let them mature.

Pruning
No regular pruning required.

Propagation
Can be raised from seed, though this is a slow process. Layering shoots near the ground is the easiest option.

Troubleshooting
Generally trouble-free.

Which variety?
S. sinensis is similar but even slower-growing with fragrant flowers. Mature specimens develop peeling bark which creates attractive, mottled patterns.

Symphoricarpos x doorenbosii

Shape and size

3m
2m
1m

5 years   10 years   At maturity

Position

Hardiness

Soil

MOST

Uses

Features calendar

Jan	Feb	Mar	Apr	May	June
July	Aug	Sept	Oct	Nov	Dec

Buying tips *Choose small plants (40-80cm/15-30in) for quick establishment. Larger plants should be cut back hard before planting to encourage branching.*

Symphoricarpos orbiculatus 'Variegatus'

Growing guide

The main feature of snowberries is their large, marble-like berries, although some are grown for their attractive variegated foliage. They are worth considering for difficult conditions as they grow well in very poor soils and under considerable amounts of shade.

S. x *doorenbosii* and its varieties make good winter interest plants, offering yellow autumn foliage and pink or white berries. To show off the berries, plant as single specimens in borders, or in groups against a background of dark foliage. Birds seldom take the berries, which are poisonous to mammals.

Variegated snowberries are worth growing for their foliage, although they rarely produce berries. They are easy to grow, but in dense shade the variegation will be less distinct. There is a lot of confusion over the naming of variegated varieties, so choose on appearance.

All varieties can be grown as an informal hedge, but 'White Hedger' is the best as it has a compact, upright growth which ultimately reaches 1.8x1.2m (6x4ft). Plant 0.6m (2ft) apart.

Pruning

Variegated snowberries occasionally throw up plain green shoots that should be cut out at the point of origin. To encourage the production of lots of new, brightly variegated shoots, prune established plants in early spring by removing one-third of the oldest branches to ground level. Prune other snowberries in the same way, but in late winter. Plants can also be cut right back.

Propagation

Take semi-ripe cuttings in early summer and root in a cold frame, or wait until autumn or winter and take hardwood cuttings and root in the ground. It is also possible to sever rooted suckers from the mother plants. Some white-berried varieties grow reliably from seed.

Symphoricarpos x doorenbosii 'Magic Berry' and S. albus

Troubleshooting

Some species (e.g. *S. albus*) eventually form thickets and it is difficult to restrict them.

Which variety?

FOR BERRIES

***S.* x *doorenbosii* 'Magic Berry'** Rose-pink berries, very free-fruiting.

***S.* x *d.* 'Mother of Pearl'** White berries with a pink flush. Purple-green leaves. The best for berries and the most widely available.

***S.* x *d.* 'White Hedger'** Good for hedging if trimmed two or three times in summer.

FOR FOLIAGE

***S. orbiculatus* 'Albovariegatus'** White and green leaves, rarely produces berries. Grows only half the size of *S.* x *doorenbosii*. **'Variegatus'** is similar with yellow and green leaves.

***S* x *chenaultii* 'Hancock'** A low-growing type, ideal as ground cover in difficult areas. Leaves are green, but turn orange-red in autumn, Flowers are prominent in late spring. Berries are purplish-pink in sun, white on their shaded side.

Avoid the vigorous, suckering types such as **S. albus** (*S. racemosus*) or **S. orbiculatus** (*S. vulgaris*) as they can be very invasive. They are really only suitable for large, semi-wild areas.

Syringa varieties

Shape and size

		6m
		4m
		2m

5 years 10 years At maturity

Position

Hardiness

Soil

ACID   NEUTRAL

Uses

Features calendar

Jan	Feb	Mar	Apr	May	June
July	Aug	Sept	Oct	Nov	Dec

Buying tips *Look for a balanced shrub with at least three or four branches starting not more than 15cm (6in) above soil level. Avoid any plants which already have suckers.*

Syringa x josiflexa 'Bellicent'

'Primrose'

Growing guide

Lilacs are common, summer-flowering shrubs noted for their fragrance. The common lilac (*S. vulgaris*) with its large, straggly habit and unsightly suckers puts many people off lilacs. However, by choosing the variety carefully, you can get a compact and attractive shrub.

The major drawback is the short-flowering season, which is over after three weeks. To overcome this, you could choose *S. microphylla* 'Superba' which has a second flush of flowers in late summer and looks attractive out of flower, or you could extend the season by planting varieties with different flowering times (e.g. 'Charles Joly' tends to flower several weeks before 'Madame Lemoine'). Some lilacs, like *S. x josiflexa* 'Bellicent', have attractive dark green foliage and a graceful habit.

Pruning

Proper pruning is essential to prevent lilacs from growing tall and straggly with all the flowers on the top. Prune immediately after flowering in early summer and again in the winter. As soon as the flowers start to fade, prune back all the flowering shoots to the first leaves below the flower cluster. In winter, cut any weak branches right back to the main stem and thin out a few of the older stems. Also remove any new shoots that develop at the base of the shrub.

The first year after planting, remove the flowers before they open to encourage vigorous shoot growth. Cut back all the stronger shoots in February by about two-thirds to just above a pair of dormant buds. At the same time, cut off any weak shoots right back to the main stem.

Neglected lilacs can be rejuvenated by cutting them right down in late winter. Remove all but about six of the most vigorous and well-spaced younger stems. Flowers will appear on the new growths after two or three years and regular summer and winter pruning should ensure a well-shaped bush.

Propagation

Named varieties of *S. vulgaris* are usually grafted, but the species can be propagated by taking cuttings

'Charles Joly'

from the new shoots in summer and rooting them in a cold frame.

Troubleshooting

Varieties of *S. vulgaris* may be grafted on to the roots of privet or common lilac, so suckers can be a problem. Tear or cut them out.

Varieties of *S. vulgaris* can take between three and five years to flower. Sometimes birds remove the flower buds during a harsh winter, so it can be worth netting them.

Lilac blight can cause browning of the leaves and shoots. Severe pruning will get rid of the infection. Burn any infected shoots.

Less common is the lilac leaf miner which can be controlled by a dimethoate-based insecticide.

Which variety?

S. VULGARIS VARIETIES

'Charles Joly' Upright habit, dark purple, double flowers, early flowering.
'Katherine Havemeyer' Dark lavender-purple, double flowers. Good scent.
'Madame Lemoine' White, double flowers. Good scent.
'Michel Buchner' Pale rose-mauve flowers.

'Mrs Edward Harding' Red to rose-purple, double flowers.
'Primrose' Less vigorous variety; 1.2x1m (4x3ft) after five years. Pale yellow flowers, little scent.
'Souvenir de Louis Spaeth' ('Andenken an Ludwig Spath') Long, wine-red flowers. Good scent.

OTHER SYRINGA SPECIES

The following are worth considering as they are usually smaller, although not many are strongly scented:
S. x *josiflexa* 'Bellicent' A graceful habit with attractive dark leaves. Vigorous and bushy habit, reaching 2x1.8m (7x6ft) after five years. Pink flowers.
S. *meyeri* 'Palibin' (*S. palibiniana*) Ideal for smaller gardens as it is compact; 0.8x1m (2½x3ft) after five years. Scented, purple-pink flowers.
S. *microphylla* 'Superba' Good for smaller gardens. Upright habit, reaching 1.5x1.2m (5x4ft) after five years. Rose-pink flowers in early summer and again in September. Good scent.
S. x *persica* Good for smaller gardens as it is only 0.9x0.9m (3x3ft) after five years. Pale purple flowers.
S. *reflexa* Has large leaves but is free-flowering. Rose-purple flowers, very little scent. 2.4x1.8m (8x6ft) after five years.

Close-up of the flowers of 'Madame Lemoine'

'Madame Lemoine'

Tamarix

Shape and size

6m
4m
2m

5 years   10 years   At maturity

Position   Hardiness   Soil

ACID   DRAINED

Uses

Features calendar

Jan	Feb	Mar	Apr	May	June
July	Aug	Sept	Oct	Nov	Dec

Buying tips *Look for plants with plenty of shoots as these are likely to form the most attractive specimens.*

Tamarix pentandra flowers in late summer

Growing guide

There are two widely grown species. They look quite similar but *T. pentandra* flowers in August and *T. tetrandra* flowers in May. Both have feathery pink flowers though those of *T. pentandra* are longer. Tamarix are most commonly grown as windbreaks or informal hedges in coastal gardens. *T. pentandra* can also be clipped as a more formal hedge. Plant 0.9m (3ft) apart for a screen or 0.6m (2ft) for a denser hedge. They will also do well in inland gardens if the soil is well-drained – they are commonly killed by waterlogging.

Pruning

Prune *T. pentandra* between October and February and *T. tetrandra* after flowering in early June. In both cases, cut all the shoots back by a third to a half. If growing *T. pentandra* as a hedge, cut back the shoots to 30cm (12in) after planting and tip back the resultant new shoots when they reach15cm (6in). In subsequent years, cut back all the new growth to 15cm (6in) in the winter.

Propagation

Take 23cm (9in) hardwood cuttings in October or November. Insert to two-thirds their depth in a sand-lined trench. Wait until the following autumn before moving them to their final positions.

Troubleshooting

Avoid waterlogging and lime-rich soils. Provide a more sheltered position in exposed, inland gardens.

Which variety?

'Pink Cascade' has a longer flowering season, from July to August. **'Rubra'** has deeper pink flowers. These are often sold as varieties of *T. ramosissima* but for garden purposes should be treated like *T. pentandra*.

Tamarix tetrandra flowers in spring

Vaccinium, deciduous

Shape and size

| | | 3m |
| 2m |
| 1m |

5 years | 10 years | At maturity

Position

Hardiness Soil

ACID

Uses

Features calendar

Jan	Feb	Mar	Apr	May	June

July	Aug	Sept	Oct	Nov	Dec

Buying tips *Look for bushy plants well-covered in foliage. Not widely available from garden centres so you may have to go to a specialist nursery.*

Vaccinium in flower

Growing guide

The deciduous vacciniums not only have berries and flowers but also striking and long-lasting autumn leaf tints. They make particularly good container plants as they have such a long season of interest. Grow them in an ericaceous compost as they like more acidic conditions than other acid-loving plants. Add a tea bag to the watering can every few weeks to prevent alkaline salts building up. Where conditions are suitable in the garden, they make excellent companions for azaleas and rhododendrons.

Pruning
None required except for an occasional tidy up.

Propagation
Layer shoots in the autumn. Rooting may take up to two years. Alternatively, divide in early spring.

Troubleshooting
Generally trouble-free provided the soil remains acidic and moist.

Which variety?

V. arboreum (farkleberry) Leathery leaves with a bluish sheen and white flowers borne singly or in clusters. The blue-black berries are not edible. Long-lasting autumn leaf tints.

V. arctostaphylos (whortleberry) The young shoots are red when young, turning green to reveal the finely toothed leaves. The foliage turns purplish-red in autumn and may remain until the end of the year. The white flowers (which often have red tinges) are bell-shaped and come in two distinct flushes – in early summer and early autumn. The berries are purplish-black and shiny and edible.

V. corymbosum (swamp or high bush blueberry) Bright green leaves turning scarlet and bronze in autumn. The flowers are pale pink or white and borne in clusters. The fruit is large, like small black grapes, and sweet and edible. ***V. angustifolium*** (low bush blueberry) is similar, but low-growing.

Evergreen vacciniums

There are many species of evergreen vacciniums, some of which, including the cranberry and cowberry, are natives to Europe. They like very acid soils (around pH 5.5 or less) and have the same growing requirements as the deciduous varieties. If you have suitable conditions, they are neat plants that are ideal for combining with azaleas and rhododendrons.

Most have white flowers in May and June followed by red or black berries in late summer. On some species, such as the cowberry, the berries last well into the winter.

Which variety?
V. floribundum The new growth starts out red, turning purplish and finally dark green. The pink flowers are formed in clusters in June followed by edible red berries in late summer.

V. glaucoalbum The leaves are green on top and a bright bluish white below. The clusters of white flowers sometimes have a pink tinge and the berries are blue-black. The new leaves of this species can be damaged by late spring frosts so protect with a double layer of horticultural fleece if necessary.

V. oxycoccos (European cranberry) A prostrate shrub, growing only 5cm (2in) tall with wiry stems covered in small pointed leaves. The pale pink flowers hang from thread-like stems and open over a long period, from June to August. The red berries are edible and good for cranberry sauce.

V. vitis-idaea (cowberry) A prostrate shrub, growing to 15cm (6in) in height, with glossy, oval-shaped leaves and white or pale pink flowers at the ends of the shoots. The berries are dark red.

Viburnum, deciduous types

(e.g. V. x bodnantense 'Dawn')

Shape and size

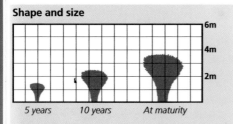

| 5 years | 10 years | At maturity |

Position

Hardiness

Soil

MOST

Uses

Features calendar

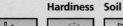

Jan	Feb	Mar	Apr	May	June
July	Aug	Sept	Oct	Nov	Dec

The berries of Viburnum opulus

Growing guide

This is a large, varied group of shrubs that can provide flowers, autumn foliage colour and berries. The information in the icons refers to *V. x bodnantense* 'Dawn'; where other deciduous viburnums differ, see the variety guide.

One of the best features of viburnums is their long-flowering period. *V. x bodnantense* 'Dawn' produces masses of flowers from January until March. In the Southwest of Britain they can flower from October to December and again in February. In winter, sprays from *V. x bodnantense* 'Dawn' and *V. farreri* can be picked so the scented flowers can be enjoyed indoors. Alternatively, plant near the house with winter-flowering heathers and spring bulbs to cheer you up in the colder months.

There are the early spring varieties like *V. carlesii*. For a really striking display in May and early June, there are several varieties of *V. opulus* and *V. plicatum* to choose from. Depending on the variety, you can have delicate, flat lacecap flower heads or round pom-pom flowers. The latter are sterile and do not produce berries.

The native guelder rose, *V. opulus*, provides good colour in the autumn with both foliage and berries. The maple-like leaves turn bright orange-red. It does grow rather large, so if you don't have a wild area in your garden, try to get hold of the dwarf variety 'Compactum'.

The smaller, more compact viburnums are useful in mixed borders. For example, *V. plicatum* 'Watnabe' has a compact, upright habit and lacecap flowers from June off and on until October.

Pruning

Varieties of *V. opulus* and the winter-flowering varieties like *V. x bodnantense* 'Dawn' can become congested after five years. To prevent this and improve flowering, cut out two or three of the oldest shoots every one or two years. To maintain the tiered habit of *V. plicatum* 'Mariesii' and 'Lanarth' cut out misplaced branches.

Propagation

It is easy to layer species like *V. opulus* which produce low branches. Peg down in the spring and they should root by the autumn. Hardwood cuttings can also be taken in October. Root in peaty compost in a cold frame, burying them so the top third is showing. Liquid feed every fortnight through the summer and plant out in autumn.

Troubleshooting

Winter and spring flowers can be damaged by strong winds. For exposed gardens, the more compact types like *V. juddii* are best.

Buying tips *It is worth noting that the labelling of some types, especially* V. plicatum, *is not always consistent. It may be sold as* V. tomentosum *and the varieties 'Mariesii' and 'Lanarth' are often confused.*

The winter blooms of Viburnum x bodnantense 'Dawn'

Which variety?

V. **x** *carlcephalum* Prefers sun. Strongly scented flowers in April for 3-4 weeks. Yellow-orange autumn colour.

V. **x** *carlesii* Small (1.2x1.2m/4x4ft) after five years). Red in bud then pink, scented flowers in April for 3-4 weeks. Yellow-orange autumn colour.

V. **x** *juddii* Neat and compact (0.9x0.9m /3x3ft) after five years. Scented flowers in April for 3-4 weeks. Can suffer from blackfly.

V. farreri (*V. fragrans*) Small (0.9x0.6m/3x2ft after five years). Scented flowers from late October for 20 weeks.

V. opulus A good native shrub, reaching 1.8x1.8m (6x6ft) after five years. White lacecap flowers in June for 2-3 weeks. Red-orange autumn colour and red berries in August for 4-6 weeks. Several interesting varieties worth looking out for:

'Aureum' Bright yellow, young foliage.

'Compactum' Grows only 0.9x1.2m (3x4ft) after five years.

'Notcutt's Variety' is the same size as 'Compactum' but has the best berries.

'Sterile' ('Roseum') has showy pom-pom flowers but no berries. It grows 1.8x1.2m (6x4ft) after five years.

'Xanthocarpum' has yellow berries and grows 1.8x1.2m (6x4ft) after five years.

The *V. plicatum* varieties are known for their tiered branches and stunning flowers in May and June.

'Mariesii' Grows 1.8x1.5m (6x5ft) in ten years.

'Lanarth' is similar but stronger growing and is best as a specimen.

'Grandiflorum' is a similar size to 'Mariesii' but has pom-pom flowers and no berries.

'Pink Beauty' is slightly smaller than 'Mariesii', with pink flowers.

'Watnabe' ('Nanum Semperflorens') Grows 1.2x1m (4x3ft) after ten years and flowers intermittently until October.

V. sargentii **'Onondaga'** has maple-like leaves that are bronze when young. Creamy, lacecap flowers in May. Bronze-red autumn colour and red berries.

The lacecap blooms of Viburnum plicatum 'Mariesii'

Viburnum, evergreen types

(e.g. V. davidii)

Shape and size

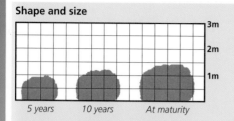

5 years   10 years   At maturity

3m
2m
1m

Position

Hardiness

Soil

MOST

Uses

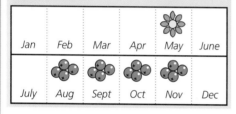

Features calendar

Jan	Feb	Mar	Apr	May	June
				✿	
July	Aug	Sept	Oct	Nov	Dec
	●●	●●	●●	●●	

Buying tips *Buy V.* davidii *in the berrying season (August to November) so you can be sure of getting the right sexes. Buy one male to five females.*

Viburnum tinus 'Variegatum'

Viburnum x burkwoodii

Growing guide

This is a large and varied group of shrubs that can provide winter flowers, bold foliage and berries. The information in the icons refers to *V. davidii*; for details of where other evergreen viburnums differ, see the variety guide.

Evergreen viburnums have a wide range of uses around the garden and are easy to grow. Where the soil is very dry, add plenty of organic matter and mulch regularly. Least tolerant of extremes of dryness or waterlogging are *V. tinus*, *V. davidii* and *V. x burkwoodii*.

The winter flowers of *V. tinus* are welcome from November to March. It can be grown as a hedge as well as a specimen or in a mixed border. For a hedge, plant 45cm (18in) apart; if it is grown informally it will provide a good, dense screen as well as winter flowers.

V. davidii has the most unusual turquoise berries on female plants from August to November and these combine well with the bold foliage. However, to get berries, you need to plant one male plant to every five females. This shrub will grow well in less favourable parts of the garden, such as beside a north-facing wall or fence, under deciduous trees or even in a wind tunnel. It is also a useful ground cover plant.

Both *V. tinus* varieties and *V. davidii* have enough year-round interest to grow in large tubs, although you may need to prune them.

Consider *V. rhytidophyllum* for its bold, corrugated foliage. The leaves can reach 20x8cm (8x3in) and have the curious habit of drooping in cold weather. The upper surfaces are a dark glossy green and underneath they are grey and felty.

Pruning
Pruning is not essential but may be needed to restrict the size. Cut back over-vigorous branches to a side branch in early spring each year.

The berries of Viburnum davidii

Viburnum rhytidophyllum in berry

Cut back *V. rhytidophyllum* every year in March if you want it to produce extra large leaves and to restrict its size to around 0.9x0.9m (3x3ft). However, such drastic pruning means that it will not produce either flowers or fruits. As a compromise, you could prune out one-third of the stems every year but expect it to grow to at least twice the size eventually.

Propagation

Take cuttings from the side shoots in September and root in a cold frame using peaty compost. Pot on or plant out in spring. Cuttings can also be taken in summer from young shoots. Root these in a pot covered with a polythene bag. Pot on in early autumn and overwinter in a cold frame.

Troubleshooting

Generally trouble-free.

Which variety?

V. x burkwoodii Semi-evergreen. Scented flowers in April. Avoid shade. 1.8x1.2m (6x4ft) after five years.

V. rhytidophyllum Grown for its bold leaves that droop in cold weather. Red-black berries. 1.5x1.2m (5x4ft) after five years.

V. tinus Flowers from October for 16-20 weeks. Blue-black berries in spring. Tolerates shade. 1.2x0.9m (4x3ft) after five years. You may come across the following varieties:

'Eve Price' Pink flowers from February for 8-10 weeks. 0.9x0.9m (3x3ft) after five years.

Gwenllian' Flowers from November for 16-20 weeks.

'Variegatum' Green and cream leaves. Flowers from November for 16-20 weeks. Needs a sheltered, sunny spot.

Viburnum tinus trained as a standard

Vinca

MINORS: shape and size

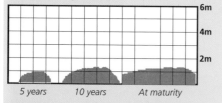

5 years	10 years	At maturity

MAJORS: shape and size

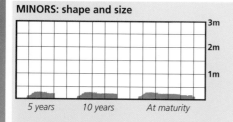

5 years	10 years	At maturity

Position

Hardiness

Soil

MOST

Uses

Features calendar

Jan	Feb	Mar	Apr	May	June
		🌼	🌼	🌼	
July	Aug	Sept	Oct	Nov	Dec

Vinca major 'Elegantissima'

Ground cover of Vinca minor

Growing guide

Periwinkles are reliable stalwarts for parts of the garden where little else will grow. But in the wrong situation their rampant nature can be a nuisance. Whether you should opt for the greater periwinkle (*V. major*) or lesser periwinkle (*V. minor*) depends how large an area you want to cover.

Greater periwinkles spread around 0.9m (3ft) in a single growing season. They are useful for under-planting between trees and large shrubs where conditions are dry and shady. Their toughness and vigour can be harnessed to cover banks or cold, wet corners. For ground cover in a shady position, plant 0.9m (3ft) apart; on heavy, wet soils reduce the spacing to 0.6m (2ft). The flowers are more prolific in the sun.

The lesser periwinkles are more restrained in their growth and offer a wider range of flower and foliage colours. They can be used as ground cover planted 45cm (18in) apart. Interplant them between deciduous shrubs, roses or herbaceous plants. They are tough enough to survive shade and will suppress weeds too. They are also useful for baskets and containers in the shade.

You can use periwinkles to cover up climbers or conifers that have become bare at the base. Tie the new shoots to the bottom 0.6m (2ft) of the climber or conifer.

Pruning

Once established, improve flowering and density of cover by cutting all shoots back to ground level in February or after the main flush of flowers. Use shears or a trimmer.

Propagation

In spring, split up into small pieces and replant immediately. Stem cuttings can also be taken in October, root in peaty compost in a cold frame and plant out in spring.

Troubleshooting

Stems can rot if they are planted too deep (the new buds at the base of the stem should still be visible).

Periwinkle rust can be a problem in very dry summers. The leaves turn yellow and develop small raised brown spots on their undersides. Cut back affected parts and burn prunings.

Despite their rampant nature, periwinkles often put on very little growth in the first year after planting. They soon make up for it in subsequent years.

> **Buying tips** If you are buying plants for hanging baskets, choose the largest plants you can find as they will not grow very much – especially in winter-interest baskets. Small plants or rooted cuttings are generally the best value for ground cover .

Vinca minor 'Atropurpurea'

Which variety?

In many cases, the same variety of periwinkle may be sold under different names. Alternative names are given in brackets.

VERY RAMPANT
(i.e. spread 90cm/3ft a year)
V. difformis Narrow, green leaves. Very pale blue flowers October to November, with a second flush from March to May after a mild winter.
V. major (*V. acutiflora*, *V. acutifolia*). Broad, shiny leaves. Large, pale blue flowers March to May and intermittently throughout the year. Widely available.
V. major **'Elegantissima'** ('Variegata') Cream margins to leaves. Very large, pale blue flowers March to May.
V. major **'Jason Hill'** Deep blue flowers with a white eye March to May and sporadically throughout the year.
V. major **'Oxyloba'** ('Dartington Star', *V. hirsuta*, *V. pubescens*) Large blue flowers with narrow petals March to May.

QUITE RAMPANT
(i.e.spread 60cm/2ft a year)
V. major **'Maculata'** ('Surrey Marble', 'Oxford Marble') Pale green splashes on leaves. Large, pale blue flowers March to May.
V. minor Blue flowers March to May, and October to November. Also sporadically through the year.

V. minor **'Alba'** Broad green leaves. White flowers March to May. Widely available from specialist nurseries.
V. minor **'Argenteovariegata'** Leaves have silver margin. Blue flowers March to May. Widely available.
V. minor **'Aureovariegata'** Leaves have golden margins. Blue flowers March to May. Widely available.
V. minor **'Azurea Flore Pleno'** ('Caerulea Plena') Double, blue flowers March to May.
V. minor **'Multiplex'** Double, purple flowers March to May.

SLIGHTLY RAMPANT
(i.e. spread 45cm/18in a year)
V. minor **'Alba Variegata'** ('Alba Aurea Variegata') Leaves have golden margins. White flowers March to May.
V. minor **'Atropurpurea'** ('Burgundy', 'Purpurea', 'Rubra'). Purple flowers April to May.
V. minor **'Bowles' Variety'** Very large, blue flowers with broad petals March to May.

LEAST RAMPANT
(i.e spread up to 30cm/12in a year)
V. minor **'Gertrude Jekyll'** Narrow leaves. Delicate-looking white flowers with narrow, white petal March to May. Rounded habit.
V. minor **'Oland Blue'** Narrow leaves. Delicate-looking white flowers with narrow, white petal March to May. Rounded habit.

Vinca minor 'Alba'

Vinca minor

Weigela
(e.g. Weigela florida 'Variegata')

Shape and size

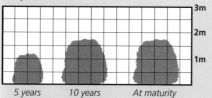

5 years	10 years	At maturity

Position   Hardiness   Soil

MOST

Uses

Features calendar

Jan	Feb	Mar	Apr	May	June
					✤
✤					
July	Aug	Sept	Oct	Nov	Dec

Weigela 'Dropmore Pink'

Weigela florida 'Variegata'

Growing guide

Weigelas are trouble-free shrubs, providing early summer flowers and, in some cases, attractive foliage too. They range in size from 0.6m (2ft) to 3m (10ft), so will fit any border.

Weigelas are tolerant shrubs but a few have special requirements. Gold-leaved varieties prefer partial shade as their leaves tend to scorch in strong sunshine; while the purple-leaved ones need full sun to develop a good colour. Also, although most are hardy, an exception is the beautiful *W. middendorffiana* which is slightly tender. This would be ideal for a south-facing wall or fence. Its early pale yellow, foxglove-like flowers would make an attractive combination with spring irises.

Most weigelas are best suited to mixed borders, but the free-flowering 'Abel Carrière' needs plenty of space for its graceful form to be seen, so would be better as specimen plant.

Pruning

At planting time, shorten the long growth from the previous year by two-thirds to encourage branching lower down. Cut out one in three stems after flowering each year once the plant is well established, i.e. after three or four years.

Propagation

Take cuttings from the new shoots in July or August. Root in a pot covered with a clear, polythene bag. Alternatively, take hardwood cuttings in autumn and root in a cold frame.

Troubleshooting

Variegated varieties may sometimes produce all-green shoots. Remove these as soon as they are noticed.

Buying tips *Look for plants with at least four or five stems so that they will put on a good display in the first year.*

Weigela 'Victoria'

What happens if you do not prune

Which variety?

You will find a handful of varieties in most garden centres - usually **W. florida 'Foliis Purpureis'**, **W. florida 'Variegata'** and the two red-flowered varieties **'Bristol Ruby'** and **'Newport Red'**. If you are short of space, it is worth remembering that these last two are amongst the largest. To obtain some of the smaller ones you may have to go to a specialist.

FOR FLOWERS

'Abel Carrière' 1.8x1.8m (6x6ft) after five years. Arching habit, rosy-pink flowers .

'Bristol Ruby' 1.5x1.5m (5x5ft) after five years. Red flowers.

'Newport Red' Very similar to 'Bristol Ruby'.

W. japonica 'Dart's Colour Dream' 0.9x0.9m (3x3ft) after five years. Pink, red and white flowers on the same plant June to July.

'Evita' 30x30cm (12x12in). Red flowers June to July. Flowers on mature wood only, prune sparingly.

'Minuet' 0.6x0.6m (2x2ft). Slow-growing with dark green leaves and red flowers.

W. middendorffiana 0.9x0.9m (3x3ft) after five years. Pale yellow flowers April-May. Needs a sheltered position.

'Victoria' 0.5x0.5m (1½x1½ft) after five years. Dark green foliage flushed with purple. Flowers deep pink June to July. Often a second flush of flowers in late summer.

FOR FOLIAGE

'Briant Rubidor' ('Olympiade') Striking introduction with red margins to the golden leaves. Dark red flowers in June and July.

W. florida 'Aureovariegata' 0.9x0.9m (3x3ft) after five years. Green and gold foliage. Flowers dark pink June-July.

W. florida 'Foliis Purpureis' 0.6x0.6m (2x2ft) after five years. Slow-growing variety with purple foliage and dark pink flowers.

W. 'Looymansii Aurea' 0.9x0.9m (3x3ft) after five years. Lax growth with very bright, gold foliage and pink flowers.

W. 'Praecox Variegata' 0.9x0.9m (3x3ft) after five years. Green and cream foliage. Pink flowers.

Weigela 'Looymansii Aurea'

Yucca filamentosa

Shape and size

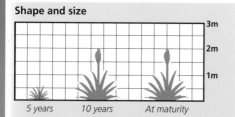

5 years | 10 years | At maturity

Position

Hardiness

Soil

DRAINED

Uses

Features calendar

Jan	Feb	Mar	Apr	May	June
✸	✸				
July	Aug	Sept	Oct	Nov	Dec

Buying tips *Yuccas are slow-growing so it is worth buying a large plant even though it is likely to be expensive.*

Yucca filamentosa

Flower spike of Yucca flaccida

Yucca gloriosa 'Variegata'

Growing guide

Yuccas are ideal architectural plants and the hardier types are worth trying outdoors in milder parts of the country. If you are worried about losing an expensive plant over winter, try growing them in containers. Think of them as foliage plants, at least initially, as they do not generally flower for the first five to ten years. Once they start flowering, however, they should flower every year.

They will thrive in poor soils; their main requirement is good drainage. Yuccas look effective in gravel areas and do well in seaside places.

The pointed leaves have sharp tips and serrated edges, so avoid planting in areas where people walk by or children play. When working near yuccas, wear glasses or goggles to protect your eyes.

Pruning

Remove dead or damaged leaves in spring.

Propagation

Young offsets can be removed in spring using a sharp knife. Grow on in sandy compost until well-rooted.

Alternatively, lift the plant and look for small swollen buds at the tips of the roots. Remove with a sharp knife, pot up and grow on in the greenhouse.

Troubleshooting

Generally trouble-free.

Which variety?

Y. flaccida has foliage which droops at the tips and has 0.6-1.2m (2-4ft) flower stalks.
***Y. flaccida* 'Golden Sword'** has yellow-striped leaves.
Y. filamentosa has erect leaves and flower stalks of 1.2-1.8m (4-6ft). There are two varieties you may come across: **'Bright Edge'** (yellow-edged leaves) and **'Variegata'** (cream-edged leaves).
***Y. gloriosa* 'Variegata'** has leaves with broad yellow margins.

Zauschneria californica

Shape and size

5 years	10 years	At maturity

3m
2m
1m

Position

Hardiness

Soil

DRAINED

Uses

Features calendar

Jan	Feb	Mar	Apr	May	June
✸	✸	✸	✸		
July	Aug	Sept	Oct	Nov	Dec

Buying tips *Most likely to be available from nurseries specialising in conservatory plants.*

Zauschneria californica

Zauschneria latifolia

Growing guide

Well worth growing for its prolific sprays of bright red tubular flowers. Although it is not reliably hardy, you can grow it outdoors in a sheltered position, such as at the foot of a south-facing wall. In winter, protect the crown with a 15cm (6in) layer of bracken or bark chippings. Alternatively, grow it in a 30cm (6in) container, using a John Innes No 2 compost, and take it into a conservatory or frost-free greenhouse for the winter.

Pruning

The top growth dies back in winter and it should be cut back to ground level before the new shoots appear in spring.

Propagation

Take cuttings from the new shoots in May when they are around 5cm (2in) long.

Troubleshooting

Watch out for aphids on the young growth and spray with an insecticide if seen. If not controlled, the shoots and leaves will be distorted and the plant's appearance ruined for the whole season.

Which variety?

***Z. californica* 'Dublin Bay'** (also called 'Glasnevin') has green leaves (the species has grey-green leaves) and brighter red flowers.
Z. latifolia is very similar to *Z. californica* but has broader leaves.

Shrub selector

Grow witch hazels, or Hamamelis, where you can appreciate the spicy scent and curious appearance of the flowers

Fragrant flowers

To get the full scent from these shrubs, plant in a warm, sheltered position. Make use of any south- or west-facing walls near doors or windows. Smaller scented shrubs can be grown near patios or as an edging to paths. Larger shrubs can be trained over arches or pergolas.

Buddleia
Chimonanthus praecox
Choisya ternata
Cytisus battandieri
Daphne
Elaeagnus
Genista cinerea
Hamamelis mollis 'Pallida'
Lavandula
Mahonia japonica
Myrtus communis
Osmanthus
Philadelphus
Rhododendron, some (e.g. R. luteum)
Sarcococca
Syringa
Viburnum

Dry shade

The combination of shade with a dry soil makes it difficult for shrubs to establish without help. Water and mulch them well for the first two seasons and expect a slightly more lax habit in shady positions.

Aucuba japonica
Berberis darwinii, B. linearifolia
Buxus sempervirens
Chaenomeles
Cornus canadensis
Cotoneaster
Elaeagnus
Euonymus
Fatsia japonica
Ilex
Mahonia
Rubus
Symphoricarpos
Vinca

Boggy soils

In ground that is waterlogged over winter and early spring, it is generally best to wait until late spring or early summer before planting. Even plants that can tolerate permanently wet soils need some air in the soil, so when planting, add plenty of well-rotted organic matter.

Cornus alba
Rhamnus
Salix
Sambucus
Spiraea
Symphoricarpos
Viburnum opulus

Thrive on chalk

Soils over chalk usually have a pH of 7.5 or more. At this level of alkalinity, some shrubs cannot take up certain nutrients from the soil, resulting in yellowing of the leaves (a condition known as lime-induced chlorosis). There are benefits to chalky soils – they warm up quickly in the spring, are light and easy to work, and are well-drained. Many more shrubs than are listed below will tolerate chalk, particularly if plenty of well-rotted organic matter is dug in each year. However, the following shrubs will thrive in chalky soils.

Aucuba japonica
Berberis darwinii, B. x stenophylla
Buddleia davidii
Buxus sempervirens
Caryopteris
Cistus
Cytisus x praecox
Cotoneaster
Deutzia
Euonymus
Forsythia
Hebe (some)
Helianthemum
Lavandula
Philadelphus
Potentilla
Rosmarinus
Syringa
Viburnum tinus
Yucca

Dogwoods, such as Cornus alba varieties provide colour in boggy soils

Helianthemums, or sun roses, thrive on chalky soils

Vandal-resistant

While no plant can withstand a determined effort to damage it, many shrubs are tough enough to form a deterring barrier. Some have spines or thorns which can deter animals and vandals. Others can regrow quickly if damaged.

Berberis
Buddleia
Chaenomeles
Corylus avellana
Cotoneaster microphyllus
Elaeagnus x ebbingei
Euonymus
Forsythia
Ilex
Mahonia
Senecio 'Sunshine'

No pruning

One of the best ways to reduce work in the garden is to plant a shrub border. By choosing shrubs that do not need regular pruning, the border will be even more low-maintenance. A few may need trimming back if they outgrow their allotted space.

Abelia
Acer palmatum 'Dissectum'
Berberis
Daphne
Elaeagnus
Euonymus fortunei
Fatsia japonica
Genista
Hamamelis
Ilex
Lonicera nitida
Magnolia stellata
Osmanthus burkwoodii
Phormium
Sarcococca
Syringa, some (e.g. S. meyeri 'Palibin', S. microphylla 'Superba')
Viburnum (some)
Yucca

Autumn colour

The intensity and range of leaf colours, as well as how long the display lasts, vary considerably from species to species and are also affected by climate and soil type. For example, the best red and orange leaf tints are produced when days are bright and warm and the nights are cold, but with no severe frosts. High winds and heavy rain can make autumn leaf displays very short-lived, as can early sharp frosts.

Acer palmatum 'Dissectum'
Amelanchier lamarckii
Berberis thunbergii varieties
Cornus kousa
Cotinus coggygria
Cotoneaster bullatus, C. divaricatus
Euonymus europaeus
Rhus typhina
Viburnum opulus

Winter/early spring flowers

Many of these early-flowering shrubs also have fragrant flowers. This is to attract the limited number of pollinating insects around at this time. The winter and spring interest of these shrubs can be enhanced by under-planting with spring flowering bulbs, winter ground cover such as ivies and heathers.

Chimonanthus praecox
Cornus mas
Corylus avellana
Daphne mezereum, D. odora
Erica carnea, E. x darleyensis
Hamamelis
Jasminum nudiflorum
Mahonia
Salix
Sarcococca
Viburnum, some (e.g. V. bodnantense 'Dawn', V. farreri)

Acer palmatum 'Dissectum' is hard to beat for autumn colour

Viburnum x bodnantense 'Dawn' produces fragrant blooms all winter

Seaside gardens

Note that while these shrubs will tolerate salt-laden air, they may need some shelter while they get established – especially on exposed cliff-side gardens.

Buddleia
Calluna
Caryopteris
Ceanothus
Chaenomeles
Cotoneaster
Cytisus
Elaeagnus
Erica
Escallonia
Forsythia
Fuchsia
Garrya
Genista
Griselinia
Hebe
Helianthemum
Hippophae
Hydrangea
Hypericum
Ilex
Lavandula
Olearia
Phlomis
Pittosporum
Potentilla
Romneya
Rosmarinus
Salvia
Santolina
Senecio
Spartium
Spiraea
Tamarix
Ulex
Yucca

Yucca gloriosa 'Variegata' makes a good specimen plant for a seaside garden

Heavy clay soils

Aucuba
Berberis
Chaenomeles
Choisya
Cornus
Corylus
Cotoneaster
Hypericum
Kerria
Osmanthus
Philadelphus
Potentilla
Prunus laurocerasus
Pyracantha
Ribes
Rubus
Salix
Skimmia
Spiraea
Symphoricarpos
Syringa
Viburnum
Vinca
Weigela

Sandy and free-draining soils

Amelanchier
Berberis
Ceratostigma
Cistus
Clerodendrum
Convolvulus cneorum
Cotoneaster
Cytisus
Elaeagnus
Genista
Hibiscus
Hippophae
Hypericum
Indigofera
Lavandula
Lespedeza
Perovskia
Phlomis
Potentilla
Rhus
Rosmarinus
Salvia
Sambucus
Spartium
Spiraea
Stephanandra
Symphoricarpos
Tamarix
Ulex

Pyracanthas thrive on heavy clay

Spanish gorse, Genista hispanica, makes good ground cover for sandy soils

Hot, dry spots

These shrubs should all withstand baking conditions, such as the base of a south-facing wall. But remember that all shrubs need watering for the first season while they get established.

Buddleia
Ceanothus
Cistus
Convolvulus
Cytisus
Genista
x Halmiocistus
Helianthemum
Lavandula
Rosmarinus
Salvia
Spartium
Yucca

Cistus x corbariensis loves hot, dry spots

Good windbreaks

Berberis x stenophylla
Buxus sempervirens
Cotoneaster 'Cornubia'
Cotoneaster simonsii
Elaeagnus
Erica arborea
Escallonia
Euonymus japonicus
Griselinia
Hippophae
Ilex
Ligustrum
Prunus laurocerasus
Prunus lusitanica
Viburnum tinus

Exposed, windswept gardens

Calluna
Cistus
Cotoneaster, prostrate and
    low-growing types
Erica
Fuchsia
Helianthemum
Hydrangea macrophylla
Lavandula angustifolia
Olearia (milder areas only)
Pittosporum (milder areas only)
Santolina
Senecio
Spartium junceum

Heavy industrial pollution

Amelanchier
Aucuba
Berberis
Buddleia
Ceratostigma
Cistus
Colutea arborescens
Cotinus
Cotoneaster
Cytisus
Deutzia
Elaeagnus
Euonymus fortunei varieties
Erica
Escallonia
Genista
Hydrangea
Kerria
Kolkwitzia
Leycesteria
Magnolia
Mahonia
Pernettya
Philadelphus
Potentilla
Rhus
Ribes
Sambucus
Sarcococca
Spartium
Spiraea
Syringa
Viburnum tinus
Weigela

Brooms and ceanothus make attractive companions for a hot spot with free-draining soil